ONE THOUSAND HOMOSEXUALS

BOOKS BY DR. EDMUND BERGLER

ONE THOUSAND HOMOSEXUALS (1959)
MONEY AND EMOTIONAL CONFLICTS (1959)
PRINCIPLES OF SELF-DAMAGE (1959)
THE PSYCHOLOGY OF GAMBLING (1957)
HOMOSEXUALITY: DISEASE OR WAY OF LIFE? (1956)
LAUGHTER AND THE SENSE OF HUMOR (1956)
THE REVOLT OF THE MIDDLE-AGED MAN (1954)
KINSEY'S MYTH OF FEMALE SEXUALITY
(in coll. with S. Kroger, 1954)
FASHION AND THE UNCONSCIOUS (1953)
THE SUPEREGO (1952)
COUNTERFEIT-SEX (1951)
THE WRITER AND PSYCHOANALYSIS (1950)
CONFLICT IN MARRIAGE (1949)
THE BASIC NEUROSIS (1949)
DIVORCE WON'T HELP NEUROTICS (1948)
THE BATTLE OF THE CONSCIENCE (1948)
UNHAPPY MARRIAGE AND DIVORCE (1946)
PSYCHIC IMPOTENCE IN MEN (1937)
TALLEYRAND-NAPOLEON-STENDHAL-GRABBE (1935)
FRIGIDITY IN WOMEN (in coll. with E. Hitschman, 1934)

EDMUND BERGLER, M.D.

ONE THOUSAND HOMOSEXUALS

*Conspiracy of Silence, or
Curing and Deglamorizing Homosexuals?*

PAGEANT BOOKS, INC., Paterson, N. J., 1959

Published by Pageant Books, Inc.
128 Oliver Street
Paterson 1, New Jersey

Printed in the United States by
Rae Publishing Company
Cedar Grove, New Jersey

Library of Congress Catalog Card Number: 59-13249

First Edition

Contents

Preface

In December, 1942, I delivered a lecture on homosexuality before the New York Psychoanalytic Society.* In the course of the lecture I stated: "The prognosis of analytical treatment of homosexuals is a favorable one," provided the patient really wants to change, mistakes in the selection of cases are avoided, and treatment penetrates to the deep masochistic layers of the unconscious. This was a new thesis; at that time all of analytic-psychiatric literature on the subject of homosexuality was permeated with unmitigated pessimism, as far as curability was concerned.

In 1951, fortified by additional clinical material, I reasserted my conviction in my book, NEUROTIC COUNTERFEIT-SEX.** In 1956, again, I presented new confirming proofs in another book, HOMOSEXUALITY, DISEASE OR WAY OF LIFE?*** On page 188 of the latter book I reviewed the cases I had seen:

> In nearly thirty years, I have successfully concluded analyses of one hundred homosexuals (thirty other analyses were inter-

* "Eight Prerequisites for the Psychoanalytic Treatment of Homosexuality," December 22, 1942. Published under this title in The Psychoanalytic Review, 31:253-286, 1944.

**COUNTERFEIT-SEX. Second, enlarged and revised edition. Grune & Stratton, New York, 1958. The book represents a triple monograph on homosexuality, impotence, frigidity.

*** Hill & Wang, New York, 1956.

rupted either by myself or by the patient's leaving), and have seen nearly five hundred cases in consultation (cases referred to colleagues, or judged unsuitable for treatment, or refusing treatment, or seen against their own will because of parental pressure, or unable to go into treatment for financial reasons or because they lived out of town, etc.).

HOMOSEXUALITY: DISEASE OR WAY OF LIFE? had an unexpected fate. Both the United Press and Time Magazine reviewed it, thus bringing it nationwide publicity. The Pastoral Psychology Book Club selected it as one of its monthly choices for distribution to its members. Suddenly, the fact that homosexuality can be cured became known to diversified groups of people. In the two years since publication of this book I have seen more than three hundred and fifteen homosexuals in consultation, treated and cured twelve additional cases, and received hundreds of letters from all parts of the country asking for information or for referrals to psychiatrists who agreed with my view of the problem. It is ironic that the number of homosexuals I saw during these two short years came to nearly half as many as I had had the opportunity of observing in the previous thirty years.

These figures take no account of the tangential impressions received from reports of homosexuals in treatment. These references deal with two groups: their "steady" boy friends (the small minority), and the truly amazing turn-over of five-minute-stands (the large majority). The promiscuity of homosexuals is notorious; it is not an exaggeration to state that when treating one homosexual one hears of dozens (in some cases, hundreds) of his confreres.

Nearly one thousand homosexuals provide a large cross-section, and experiences gathered from them carry some weight. The involuntary mass experiment I conducted added to my knowledge of the problem. The present volume is a report on these newer experiences.

That personal imponderabilia and "suggestion" are not involved in the cure of homosexuality, provided the "analytic instrument" is used as I have suggested, is proved by the fact that some fifty cases were cured by eight colleagues to whom I referred these patients during the last two years. The number of referrals was around one hundred and fifty; not all could enter treatment, nor could all of them continue, nor were they advised to.

I am reaffirming my conclusion, based on actual clinical cases, that homosexuality—if treated appropriately—has an excellent prognosis and *is* curable in the short period of eight months in psychiatric-psychoanalytic treatment.

So far, all non-medical attempts to cope with homosexuality have been based on severe legal restrictions, private moral indignation, and a conspiracy of silence—save for a very few distinguished exceptions—engaged in by newspapers, magazines, television and other mass media of information. None of these techniques has proved effective. I am proposing a complete departure from these methods: stripping the glamor from the disease, homosexuality, by measuring the myth against the clinical facts which prove that homosexuality *is* a disease and *is* curable. There is no more glamor in homosexuality than there is in, let's say, a case of typhoid fever. Keeping the problem under cover endows it with the masochistic allure of "glamor plus danger," and this helps provide confirmed homosexuals with ever-new teen-age recruits. The trouble is that our young people don't know it—yet. And their elders don't tell them—yet. This is because the elders themselves don't know—yet, or don't yet dare to open their mouths. It is only when a youngster becomes a homosexual, and his parents are emotionally involved, that the great lamento starts.

EDMUND BERGLER, M.D.

New York City, January, 1959.

1

The Crux of the Matter

To STATE THE PROBLEM as succinctly as possible:

Imagine a man who for some mysterious reasons unconsciously wants to be mistreated by a woman, though consciously unaware of this wish. Imagine, further, that this person inwardly fears his own wish, but instead of giving up the wish itself gives up its alleged or imagined central figure, woman. Since there are only two sexes, this leaves him only one alternative in his frantic flight: man. Officially, and as a defense against his real inner wish, he turns to man in order to find peace, quiet, love, understanding, safety. But underneath these official aims his real, compelling need remains the need to be mistreated. His retreat to "another continent" does not alter the old, unofficial conflict. Sooner or later (and sooner rather than later) he will feel that the man with whom he has sought refuge mistreats him, misunderstands him, fails to do him justice, deliberately tortures him by arousing his jealousy. Moreover, his flight in no way affected his sex glands. Since they are still working, it is inevitable that man, his antidote against the feared sex, woman, will secondarily be elevated to the status of a sexual attraction.

Simplified as it is, this account tells the whole story of homosexuality's unconscious background.* Ironically enough, homosexuality has little to do with sex proper (at best, it pertains to counterfeit-sex), but has intimate connections with psychic masochism.

To put the same story into more scientific terms: The homosexual is unconsciously a masochistic injustice collector who has shifted the "power to mistreat" from woman to man. His brother under the skin is the Caspar Milquetoast who (unconsciously on purpose) marries a shrew who soundly mistreats him. Consciously, he complains bitterly, but his apparent resentment and dissatisfaction do not affect his actions. Death, not divorce, will part him from his torturer. The Milquetoast is not a heroic figure, but at least he compares creditably with the homosexual; he does not run to "another continent" to escape his fear.

The homosexual's reaction to this account can be guessed. Furiously, he declares that of course he does not want to be mistreated; indignantly, he points out that the unconscious is a nonsensical fiction; pathetically, he protests that both his intentions and his biological makeup have been misunderstood: he represents the "third sex," and was born "that way." To make this last point absolutely clear, he goes on to explain that all human beings are made up of masculine and feminine elements; the biological endowment of the homosexual merely contains a more strongly pronounced element of femininity than that of the heterosexual male.

This string of standard disclaimers and excuses has recently been lengthened by a new and spurious argument. According to Kinsey's much touted statistics, every third American man one meets on the street has had some adult homosexual experiences. Can so many red-blooded Americans be wrong?

This maze of confusion, misinformation and outright medical balderdash has been presented to me with absolute conviction in hundreds of interviews, discussions and letters. Here is one such typical discussion. Mr. A., an intelligent young homosexual who

*For addenda, see pp. 44, 67*ff*.

had consulted me "only to do his silly parents a favor," began by making his attitude "crystal clear."

"I have no intention of changing," he said. "I like my way of life. I'm happy. I promised my parents I would see you, and I have. Can I leave now?"

"Not before you get this information: Homosexuality is invariably connected with severe self-damaging tendencies that are fully unconscious, and that must in time show up. You may not be able to see the connection at all, but it can be traced."

"Nonsense!"

"Did you ever hear of an X-ray specialist's discovery of the existence of a dangerous internal cancerous growth, even though the patient himself has not yet experienced any symptoms?"

"You can scare children! I know what I want!"

"So you believe. But you are a puppet, and your unconscious is the puppet master."

"Tell that one to the marines!"

"Provocations don't change facts. Please search in your memories, and tell me if happiness is the only emotion you experience in your homosexual contacts."

"It is!"

"And yet your parents told me they had overheard telephone conversations in which you repeatedly reproached your assortment of boy friends for infidelity, and so on. Bitterness and jealousy don't make for happiness."

"Those sneaks! Now they've been listening in on the extension!"

"Why not say that you yourself masochistically staged this situation? Making these scenes on the telephone instead of face to face was an invitation to your parents to listen in. You provoked the disclosure yourself. Isn't this a good example of the psychic masochism I'm talking about?"

"I'll just have to move out and live alone."

"At whose expense? Your parents'?"

"To hell with their silly, antiquated notions!"

"These silly antiquated notions are part of the reality you have to come to terms with. Your parents consider your homosexual perversion exactly as dangerous to you as an addiction to morphine or heroin would be, and they take it for granted that homosexuality, like drug addiction, has to be treated medically.

Now, you used your indignation over their attitude to sidestep the question I asked you a few minutes ago. Let's get back to it. How can you be so happy in your homosexuality, if you are constantly embroiled in jealous or injustice-collecting conflicts with your successive boy friends?"

"Don't heterosexuals ever have lovers' spats?"

"Occasionally, not typically. Nor do they, if they are mature people, live so promiscuously."

"I've read your silly book on homosexuality, and can only say that you totally misunderstand us."

"For instance?"

"You don't even see the glamor, the excitement, the vitality which homosexuality promotes!"

"This 'glamor' is nothing but the allure of danger, which feeds your masochism. Objectively, there is no more glamor in the disease, homosexuality, than there is in a case of any other disease."

"That's ridiculous! And besides, you don't even mention the biological factor of inborn femininity. A homosexual doesn't have any choice. Nature made him that way."

"That theory is yellow with age, which wouldn't matter if it didn't contradict elementary logic. How can allegedly inborn femininity be responsible for the masculine homosexual? Doesn't every feminine homosexual pair off with a masculine one?"

"Well . . ."

"I will note that you cannot answer this objection. For your information, the biological 'anlage' cannot account for homosexuality, simply because of therapeutic cures in psychoanalytic treatment. The records of homosexual cures through analysis provide a Q.E.D. that can't be argued away. A purely biological setup cannot be changed by therapy. The color of your eyes, for example, is all a matter of biology, without a psychic superstructure, and it can't be altered. But we can cure homosexuality with psychological-psychiatric treatment; therefore the biological argument is faulty."

"May I ask questions?"

"Of course. Please do."

"What about Kinsey's statistical argument? If one-third of all men, at one time or another, have had homosexual contacts, how can homosexuality be classed as a perversion?"

"Kinsey's statistics are totally wrong. He erroneously took his neurotic volunteers to be a cross section of the U.S.A. And, being emotional in his rejection of dynamic psychiatry—and misunderstanding its basic tenets besides—he became the voluntary or involuntary dupe of the highly efficient homosexual propaganda machine. Now, every homosexual, admittedly or not, is full of inner guilt which unconsciously pertains to his overgrown psychic masochism and is secondarily shifted to his homosexuality. He tries to relieve his guilt by telling himself—and everyone else—that homosexual wishes are universal. As soon as the homosexual grapevine carried the news of Kinsey's 'friendly attitude' towards homosexuals (and that's an understatement, since—whatever his personal reasons—he considered them 'normal'), volunteers began pouring into his office, eager to 'confess.' Kinsey made no attempt to explore the motives of these 'idealistic' people, and so of course he arrived at erroneous conclusions."

"According to you, Kinsey is all wrong?"

"If you start, psychologically speaking, with the assumption that one and one equals twenty-seven, all further conclusions are of necessity wrong. Kinsey damaged his entire project by uncritically making use of a weighted sample of the population. More than that, he worked on the premise that his volunteers were capable of giving unbiased information. That, too, distorted his findings. Even if his volunteers had wanted to be entirely frank, detached and objective, they would have failed; the unconscious is always un-conscious. This error led Kinsey to become a naive propagandist for his own preconceived notion that in sex anything goes—provided enough of the people sampled (virtually all of them neurotics) do it. A sexual outlet, in his definition, included animal contacts as well as heterosexuality and homosexuality, and he assigned all three an equal level.

"There is an ironic postscript to the well-publicized findings of Kinsey's Volume I and Volume II. Volume III was published posthumously, in May, 1958, under the supervision of Kinsey's collaborators. It deals with a half-apotheosis of abortion, declaring it psychologically harmless. In this volume, Kinsey's collaborators admit that the notorious and controversial sample—and I am quoting verbatim from page 17—'can be used as basis for inferences only for the educational upper twenty per cent of the U. S. population.' In other words, the titles of the previous volumes—*Sexual Behavior in The Human Female* and *Sexual Behavior in The Human Male*—were misleading. This is exactly what Kinsey's critics* have maintained, over his violent protests."

"I never heard of that retraction in Volume III."

"Look it up and check for yourself. Check on this, too: doesn't this retraction cancel the claim that 'every third man' is homosexual? In any case, Kinsey or no Kinsey, homosexuality is a disease with ramifications totally unknown to you. You told me that you don't want to change. Translate that: it means you haven't had enough punishment—so far. Wait until you find yourself faced with a good-sized and inexplicable depression, damage to your professional and social life, the demands of an extortionist, court actions, prospects of jail, venereal disease or another one of the inevitable penalties of your homosexuality. The self-damage that is a part of homosexuality doesn't show itself immediately. It is a kind of time-bomb, set to go off in a few years."

"I dig you, if you know the beat generation's lingo."

"'Beat' is right."

"We mean it differently: we get the beat, the beatific. One last question, Doctor. Do you or don't you have a moral prejudice against homosexuals?"

"I do not. For me, homosexuals are sick people in need of treatment."

"Then why do you call them 'perverts,' a term that has moral connotations?"

"You told me you had read one of my books on homosexuality. You should recall a fact that I always emphasize: the medical connotation of the term, 'perversion,' is diametrically opposed to its popular implications. The layman uses the word to denote a morally objectionable abomination. Psychiatrically, perversion describes a specific neurosis in which the pleasure involved is consciously experienced, in contradiction to the typical neurosis in which the pleasure is totally unconscious."

* Kinsey's medical and psychological errors are too extensive to be fully dealt with in a short discussion. In collaboration with the gynecologist Professor W. S. Kroger, I devoted a whole volume to this topic: KINSEY'S MYTH OF FEMALE SEXUALITY, Grune & Stratton, New York, 1954.

"I did not know that."

"You see what an unprecise reader you are. More important: in this incident you have shown a typical homosexual tendency to 'catch' the heterosexual in an allegedly hypocritical act or attitude. The underlying masochism here is equally typical. When you read my book, you must have registered the distinction I just explained, although you have since forgotten it. You've been here only a few short minutes, and you gave me no material; still, it has been possible to point out two masochistic actions on your part. Both your so-called mistake in talking indiscreetly on your home telephone, and in this way revealing your secret to your parents, and the form of argument you used here are samples from a bottomless reservoir of masochism."

This young man reached the high point of his anger ("Nonsense!"—"Tell it to the marines!"—"You can scare children!") when I told him that what a homosexual unconsciously wanted from his partner was "psychic masochistic pleasure," or, in other words, the pleasure of being mistreated. If he had simply said, "I know nothing about this wish," he would have been stating an exact fact. But he behaved no differently from any neurotic hearing for the first time of the "pleasure-in-displeasure pattern." The human mind cannot conceive of the possibility that a force existing within the individual should untiringly fight against self-interest and the pursuit of happiness, and as untiringly seek out humiliation, defeat, pain.

Nevertheless, psychic masochism (the pleasure-in-displeasure pattern) is a universal human trait. Everyone harbors at least traces of it; the traces rise to a superabundance in neurotics and perverts. But since the scourge is totally unconscious, even a confirmed psychic masochist feels no uneasiness when dismissing it from his consideration with a resounding "Nonsense!" This does not at all dismiss it from his daily life. For psychic masochism is—and has been from childhood—his faithful if invisible companion.

How much of a glutton for unconscious punishment the individual is depends on events which occurred behind the scenes, within his unconscious mind, during his nursery past. These events, and the way he originally reacted to them, have shaped the approaches, attitudes and conclusions attached to every minor and major crisis in his life. In neurotics, the aim of extracting unconscious pleasure from conscious displeasure invades virtually every sector of their lives; in not-too-neurotic or so-called normal people, the psychic masochistic aim is quantitatively less pronounced, and remains in ambush a good part of the time, emerging to strike a telling blow when a favorable opportunity presents itself.

There are no outward signs to distinguish the assiduous masochist from his part-time brother under the skin. The psychic masochist looks and seems to act like anyone else; his dislikes, preferences and ambitions are all familiar. Like anyone else, he appears to be trying to do the best he can for himself: to live well, to have fun, to ensure a comfortable future. But a graph of his successes and failures would immediately reveal a curious difference. Typically, the ratio of setbacks to triumphs runs at about ten to one: after a series of futile, impractical or downright inept undertakings comes one solid success. The psychic masochist, looking back at his even unhappier record, gloomily explains it in terms of "bad luck" and "the wrong breaks"; his ratio of failure is so much higher than the average that no one can help suspecting that there is "something wrong." This discouraging incidence of failure need not necessarily characterize every area of his life. In many people, psychic masochism is confined to one sector of their lives, leaving others relatively untouched. A comparatively successful business man, for example, may reveal his unconscious preference for unhappiness only in his domestic life, or in the general sourness of his attitudes.

"Bad luck" and "the wrong breaks" are of course mere rationalizations; they and all their variations and enlargements represent the best a person can do in trying to explain an unconscious process by consulting only conscious evidence. They satisfy, as explanations, because they combine immediately available facts in a form that appears to be both logical and possible. No matter how earnestly a person believes his own rationalization, however, it does not touch on the real state of affairs, for reality in all human emotional situations begins with the unconscious.

One of my patients was convinced that he owed his conspicuous failure to the bad luck of having collided with a succession of "spiteful corporation vice-presidents." He had climbed far enough up the business ladder to become a well-paid executive; he had then found himself getting, and losing in quick order, a series of excellent jobs. In the analysis, it became clear that his own provocations had invited each dismissal, but he could not be shaken from his conviction of being the innocent victim in each case. I suggested that he had unconsciously wanted to be fired from each of these jobs; in reply, he earnestly repeated that all he wanted was to be "a first-class success." He did concede that at times he yielded to his "perverse" sense of humor, perhaps applying it where he shouldn't—to his superiors. But provocation for the unconscious purpose of forcing defeat—never!

It is undoubtedly pleasanter to see oneself as the fortunate-unfortunate possessor of a "perverse sense of humor" than as a seeker of humiliation and pain. The pleasant explanation is a rationalization; the unpleasant one is the truth.

Consciously, the masochist means to be successful; unconsciously, he is determined to fail. He is not an innocent victim, but a strategist with an implausible purpose. It is this purpose that makes for incredulity in anyone who hears of psychic masochism for the first time. "Such people don't exist" is the typical response.

They shouldn't exist, but they do. They are the product of neurosis, a peculiar disease that for peculiar reasons refuses to respond to applications of that universal panacea, common sense. And neurosis has its seat in the unconscious, which in its turn should by right be a concept dissected, argued over and cherished by those eccentrics called analysts, though of no importance to the odd billions of non-analysts inhabiting the face of the earth. Again, the uncomfortable fact wins out. Unreal as the unconscious may appear to be, fantastic as its workings may seem, its existence and its ascendancy correspond to observable facts.

Psychic masochism is the most insidious as well as the most widespread of neurotic traits. The term can be most briefly defined as the unconscious wish to defeat one's conscious aims, for the purpose of enjoying one's self-made failure.

The psychic masochist achieves his unsuspected purpose by enacting a drama in three parts.

His first act consists of provocation or the misuse of an existing situation. Protected by the conscious illusion that he is behaving "normally," he actively invites a disappointment, a rebuff, a humiliating insult or an attack.

The second act is devoted to an apparent attempt at self-defense. Righteously indignant at the allegedly unprovoked and undeserved defeat just sustained (the provocative aspect of his own actions remains buried in his unconscious), he vigorously protests the other person's supposedly aggressive conduct, and launches an attack in retaliation.

In the last act he retreats from his inevitable defeat to self-pity, lamenting his wrongs. The theme of this jeremiad never varies: "Such an injustice! These things happen only to poor little me!" Still securely buried in the unconscious is his real emotion: under the surface of unhappiness, he is masochistically enjoying his self-engineered defeat.

The final result of adherence to this pattern of behavior can only be an endless chain of injustice collecting.

If the psychic masochist were to be accepted as the authoritative interpreter of human motives, we would have to see ourselves as living in a world of unalloyed wickedness, in which injustice and malice reigned unchallenged, and kindness or decency appeared only for the sake of disguising villainy.

The pattern of psychic masochistic behavior described above represents the *clinical picture* of this neurotic disease; it outlines the clinically visible facts pertaining to an already established neurosis. To understand the "how" and the "why" and the "when" of the disease, it is necessary to go over its genetic background (the *genetic picture*), and recount the historical development of the neurosis.

The entire story begins with one unchangeable—because biologically determined—circumstance: The human child begins life with a certain individualized endowment of aggression, but without the physical ability to express that aggression effectively. At birth, and during the many months before the child becomes the master of his own body, human beings are limited in their protests by the strictly limited nature of the physical actions they are capable of making. In the beginning, they can do no more than cry, vomit, spit or make uncoordinated movements of arms and legs. Later, they learn to clench their fists and direct their extremities in more purposeful, more violent movements. None of these methods succeeds in satisfying the need to express anger. Even more important, the problem is not self-correcting. When the child grows older, and gains in physical strength and motor control, he cannot use his new abilities freely because he has at the same time gained in knowledge of his environment. He has learned to understand taboos, to fear punishment and to dread guilt. Pressed by the rulers of the nursery, his upbringers, the child shifts a part of his motor activity—through which he discharges his aggression—into approved channels. This leaves a good portion of aggression still unexpended. What happens to this unused destructive energy?

Aggression is an inborn drive; like all drives, it must find expression. The preferred direction for its flow is outward; when this direction is blocked, the impulse towards "movement" still remains dynamically effective, and an alternative direction is attempted. The only alternative is to reverse the flow. Unexpended aggression therefore turns inward, against the child himself. This store of unused aggressive energy accumulates within the *inner* conscience, subsequently to be used in a manner that will be explained.

Biological and cultural factors thus combine to entrap the child in the first of his insuperable dilemmas. He cannot help the fact that he is born with the identical endowment of aggression at his disposal as an adult; he cannot help the fact that he matures too slowly to prevent his unexpended aggression from accumulating within his unconscious, where it becomes a weapon to be used against himself. Nor can his environment clear the way for him to expend his aggression fully. Restriction of the child's outward aggression must be a part of the educational process; one of the essentials of civilized living is the acceptance of boundaries.

The second of the child's conflicts also burdens him from birth. The infant comes into the world from an existence of effortless comfort: food and oxygen were supplied to him through his mother's blood vessels. This familiar fact, plus the inferences that can legitimately be drawn from observing the behavior patterns of all infants and young children, makes it possible for us to know that every child begins life with the illusion that he controls his environment magically; he has merely to express a wish, and that wish will be instantly fulfilled. Technically, this illusion is known as infantile megalomania.

More than anything, the newborn wants to go on living in the utopia he has known. Some of his "magical abilities," of course, are gone forever. He must now do his own breathing, sucking and swallowing. But to the extent that it is possible, his upbringers unknowingly do their best to maintain his fantasy. They surround him with warmth and darkness, insulate him from noise, leave him in almost unbroken sleep, feed him with warm milk.

As the infant must see it after he has adjusted to the first shock, his "magic" is still working, though perhaps not so well as it had. What he wants still materializes—in different form, to be sure—from a void. In his faulty perception of his world, he is not the dependent, painstakingly tended and watched, but the omnipotent sorcerer, in full control of his universe. Inevitably, however, his complacency is shaken. With the best of intentions, no parent can instantly and invariably fulfill all of a baby's wishes. The matter of timing is extremely important here. What a baby wants, he wants at once; a delay of a few seconds offends him as strongly as a delay that an adult would call lengthy. Obviously, the child's body is in no way harmed when he cries at eight o'clock and is fed at five minutes past. But the unaccountable interim, during which his magic has apparently failed, both frightens and infuriates him. The wait counts as a defeat, and the child reacts with fury.

Eventually, the child manages to explain these "failures" in a way that protects his fantasy of omnipotence. His magical powers, he now tells himself, provide him with everything "good"; an evil intruder (his mother!) is responsible for everything "bad."

This reformulation sets a pattern. As reality forces itself on the child, he makes his grudging concessions to it and includes a recognition of the real world in his concept of existence. But into this recognition he always weaves a reaffirmation of his cherished fantasy of omnipotence. For him, this fantasy has the full value of reality. As he grows older and bit by bit accepts the world of reality for what it is, he still keeps a guardian eye on his first and most precious illusion, losing no opportunity to prove that his magic still operates.

During the period when the child's picture of his world represents all "good" as coming from himself, and all "bad" from some unknown evil force, he builds up a septet of baby fears, in which there is but one villain, his mother. In these fears, one can discern the pattern of reformulating reality in order to protect the fantasy of omnipotence. In all of them, the child figures as the innocent victim of a witch who is capable of starving, devouring, poisoning or choking him, of chopping him to pieces, of draining or castrating him.

The fear of starvation—earliest of the septet—grows out of feeding delays; his "good" magic, the child reasons, has been overcome by his mother's evil intentions against him. The fear of being devoured has been interpreted by the English school of psychoanalysis as a projection of the baby's own aggressive designs on the breast or bottle. The theme is: "I don't want to bite; mother wants to devour me."

The fear of being poisoned represents a modification of an earlier fear; forced to concede that his mother does not starve him, the child protests: "Yes, but the food she gives me is poisoned."

The fear of being choked can be discerned in fantasies of being choked by the mother's breast or body. There is no reality basis for this fear, despite the apparent plausibility of the claim that it could be set in motion by the mother's too-energetic clumsiness in feeding, or by the child's perception of the difference between his own size and his mother's.

The mother's harmless intentions in cleaning and washing the child are misinterpreted, to give rise to the fear of being chopped to pieces. Again, the evil design is not a "logical" conclusion from the mother's clumsiness or overforcefulness.

The fear of being drained arises from the infant's feeling of helplessness when "propelling forces" impel him to eliminate urine and feces.

The fear of castration, the climax of the septet (and the one which has the least claim to the name of "baby fear," since it appears when the child has learned to walk and talk), has been shown by recent analytic literature to rest on several precursors.

The child had been deprived of his uterine paradise, had been forced to relinquish the bottle (or breast), had been "drained" of his stool, had lost his milk teeth. All these deprivations lay the foundation for the idea that "pleasure leads to the loss of the pleasure-giving organ." (F. Alexander)

Each of these baby fears becomes modified in later years, following the direction evident in the development from the fear of starvation to the fear of castration. Each in turn is subordinated to reality and translated into more or less plausible terms. In the adult neurotic, for example, the fear of starvation is represented by the reproach: "Mother (or mother substitute) refuses me love, attention, gifts." All neurotic manifestations include a reformulation of one of these fears.

To the young child, therefore, the nursery is a battleground where he stands alone, pitted against overwhelming odds. In addition to the evil motives he imputes to his "enemies," his upbringers (and it is indeed ironic that the immature child should thus misinterpret his mother's sacrificial ministrations), he sees them wielding three very real weapons: punishment, moral reproach, and the power to arouse guilt feelings. Constantly, he is forced to surrender to these weapons, and to do as he is told instead of as he wishes. This conformity presents the most dangerous threat to his illusion of omnipotence so far encountered, and to defend his illusion against further inroads the child devises an ingenious expedient. Unconsciously, he identifies himself with the commands of his educators, so that he himself seems to be imposing restrictions on his conduct. In other words, his identification enables him to claim that he is not yielding to pressure, but acting independently and of his own free will.

In this way the child puts himself, with his parents, on the side of law and order and eliminates one type of reality conflict. Actually, of course, this is a mere bookkeeping transaction. The command which had been a debit when issued by the parents becomes an asset when issued to himself by the child. But the shift yields a concrete profit none the less. The child saves face, avoids punishment, and rescues valuable remnants of his illusion of omnipotence. During this same period the child typically constructs rosy pictures of his own glorious future: a tendency which leads to future trouble, but at the moment strengthens his fading faith in his own magic powers.

The child's identification with his parents' precepts marks the establishment, within the unconscious, of what can be called "the department of don'ts and great expectations."* This department is a part of the inner structure called the unconscious conscience. Its function, as has been shown, is benevolent. Until it becomes operative only force—a frustrating and disagreeable procedure—could restrain a typically "naughty" child, but its appearance enables that same uncontrollable child to retreat with dignity from his untenable position. "Nobody has to force me to stop doing awful things," the facesaving formula runs; "I want to stop. I am good because I like it."

Benevolence characterizes only one part of the inner conscience, however. Counterposed to the department of don'ts and great expectations is the "department of torture,"** composed of the aggression which the child has been unable to express outwardly, and which therefore rebounded against him. This department has a single function: torture. Its strength is the stored aggression which has accumulated since infancy; its primary target is provided by the contents of the department of don'ts and great expectations.

The department of don'ts represents the child's idealized self-portrait. It shows him magically ruling over his contemporary environment, and projects his miracle-working abilities into his future as well by including a grandiose plan of outstanding success as an adult. This latter promise is the vulnerable spot. The inner torturer takes the boast as its measuring rod. Throughout the individual's life, the department of torture continually contrasts present achievements with childhood expectations. Since the expectations are never modest (a fantasy of omnipotence cannot give rise to moderate plans), the torturer can always point to a painful discrepancy. The punishment imposed accords with the extent of the difference between hopes and accomplishments.

This does not mean that the environment's approval, respect, or even admiration strips the inner torturer of his power to

* Freud's scientific term was "ego ideal."

** The scientific term, suggested by the late Dr. L. Jekels and myself, is "daimonion"; we borrowed the term from Socrates.

punish. The individual's actual achievements may entitle him to his eight lines in *Who's Who,* but this recognition has no standing within his unconscious. The only criteria there are provided by his own boasting statements during childhood. The rash promises he made to himself before he knew the world, before he could read or write or understand that history did not begin with the day of his birth, remain binding on him—within the unconscious—throughout his lifetime. Since he can never produce exactly what he promised, the department of torture can always reproach him for "failure." Again and again he pays for his childhood optimism with conscious dissatisfaction and guilt.

Unconsciously, the victim may plead for consideration and construct elaborate explanations; his pleas do not affect the sentence. Consciously, he may try to come to terms with his early ambitions, and persuade himself that he is contented with what he has accomplished. But conscious revisions do not register; the original promissory note remains intact. The inner torturer's demands can be modified only by clinical psychoanalysis.

How much conscious happiness the individual can extract from his existence depends on his ability to withstand the onslaughts of his inner torturer. Every human being counterattacks in some way when the inner tyrant launches its accusations and pronounces its sentences. But neurosis strips its bearer of his most effective weapon: the weapon of real aggression. The not-too-neurotic person has retained a good percentage of aggression for use both externally and in fighting his inner tyrant; the neurotic, on the other hand, has allowed the inner tyrant to come into possession of the bulk of his total store of aggression. Some part of what is left must be diverted for use in the outer world; only a pitiful trickle remains to be devoted to the unconscious battle. What appears as aggression in neurotics is mostly pseudo-aggression, a simulation in which the real purpose is not what it appears to be.

Nevertheless, even the neurotic fights back. He makes use of unconscious strategies which can best be described as alibis and refutations. Psychic masochism is the most important of these.

The young child's establishment of the department of don'ts does not, of course, eliminate all punishment and all conflict from his life. As the child's horizon expands, new factors, bearing with them new and unsuspected taboos, appear; with these changing factors come the seeds of conflict. Moreover, the child's identification with his parents' precepts has been selective; he has not taken over their code precisely and in toto. This very selectivity, in fact, largely explains the difference between a "good" and a "naughty" child. The good child has been logical rather than capricious in choosing the taboos he will make his own. He has accepted the important nursery rules, the rules most insistently emphasized. Accepting these has eliminated his major conflicts with his upbringers; his rebellions are now centered on minor matters. There are other children, however, who do not learn this important lesson about "major" and "minor" crimes in the nursery. Their identifications invariably omit one of the important points of nursery good behavior. In consequence, conflict—and its aftermath of punishment, reproach and guilt—remains very much in evidence in their lives. It is these children who become addicts to psychic masochism.

These children are no different from anyone else in their conscious desire for a pleasant and comfortable existence. But they have refused the obvious first step towards this end: they have insisted on retaining forbidden wishes and habits. Having become dependent upon a steady diet of punishment and pain, they must reconcile this need with their equally insistent need for pleasure. Only one possible solution applies: they must learn to derive pleasure from displeasure.

This is precisely the unconscious procedure of the psychic masochist. He applies a layer of unconscious satisfaction as sugarcoating to each failure, each humiliation, and in this way transforms external disappointment into inner happiness. The final formula reads: "The only pleasure one can derive from displeasure is to make displeasure a pleasure."

This pattern carries an inner bonus. As the psychic masochist sees it, his transformation of external pain into unconscious joy has been a triumph over his stupid upbringers. (Later on, the department of torture substitutes for the "stupid upbringers.") The authorities, in his view, "think they punished me; they are wrong—I, by my provocation, made them punish me!" Obviously, when punishment is ardently desired the imposition of penance (either conscious or unconscious) cannot achieve the result intended. To the presumable victim, the judge is not pronouncing sentence but acceding to an unspoken demand. The megalomaniacal profit here should not be overlooked.

The pattern of psychic masochistic behavior (clinical picture) now assumes its set form. Re-enacting, again and again, a drama that originated in childhood, the psychic masochist collects injustices, generally by creating them through his own provocations (although he does not scorn to take to himself the ready-made injustices he finds, for example, in the pages of the newspapers). He defends himself, with a fine show of false aggression, against these unjust actions; he winds up the drama with an equally convincing show of lamentation and self-pity: "Why am I always the innocent victim?"

The psychic masochist's show of aggression is not called "pseudo" because it fails to convince, because it lacks fire, or because it is powered by an insufficiency of energy. In these respects it is solid enough; its unreality betrays itself, not in its external trappings, but in its less palpable qualities. Here is a table which distinguishes between real (normal) aggression and pseudo-aggression, which is a neurotic attribute:

REAL AGGRESSION	PSEUDO-AGGRESSION
1. Used only in self-defense.	Used indiscriminately when an infantile pattern is repeated with an innocent bystander.
2. Object of aggression is a "real" enemy.	Object of aggression is a product of fantasy, or artificially-created enemy.
3. No accompanying unconscious feeling of guilt.	Feeling of guilt always present.
4. Amount of aggression discharged corresponds to provocation.	Least provocation, greatest aggression.
5. Aggression always used to harm enemy.	Often used to provoke "masochistic pleasure" expected from enemy's retaliation.
6. Timing: Ability to wait until enemy is vulnerable.	Timing: Inability to wait, since show of aggression serves as defense against inner tyrant's reproach of psychic masochism.
7. Not easily provoked.	Easily provoked.

8. Element of infantile game absent; no combination with masochistic-pseudo-sadistic feelings; the only feeling is that a necessary but disagreeable job had to be performed.	Element of infantile game present, combined with masochist-pseudo-sadistic excitement, usually repressed.
9. Success expected.	Defeat unconsciously expected.

Important as these distinctions are, none of them is likely to become evident to the spectator watching the psychic masochist going through the supercharged motions required by the second act of his private drama. What he usually concludes—often with respectful awe—is that "Mr. Bangs has a terrible temper." The psychic masochist's success in putting over this characterization undoubtedly gives him a good deal of conscious satisfaction. Yet —whether he knows it or not—this is not his primary purpose. The essential function of the pseudo-aggressive display is to sidetrack the inner tyrant.

The inner judge has by no means been deluded by the psychic masochist's transformation of pain into pleasure. A veto on the sleight-of-hand trick is invariably pronounced in no uncertain terms. Psychic masochism—the passive acceptance of external punishment for the sake of unconscious pleasure—ranks as the crime of crimes in the unconscious code-book, simply because no tyrant tolerates negation or neutralization of his techniques of torture. Aside from the straightforward defenses available only to not-too-neurotic people, psychic masochism is the only expedient which succeeds in cheating the inner tyrant out of an opportunity for torture. As such, it is invariably forbidden; in order to gain his end, somehow, the psychic masochist must provide an alibi which allegedly shows that he is not a passive seeker of pain, but an active fighter against it. The outer world's acceptance of his aggression at face value is his trump card. Using that acceptance as proof, he puts forward the claim that he is not guilty of psychic masochism, but of the lesser (intrapsychically speaking) crime of pseudo-aggression, and accepts punishment for the lesser infraction. At the same time, as an additional cover for his real crime, he constructs the consoling fantasy of "the innocent victim" (Act Three of the drama of injustice collecting).*

* It is this watchfulness on the part of the inner torturer that forces the child to make the transition from the "genetic" to the "clinical" picture in psychic masochism.

The puzzle here is the inner tyrant's apparent willingness to follow a trail that it knows is false. The answer is to be found in the structure of this inner department: its only function, it will be remembered, is torture. Its interest is concentrated, therefore, on the imposition of punishment; the pretext for condemnation is only incidental.

One must admit that psychic masochism is a solution, although the not-too-neurotic person would find the remedy as bad as the disease. But to an individual who has unconsciously adjusted his inner attitudes to the fact that he can perceive pain as pleasure it becomes the standard formula for coming to terms with his unconscious problems.

And the homosexual? He is a psychic masochist—plus. That "plus" denotes the inner twist which has delegated to man what originally pertained to the distorted image of mother—after all, a woman.

2

The First Interview

THE PATIENT'S FIRST VISIT to the psychoanalyst almost invariably provides clues important to the subsequent treatment. Homosexual patients excel in circumlocution, which means that the analyst must exercise his ability at trained guesswork. Some facts cannot be successfully buried under evasions or even outright refusals to reply to questions.

The interviews to be reproduced in this chapter of course represent only excerpts from actual dialogues between analyst and patient. Some questions and answers—essential for future treatment but not for understanding of the over-all picture—are omitted; no details of sexual activity, for example, are presented here.

These ten interviews were chosen to present as many aspects of the problem as possible. Each patient belongs to a different "type"; each type is repeatedly encountered, with, of course, its minor individual variations.

Mr. B. was a young man of twenty-six who presented himself to me under an alias. His first words were melodramatic:

"You see before you a candidate for suicide!"

"What do you consider important enough to make you throw your life away?"

"My future is a shambles. I have nothing to live for!"

"What happened?"

"I am a teacher. After a long wait, I was finally appointed to a position I had been wanting. Six weeks after I started the job, I was asked to resign. Oh, they were polite about it, but they made it plain that if I refused to resign I would be fired."

"Why?"

"They didn't say."

"But you must have known."

"Probably my homosexual record."

"A police or a court record?"

"Both. I was arrested three times, and put on probation twice."

"Was your job in a public school system? Where?"

"In a large city in the Middle West—pick any one of fifty cities. Yes, in the public school system."

"And you knew that the authorities always check on the credentials and reputation of the teachers they hire?"

"Yes, I knew, but I didn't think of it."

"Could you have applied for a position in a private school, where there would be less thoroughness about checking, because of the shortage of teachers?"

"I did have a private school job for two years, and everything was all right."

"Why didn't you stay in your safe position?"

"I wanted to better myself."

"But that meant running the risk of having your record discovered."

"My mistake."

"Has it occurred to you that you yourself, masochistically, created your own trouble?"

"Yes, but unfortunately I saw that only after I read your book."

"In your homosexuality, do you specialize on children or adults?"

The patient did not answer. After some moments of trying to get his facial and vocal muscles under control, he gave up, and handed me a clipping from the New York *Post* instead. It read:

ORDAIN DEACON ON PROBATION IN MORALS CASE

London, June 2, 1958 (Reuters)—A young man on probation for a sexual offense took up his duties today as curate in a Church of England parish in the northeast English city of Leeds.

Michael Trotter, 25, and three other young men were ordained deacons by Bishop George Chase at Ripon Cathedral, near Leeds, yesterday in a ceremony watched by millions of television viewers.

The Bishop knew that Trotter had been found guilty of indecently assaulting a boy, 9, last July and had been put on probation for two years.

The incident made newspaper headlines today and drew a critical comment from London Daily Sketch editorial commentator, Candidus.

He said: "The man who now dons the dog collar is technically a criminal—but in the eyes of the Church, apparently no sinner."

There was one dramatic moment at yesterday's ceremony.

The Bishop asked the congregation of 2,000:

"If there be any of you who know any impediment or notable crime in any of these persons presented to be ordered deacons, for which he ought not to be admitted to that office, let him come forward in the name of God."

There was silence.

Later the Bishop told reporters:

"I think it was the right thing to go ahead with Trotter's ordination. I accept full responsibility, and I am satisfied I am doing right."

Trotter said: "I am penitent about what happened last year. I trust God will help me to resist temptation in the future."

"Well?" I asked Mr. B. after I finished reading the clipping.

"I think that's the civilized way of handling such cases."

"The deacon mentioned in the news item used a boy of nine. Am I to understand that you did likewise, but on a larger scale?"

There was no answer.

"There is no point in arguing whether or not teachers and pastors who seduce children should be put in positions of authority over children," I said.

This flat statement aroused Mr. B., and he shouted indignantly: "Are you on the side of the philistines?"

"I don't know whether one must be a philistine to object to the homosexual seduction of children by educational and religious authorities. But let us get back to the important point; let's talk about reality instead of theory. In this country, school authorities do not accept your neurotic behavior as standard."

"And that's why there's nothing left for me but suicide!"

"By no means. You could look for a job in another field, save some money, and ask me for a recommendation to a colleague who would treat you for a modest fee."

"Why should I try another field?"

"Because another teaching job would immediately bring you into contact with children again."

Bitterly, as though I had done him an injustice, Mr. B. inquired: "And I should avoid children, is that it?"

"Exactly. At least, till you are cured."

*

Mr. C. was a very shy and depressed young man in his late twenties. In a whisper, he explained: "I am consulting you because of your book."

"I have published eighteen books; which book do you mean?"

"You know."

"I assume you are talking about homosexuality."

"Yes."

"Are you a man of fantasies or actions?"

"Mostly fantasies."

"What fantasies and what realities?"

"Passive fantasies, and a few casual realities."

"Were the latter satisfactory?"

"No. I was scared and disgusted."

"More scared or more disgusted?"

"More disgusted. I don't know why."

"Why do you want to change?"

"It's no life; it's torture and disgust. I was thinking about ending it all. I asked around, and was told there is no cure. Then I read your book; it was the first positive statement I received. Please help me!"

"If you want to be helped, you can be helped. There is no tragedy involved."

"If I could only believe that!"

"Then the extensive material in my book did not convince you?"

"It did. But I am such a hyper-hyper-masochist that I don't know if anyone can help *me*. Perhaps I'm too far gone."

"Why do you consider yourself a 'hyper-hyper-masochist?'"

"Because I can give you so many examples of how I always manage to get into trouble."

"For instance?"

"Everything! I hate living at home with my shouting mother and stepped-on father. I could afford to move out, but I don't. Again and again I've fallen in love with young men who won't even look at me. But a nice fellow was attracted to me and ran after me; I turned him down, probably because he was halfway decent. In my business, I make one mistake after another. When I should be forward, I am shy; when I should act modest and polite, I put myself forward and become provocative. You asked whether your book convinced me. It convinced me one hundred per cent that I'm a masochist. So much so that I concluded I must be all masochism—nothing else!"

"Knowing about masochism is just a beginning; that knowledge can be used for two very contradictory purposes. It can be used preventively, so that you catch yourself in time to avoid masochistic actions, or it can be misused—as you seem to be doing—for the sake of increasing self-torture."

"I didn't know that. I assumed that the more I thought about my mistakes, the more I blamed myself for them, the better."

"That merely means that you are using your knowledge to cash in on an extra payment of interest on your large capital investment in masochism. Isn't it grotesque that knowledge of the existence of a neurotic mechanism can be misused to such a degree?"

"You see, I *am* a hopeless case!"

"I did not say that or even hint it. You need help, that's all."

*

Mr. D., a lawyer of thirty-four, began our interview with a provocative question:

"Doctor, do you believe in magic?"

"What kind? The magic of witch doctors, advertising slogans or dictatorial edicts?"

"Your own magic."

"I didn't know that I have magical powers."

"You do—written magic. I read your book on homosexuality and fell under its magic spell."

"Am I to understand that you read the book because you are personally involved?"

"Correct."

"Where does magic come into it?"

"Well, I am a homosexual who doesn't give a damn about other people's opinions. I know what's good for me, and what I like. I made a voluntary decision; I chose my way of life. After I read your book I began to doubt myself and to worry about my sex life. Isn't that magic?"

"All right, you have had your joke. If you want to be serious for a moment—can you be?—the book you read certainly did not perform 'magic.' But it may have performed the task of a catalyst, bringing into consciousness doubts that you must have had for some time."

"I don't think so."

"If you had no doubts, why did you read the book in the first place? Just to find out what 'the opposition' is saying? Are you generally so objective?"

"That's a good question. Why, indeed, did I read the book?"

"This game of answering questions with questions is not very enlightening. Please give me a responsive answer."

"I don't have one; all I can say is that I was interested."

"Did you have any idea of the book's theme?"

"Yes; I read about it in a United Press story in the *World-Telegram*."

"And still you read the book?"

"I did."

"What conclusions would you draw from these two facts?"

"None. I know yours by now, and I can't decide whether you are bluffing or whether you happen to be right."

"Your joke about my 'written magic' shows that you prefer to explain what you did by shifting the responsibility to an outside source, instead of admitting that it points to your own doubts about the sex life you have chosen. By the way, this is another of your mistaken assumptions. You did not voluntarily choose your kind of sex life. Homosexuality appears as a result of inner conflicts, which means that there must be inner defenses. In other words, it was your unconscious ego and not you who made the decision. You, personally, were not even invited to be present at the signing of covenants not openly arrived at. Without knowing what you were doing, you merely took over as your 'voluntary' choice a decision already—unconsciously—made. To anyone who doesn't know how the unconscious works, this may look like 'magic.' Confronted with something tangentially 'magical,' you call that 'a voluntary decision.' And then, confronted with your own latent doubts concerning homosexuality, you explain that they arose because of the 'magic of a book.' Wouldn't you say that you are slightly mixed up about magic?"

"My homosexual friends warned me not to see you; they told me you are a dangerous fellow!"

"We don't have to go into a discussion of that nonsensical judgment. Dangerous to whom? To neurosis, perhaps."

"Do you seriously claim that I don't know whether or not I want to continue my way of life?"

"Why are you here? Did you—and your homosexual friends—assume that I would strengthen your homosexuality?"

"They knew the danger, but I didn't. Actually I assumed that nobody, yourself included, could out-talk a lawyer."

"Why do you constantly sidestep the real problem? First you discussed magic; now you want to start measuring verbal facility. Who is interested in out-talking you? Or in talking you into something, for that matter? Recently I read in a homosexual magazine the estimate of sixteen million as the number of homosexuals in the United States. Do you seriously believe that I am vitally interested in diminishing that number—by removing you from the ranks? It's up to you."

"O.K. So I have doubts. Do you think these doubts are strong enough for successful treatment?"

"Only a trial treatment of four to six weeks can decide that question. If you wish, I can recommend a colleague."

"Are you so disgusted with me, already, that you won't take me as a patient?"

"That's a good example of injustice collecting. I suggested a colleague for three reasons. First, so that you wouldn't twist what

I told you into a scheme planned for my personal advantage. Second, because I took it for granted that a struggling young lawyer would not be able to afford my fee, and I wanted to save you money. Third, because I have no time at the moment, and you need treatment now. All three reasons were unselfish, if not altruistic. My suggestion was to your advantage; you saw it as exactly the opposite. Is this, or is it not, psychic masochism?"

Rather shamefaced, the patient confessed that exactly "this damned masochism" had impressed him in reading my book. "My provocations—as you would probably say—lost me an important client. I keep getting into idiotic conflicts with my lover. Etcetera, etcetera."

"I see. Better think this over, and let me know if you want a recommendation."

"What do you think: when will I enter treatment?"

"In a few years."

"I hope you are exaggerating."

"Who knows; perhaps magic will shorten the time. You know that magic is powerful."

"I don't blame you for making fun of my 'magical argument.' You will hear from me soon."

*

My first knowledge of Mr. E. was contained in a letter that reached me from a small town in the Southwest:

Dear Sir:

I am writing this letter to you as I have finally decided that the only way I will be able to solve some of my personal problems is by seeking the help of a psychiatrist. I have just recently finished reading your book, HOMOSEXUALITY: DISEASE OR WAY OF LIFE? I would like to say that I find it a Godsend. I have spent half my life, nay, it would seem all of it, wondering if this disease would continue to haunt me for the entire length of my life. At last I have the answer to the problem. Now, finding someone to help me seems to be the most pressing problem on earth. Nothing can compare with it in respect to urgency . . . I confess that I would rather be dead than continue living my life in this unnatural way. I believe in your judgment and discretion and would make practically any sacrifice in return for some kind of help.

After some complications, an appointment was arranged. The young man confirmed the impression made by his letter; consciously, he desperately wanted to change.

This case was interesting because of E.'s conscious recollections. They stood out in sharp contrast to the superficial conscious memories of most homosexuals, who describe their mothers as having been strong and dominant, their fathers as weak nonentities. This tendency had in the past led some observers to assume that the absence of a strong father had made it difficult for the boy to identify normally with a masculine image. Later experiences showed that this apparent clue to the development of homosexuality explained nothing: the boy's masochistic propensities develop during the first eighteen months of life, before the father becomes important in the child's picture of reality.

A case that clearly illustrated this point was described at some length in the book Mr. E. had read and found so impressive. "Mr. O." (pp. 224-233) had been to three other psychiatrists before coming to me. Each of these had stressed the patient's "feminine identification": in childhood the boy had been confronted with a "shouting tyrant" of a father. Six years of treatment with these three colleagues had achieved no results whatever. When the deeper layers were stressed, by myself, the outcome was full therapeutic success. To quote from a discussion with this patient, early in his analysis:

"I'm a living example of the fallacy of the theory that a homosexual develops in families where the mother is dominant and the father is a weakling, or absent altogether," Mr. O. said.

"For your information, the theory is outdated. It was constructed at a time when homosexuality was considered an aberration of the Oedipus complex. Being faced with a contradiction—why doesn't the boy identify himself with the father—the theorists took the convenient way out: When a strong mother dominates the home, there is no model for such identification, since the father is a weakling. Today, we know that this problem is a sham. The homosexual's conflict pertains to the unsolved masochistic relationship with the earliest image of the mother, the so-called mother of the pre-Oedipal period; the Oedipus complex itself, since it is a much later development, is without basic importance in homosexuals. Another proof of this is the fact that homosexuals use pseudo-Oedipal traits as camouflaging defenses. In their rare, comparatively durable affairs, they often act the roles of husband and wife. Since the unconscious *is* unconscious, a consciously approved camouflage cannot be 'the real thing.'"

"I'm glad to hear that. In my family, my father was a shouting tyrant; my mother was a subdued, meek female-ette. Of course, this opens up a new contradiction. How could such a meek and submissive person have been elevated to the role of the witch, which I understand is the part ascribed to the 'Giantess of the Nursery?'"

"The answer is simple. You are mixing up your chronology. Your opinion of your mother's submissiveness was formed at a later period, a period you remember. The image of the giantess pertains to the nursery; that period is repressed and cannot be remembered. No recollections that can be verbalized go back as far as the first eighteen months of life. This period can be reconstructed only from later actions."

Mr. E.'s external childhood situation had been very similar: his father was a shoving, brutal fellow, and his mother kind and understanding.

There is hope that an arrangement can be made for future treatment of Mr. E., whose prognosis I consider highly favorable.

*

Mr. F. was nineteen, homosexual, and serving in a branch of the Armed Services. He consulted me in despair. At the age of seven, his much older brother had seduced him. Their relations continued for two years, until the brother left home. The boy's homosexual experiences had then been limited to fantasy, until, when he entered the service, he discovered that his homosexuality was still "very much alive." He had scraped together every cent he could get to travel the three hundred miles that separated his base from my office in New York.

"Do you have affairs now, while you are in the service?" I asked. "Do you realize how dangerous it is to be caught?"

"The worst they can do is give me a dishonorable discharge. Who cares? Why should I waste any more years in uniform?"

"Are you taking your own desperation seriously? What you say sounds like cynicism, but you give the impression of being a decent fellow."

"Well, I am desperate, and sometimes I say foolish things."

"It doesn't matter here, but you had better be careful outside. Has it occurred to you that a dishonorable discharge might ruin your entire life? When we spoke on the telephone, you told me that your home is in a small rural community. How small is it, and do you intend to go back there?"

"Population one hundred and twenty. Yes, I intend to go back."

"Do you know that draft boards are automatically notified of a dishonorable discharge, and of the reason for it? The whole one hundred and twenty would know about your homosexuality."

The boy was appalled. Obviously his mental masochism had kept him from making that simple deduction.

We discussed plans for treatment, after his term of service was completed. Because of the boy's pitiable situation, I refused to accept a fee, and he thanked me tearfully. I was "the only fellow who had been really nice," he said earnestly, again and again.

One night approximately seven months later, my telephone rang. The long-distance operator inquired whether I would be willing to pay reverse charges on a call from Mr. —, in a town about five hundred miles from New York. Neither the man's name nor the town's registered as familiar, and I refused to accept the call. Still curious about the call the next day, I went through my files looking for a clue. The clue proved to be that of the young serviceman, although the address was not the one he had given me. Evidently he had been transferred, or was AWOL.

The incident shows that one cannot be nice to some (unfortunately, most) masochists: they take kindness as a sign of weakness, and work on the "soft touch" they have found until they eventually provoke the refusal they inwardly crave. It took seven months, but young F. finally figured out a way to obtain a "disappointment" from the only fellow who "had been really nice" to him. You cannot win with these people!

Mr. G. was a successful business man of thirty-eight, a confirmed homosexual ("no bones about it") who liked his way of life but, to his deep distress, had recently become "impotent in my exciting favorite sport, my homosexuality." Anxiously, he asked: "What should be done about this? And more important, what does it mean, and why should it happen?"

"Potency disturbances within the framework of homosexuality are not at all rare, although nobody talks about them; you will find no mention of them in the scientific literature, nor hear about such things from homosexuals. There are descriptions of such cases in the second, enlarged edition of my monograph, COUNTERFEIT-SEX."*

"What does this disturbance mean?"

"The same thing that a potency disturbance denotes in heterosexuality: an unconscious conflict."

"Can this be cured in psychiatric treatment?"

"No, it cannot."

"But a potency disturbance in a heterosexual can be cured, you have said."

"Yes, certainly."

"Then why not in homosexuals? Now you show that you're a holier-than-thou hypocrite; you don't want to do it!"

"Excitement and accusations don't help. Let me explain. A potency disturbance in heterosexuality means that an inner conflict inhibits a biologically preformed function. Removing the inner conflict unblocks the already formed passageways, and restores the ability to function. A potency disturbance in homosexuality shows that an inner objection to a neurotic trait—homosexuality—has been built up, and is being propelled by inner guilt. There is no normal preformed basis for removing the block. Psychoanalysis is incapable of improving homosexuality."

"That's a lot of eyewash! You psychiatrists are just stinking moralists!"

"You are quite mistaken. Personally, your homosexuality doesn't offend me on the one hand, nor rouse in me any missionary zeal for reform on the other hand. I have been explaining a simple fact to you—a neurosis within the framework of neurosis cannot

* Pp. 211-15.

be treated—and you are refusing to grasp that fact."

"O. K. I think I can catch you in your own hypocrisies. What would have happened if I had gone into analysis?"

"Gone into analysis for what purpose?"

"Just suppose I had lied and told you I was a willing candidate for the change from homosexuality to heterosexuality."

"You would not have survived the first four weeks—the trial treatment. At the end of that time you would have been asked to leave."

"Because I had committed the crime of telling a lie?"

"No. Because, never having wanted to change, you would have been an unrewarding case."

"And you wouldn't want to spoil your statistics?"

"Wrong again. If you read my books on homosexuality, you can check this statement: often I have taken on what seemed to be hopeless cases."

"Keep your troubles to yourself—what do I care about them! What happens to *me*? What am I going to do?"

"What kind of potency disturbance is involved?"

"I have a wonderful friend who is slipping through my fingers —or, well, whatever you want to call it. He wants anal penetration, and I can't satisfy him. Suddenly I found myself unable to perform, although in the past, with other people, I had no difficulty."

"There you are: the same masochism that pushes you into homosexuality is now preventing you from satisfying your 'wonderful friend.' Obviously, unconsciously, you want to lose him."

"Nuts! I want to keep him!"

"Consciously."

"I can only repeat: Nuts!"

"Is your 'wonderful friend' financially independent?"

"I gave him a job in my firm, and besides that . . ."

"In other words, he is a male prostitute?"

"How dare you say that? What's wrong with accepting presents? Whole industries exist to produce gifts—for women *and* men!"

"Does your friend keep regular business hours?"

"Well, yes. Sometimes, when he is too tired, he doesn't come to the office."

"In short, he takes advantage of the fact that he is, let's say, connected with the boss?"

"Well, once in a while."

"And you don't see the handwriting on the wall? The next steps are a lot more expensive: threats, extortion, blackmail, and what not."

There was no answer, not even an outburst. A very depressed Mr. G. asked quietly, "What am I to do?"

"You have two choices. You can indulge yourself with another outburst against me, calling me a hypocrite and a faker and whatever else you can think of. Or you can understand that what you are really trying to get out of this affair is a grand masochistic fiesta. If your friend is really as important to you as you claim he is, then you yourself, by means of your newly-developed potency disturbance, are making sure that he will leave you—at least, sexually. He may continue to exploit you financially, anyway. Your inability to give him what he wants, sexually, is driving him into the bed of your successor. And all you see is the 'tragedy' of the situation. What you don't see is that unconsciously you are aiding, abetting and speeding up the tragedy."

"What's your conclusion?"

"That without knowing it consciously you are approaching the point of no return in your homosexuality. Sooner or later this inner development will penetrate to consciousness. When it does, come and see me again. Perhaps then you can be cured of the disease of homosexuality."

Mr. G. left without a word. The next chapter in his drama may be written in a few years, or even months.

*

In the past I have repeatedly observed that homosexuals, when exposed for the first time to the concept of psychic masochism, react as if they belonged to one of two distinct categories. Some are diehards who furiously deny any trace of appetite for self-damage; Mr. A. belonged to this category. The others, corroded by inner doubts, are half-willing to accept the fact that masochism exists, and even acknowledge that it exists in themselves, but stubbornly maintain that it can have no connection with homosexuality per se.

This impression was confirmed on a larger scale after my book, HOMOSEXUALITY, DISEASE OR WAY OF LIFE?, became widely known.* I had never expected, however, to see a prospective patient—even a member of the group corroded by inner doubt—whose understanding could be as clear on the one hand and as unclear on the other as that exhibited by Mr. H., a young scientist.

Mr. H. had accepted a job in a scientific organization on the West Coast on an interim basis; the grant it carried, though low, would enable him to finish his Ph.D. dissertation, after which he could be sure of getting a well-paid position in his field. His superior, a woman, made his life intolerable, and he could not at first see that he had any recourse. At length he decided to cut the Gordian knot (or, as he ironically added, "perhaps the umbilical cord") by suggesting to the president of the scientific organization (also a woman) that a part of his grant be used to pay the salary of a secretary for his immediate superior. The woman who headed the organization was obviously a reasonable person; she had two comments to make to this suggestion. First: "Is she (the department head) really as bad as her reputation?" ("Worse," the patient answered.) Second: "The grant is small enough as is; you couldn't live on half of it." She then arranged to hire a secretary, providing her salary from another source. At the same time she transferred the patient into a department which she herself controlled directly.

"That meant," the patient went on, "that my problems were unexpectedly solved, and livable—even agreeable—working conditions established. But this was the tragic part of it: I had originally accepted that silly grant only to tide me over until I could finish my Ph.D. thesis. As long as I was under the thumb of that insufferable old witch, I did a lot of work—good work—

* Publisher after publisher rejected this book as "premature" ("A good book, but the public isn't ready for it; let me see it again in twenty years") before it reached the public under the imprint of a more intelligent and farsighted firm than most. After publication, it established a peculiar record: it became a *hidden* best seller. The best-seller lists published in the newspapers are compiled from reports submitted by leading book stores. Most of the buyers of my book were homosexuals, or relatives of homosexuals, who hesitated to show their interest openly by purchasing it in a store. Instead, they ordered the book directly from the publisher; these sales never figured in the weekly reports.

on it. As soon as my office problems were cleared up, I found myself totally blocked on my thesis.

"I thought about it and thought about it, and couldn't figure out the paradox. Just about then, I got hold of your book on homosexuality. I am a homosexual, mildly troubled by it, but not enough—before I read it, anyhow—to think of entering psychiatric treatment. After I read the book, I got the answer to my riddle in a flash: as long as that bitch tortured me, my masochism was satisfied and the more normal part of me could assert itself in my work on the thesis. After this deposition of masochism was removed by my transfer to another department, my masochism—to use one of your phrases—became homeless, and was shifted to my dissertation. Now I am completely convinced of the existence of psychic masochism, and I want to enter treatment. My grant ends in a few months. I will come to New York, look for a job, and start my analysis. That's my plan."

I told him: "I have only one thing to add to your excellent deduction. You seem to accept the precept of psychic masochism, as far as your total psychie household is concerned, but you appear to doubt whether it applies to a specific sector of this totality: your homosexuality."

"When you put it that way, I seem slightly ridiculous."

"Only inconsistent. Analysis can show you why you are inconsistent. If you come to New York for a definite stay, please get in touch with me, and I will make arrangements for your treatment by a colleague."

*

Mr. I., a man in his early thirties, consulted me in what he described as "a despondent, suicidal mood."

"Here's my situation. For five years I have been assistant to the president of a big firm in a big industry. An important job, and I did well. The old goat liked me. Then one day he called me in and without leading up to it or softening the blow told me that I was through. After this brutal beginning he came out with his so-called facts: someone had told him that I'm a homosexual."

"Are you?" I inquired.

"Of course. But listen to this: the old goat didn't even check on the information he got. Just on the strength of a rumor, he fired me!"

"What was the real reason?"

"I suspect he must have heard the same kind of rumor about his beloved son, and he used me to get the anger out of his system."

"Was there any connection between you and the old man's son?"

"He works in the firm, too, and I know him. In fact, I was just about to make him—he was still a virgin."

"Did you consider it good policy to 'mix business with pleasure,' especially if that 'pleasure' hit so close to home?"

"I thought we lived in an enlightened century! Who would believe that in the age of Kinsey there were still people who hung on to this old-fashioned nonsense!"

"You seem to have a good many illusions: about Kinsey, about our era, about the disappearance of objections to homosexuality, and so on. Are you really so naive?"

"What do you mean, naive? Is it naive to believe in progress?"

"What kind of progress are you talking about? Progress in understanding that homosexuality is a disease, or 'progress' in accepting homosexuality as equal with heterosexuality? People are learning to understand that homosexuality is a neurotic disease, but homosexuality is no nearer than it ever was—and for good reason—to being put on a par with heterosexuality."

"So you're another old fogey, like my ex-boss!"

"What did he tell you?"

"That homosexuality is a goddam vice that can be cured by clean living; that homosexuals ought to be whipped, and all the rest of that."

"Did you deny his accusation in the first place? What proofs did he produce?"

"None. I was so outraged that I admitted I was a homosexual."

"Why did you?"

"My sense of justice rebelled!"

"That's a new way of proving your masochism without admitting it. What was your real reason for confessing?"

"How should I know? I'm fighting for full equality for homosexuals."

"You are deluding yourself. You are fighting for the inalienable right to damage yourself."

"Oh, go jump in the lake!"

"That friendly suggestion wouldn't solve your problem. Seriously, do you think you could have appeased your ex-boss by explaining that his recipes—clean living, whipping, and so on—are out of date, and that psychiatric treatment can change homosexuality? Would he take you back if you went into treatment?"

"Maybe. But I wouldn't give the old goat the satisfaction of asking!"

"Do you want your job back?"

"Of course. In fact, I *have* to get it back; the chances are he won't give me a decent recommendation, and I know what he'll answer if I apply somewhere else and they ask him about my work. And I know employers ask."

"I don't quite understand your excitement. What happened to you threatens every homosexual in our biased society. If you want to be a hero and a fighter, you have to take risks and be prepared to lose. Of course, not every homosexual conducts his daily business of living along such fantastically masochistic lines. Why did you confess? Why did you try to 'make' the son of your employer?"

"I'm just an honest guy, I guess."

"You are just an overgrown masochist, I guess."

"I'm really in a bad fix."

"There's no disagreement on that point. By the way, how did you come to me?"

"I discussed your shitty book with a friend. He saw things the same way you do: he told me to go back to the old goat, show him the book, beg forgiveness, and promise to go into treatment."

"There's one hitch. Analysis cannot change a homosexual who does not have the inner wish to change. The anal compliment you just paid my book, and your whole self-righteous attitude, aren't very promising indications. Or do you disagree?"

"Now you are making trouble, too! Why should I give up homosexuality?"

"Nobody is asking you to. If you just want an excuse that will enable you to get your job back, that bubble will collapse after four to six weeks of trial treatment."

"You mean, whoever would treat me wouldn't cooperate?"

"Cooperate in what? In continuing to treat a patient who

doesn't want to change, and who is just using analysis as a decoy? Of course not!"

"What the hell, you mean I should *really* change?"

"I doubt whether you are ready for that."

"Your book is full of the unconscious stuff, and here you are forgetting about it. How do you know that unconsciously I don't want to change?"

"Nobody can know that without a trial treatment."

"There you are. Trial treatment means four to six weeks, you said. What makes you think that whoever treats me (I say that because I doubt if the old goat would be willing to pay your prices—and, so help me, he's going to pay for this) will be able to get started right away? Some of your patients had to wait three or four months; you said so in your book, and I can show the old man those passages. That gives us at least four—maybe five—months. Do you know the story of the white elephant?"

"I do, but I don't want to spoil your effect. Tell it again."

"Well, an Indian maharajah promises a hundred thousand pounds to anyone who can teach his white elephant English. There is only one hitch: if he tries and fails, off comes his head. No volunteers show up until finally an old wise man takes the job. All his friends come to condole with him. 'Why be so sad?' he asks them. 'I told the maharajah it would take ten years. In ten years, many things can happen: I can die, the maharajah can die, the elephant can die, and—who knows—perhaps the white elephant can learn English!"

"If you were as adept in avoiding masochistic trouble as you are in getting out of the noose after it is around your neck, you would be better off. You are an amusing, cynical, and probably slightly or not so slightly psychopathic fellow, and I think we can help you get your job back—temporarily. But you cannot cheat on analysis. In treatment you will be up against something smarter than you are . . ."

"You mean a psychiatrist?"

"No. I mean your own pattern of self-damage."

*

When I first saw Mr. J., a man of thirty-five, he was flaming with fury and indignation. "You damaged me!" he accused without preamble.

"I don't remember ever having met you. Or have we met before?"

"No. You damaged me by appearing on television. You were interviewed about this criminal book you wrote on homosexuality, where you said that homosexuality can be cured."

"And the possibility of cure damaged you?"

"Definitely. I spent a good deal of time and money in psychiatric treatment in Chicago—three years of time. Thirty-six months of working to adjust myself to my condition. And finally I did, and I've lived on that basis for the last five years. Now you come along and say that homosexuality can be cured. It isn't fair!"

"Why does this disturb you so much? Why not disregard what I say altogether?"

"Why should I? You are quite convincing."

"Then why do you call my book 'criminal'?"

"Because it damages so many people—the analytic ex-patients who could have been cured, but were only 'adjusted.'"

"Are you against medical progress?"

"No, of course not."

"But according to your reasoning the discovery of penicillin 'damaged' any surviving Civil War veteran who lost a leg, because of infection, almost a century ago. After all, if the 'criminal' inventors had only hurried, the amputation could have been avoided."

"That's tricky, but you still know what I mean!"

"Look: I don't know you from Adam; I am not responsible for the slow progress of our science; though I sympathize with your predicament, I am not in any way responsible for it."

"That's easy to say."

"Those are all facts . . . Do you wish to change?"

"Are we going to start all over again? We were damaged . . ."

"What is this 'we?' Who appointed you spokesman for all the other 'adjusted' or 'unadjusted'?"

"Well, there must be countless others."

"Let them speak for themselves. Do you want to talk about continuing your analysis, or shall we talk about your injustice-collecting approach in this interview?"

"I really feel lousy."

"But don't you see that inner guilt is prompting you to voice your nonsensical accusations? If you were as fully 'adjusted' as you claim to be, you wouldn't pay any attention to what I said, or what I conceivably could say in the future."

"Why this guilt?"

"Because it pertains to your flourishing masochism, a sample of which you have just displayed here."

"What a situation!"

"Not so unusual as you seem to think. My book describes cases in which people were unsuccessfully treated by three therapists before they came to me."

"Thanks, not for me!"

"By the way, since you are riding the high horse of humanitarianism and indignation, have you thought of all the misery that would be alleviated if the technique that I use for treating homosexuals were to become standard? Do you think these people would cry out, as you do, 'We are damaged!'—if they were cured?"

"Why should I care about other people?"

"Then why do you speak as if you were representing countless others?"

"You are just trying to confuse me!"

"Another question: Would you have entered analysis, eight years ago, if your analyst had known, then, that homosexuality can be cured? Did you want to change at all, or only to eliminate the trimmings?"

"I don't know."

"Here is the answer to your excitement: As long as you believed that 'nothing can be done for homosexuals' your guilt could be kept at least partially under control. As soon as that defense collapsed, your guilt increased. Instead of understanding what is going on—and you should, since you've been in analysis—you shift the responsibility, and storm into my office to launch your accusation. Think this over, and some day in the future go back into analysis with an analyst of your own choice. But don't pick an 'adaptor' or 'adjuster' again."

*

Mr. K. was a mild-mannered man of about forty who refused to give his name or state his occupation. His reticence matched his apologetic opening remarks: "I am not at all sure," he said, "that I didn't ask for this appointment under false colors. I am not a patient, or a prospective patient. All I want is information, and if you agree, some discussion."

"On what topic?"

"Homosexuality."

"Go ahead."

"I am familiar with the literature on the subject; I am a homosexual myself. I have read your publications and books on homosexuality. My friends are all terribly indignant with you, but I don't agree: everyone is entitled to his opinion."

"One moment, please. You are not talking about an a priori 'opinion,' but about clinical deductions based on actual cases."

"I accept that. I listened to my friends shouting and ranting against you, and while I listened took stock of myself and of them. You are right on one point, anyway: all our lives are permeated with masochistic self-damage."

"You are lucky that your friends can't hear you say this. You would be considered a traitor to the cause."

A thin smile appeared on Mr. K.'s face; it could have expressed either irony or contempt.

"You may not believe it, but my methodical mind doesn't search for self-confirmation, but for facts. There is no law forcing anyone to tell his friends what he has found out," Mr. K. said.

"A private investigation, with the result sealed, to be opened only after death?"

"Something like that . . . Well. As I said, I established to my own satisfaction the fact that self-damaging tendencies are present to an enormous degree in myself and the other homosexuals I know. Then I had a startling and uncomfortable thought. So far, you had proved to be right: wasn't that an argument in favor of your other conclusions, too? I am inclined to believe that, but one thing has to be cleared up. Do you, or do you not, underestimate the external difficulties that face the homosexual? May I have your opinion?"

"I don't underestimate them. In some circles in large cities the external obstacles hardly count these days. In the theatre and the movies, in interior decoration, in some scholarly and literary circles, the homosexual does not encounter prejudice; quite the contrary. Still, the amount of neuroticism among people in these circles has not diminished. I believe that homosexuality carries with it its own seed of conflict. More often than not external circumstances are misused, becoming an added stimulant; danger is alluring to some personalities."

"You believe, then, that external legal and social impediments, and prejudice in general, do not explain anything?"

"Correct. Take this as an example: Homosexuals, by and large, are unable to produce anything better than a shortlived imitation of a bad marriage. What explains the promiscuity predominant among them? Living with one partner for a long period would eliminate a good many of the external dangers homosexuals face, and yet such partnerships are rare. The real obstacles to contentment for homosexuals are internal, not external."

"I'm sure you are familiar with the arguments pointing to the acceptability of homosexuality in past civilizations."

"Yes. The star argument is based on scanty reports of mores in specific regional sectors of ancient Greece. I say 'scanty' deliberately, because we have to take Plato's reliability, for example, entirely on faith. Even as far as Plato goes, some suspicions arise. If one regards Socrates' *Apologia,* as described by Plato, one gathers the impression that the popular rejection of homosexuality actually underlay the general animus against the old philosopher. This whole business of 'corrupting the youth,' one of the basic arguments in the trial, is suspect. Don't forget that 'euphemism' is a word created by the Greeks. Do you recall the sentence in Plutarch's *Lives*: 'The ancient Athenians used to cover up the ugliness of things with auspicious and kindly words. Thus, they called harlots 'companions,' taxes 'contributions,' and a prison a 'chamber.' "

"However," I went on, "it is very likely that in times of social disintegration, as in the hundred years preceding the collapse of the Roman empire, homosexuality was more 'fashionable' than in the periods of empire-building."

"What about the argument that the whole Judeo-Christian rejection of homosexuality is based on the historical fact that the Jewish tribes, surrounded by barbarians practicing polytheism and homosexuality, had to defend themselves psychologically by establishing strong taboos against homosexuality—taboos that actually aimed at preventing backsliding into polytheism?"

"An interesting and unprovable pseudo-historical assumption that makes no particular point when used as an argument for the present situation."

"You definitely believe that happiness and homosexuality are incompatible?"

"I do. Take your own observations as the key; they led you to the conclusion that your own life and the lives of your friends are permeated with *internal* self-damage."

"Don't homosexuals want love and affection?"

"Officially, yes. Unofficially, no. Basically, they act out the unconscious situation: cruel mother mistreats the innocent baby. Some of them prefer the *active* role of mother; some the *passive* role of baby. Internal masochism and external contentment cannot go hand in hand."

"I have to make still another admission, and confirm another of your statements. It is true that there are more conflicts in the best homosexual relationship than in the worst heterosexual one."

"If you go on making these admissions, you will find yourself acknowledging that homosexuality is your lost cause," I remarked. "In the meantime, how do you manage, in the face of your disillusionments?"

Once more that thin smile appeared on Mr. K.'s face.

"I found a solution a couple of years ago: I retired into homosexual fantasy. Now my lovers are always kind and considerate; they never make trouble."

"That is the strongest argument against homosexuality—the strongest indictment of it—I have ever heard. If a form of sexual activity cannot be lived out in reality, but can only be executed through masturbation and fantasy, that form of sex is just unusable!"

"It's good enough for me."

"This I doubt. Why did you consult me? Do you really believe your rationalization—that you came here merely for a 'discussion'?"

"What else?"

"Guilt because of your 'solution.' You probably wanted

approval of some kind for your—you hoped—harmless outlet."

"Why should I feel guilty?"

"Because your fantasy of improved homosexuality, stripped of conflict, is just a defense against more deeply repressed masochistic tendencies."

"In other words, you think you will see me on your couch one of these days?"

"What I said was that your rarefied technique of making unusable homosexuality into a usable instrument of sexual contentment cannot work."

"Why not?"

"Look at the parallel in heterosexuality: would you say that the *chronic* adult masturbationist, who avoids women, is a healthy specimen?"

"Who cares about labels?"

"True. But does the system work? No, it doesn't, because of inner guilt."

"But that guilt is purely conventional."

"Not at all. The guilt pertains to repressed fantasies of a masochistic nature and is only secondarily fastened to convention."

3

Those Who Want to Change and Those Who Don't

MR. A. WAS INTRODUCED in Chapter One; he consulted me only because he was willing "to do his silly parents a favor," and—thinking that his mere appearance in my office meant that he had carried out his share of the bargain—wanted to leave after speaking his first sentence. Chapter Two introduced ten other homosexuals—all of them dejected, unhappy, desperately asking for help. What distinguishes Mr. A. from these others?

Judging only from externals, one would be tempted to say that guilt makes the difference; that guilt does not appear at all in Mr. A. ("I am happy," he said with certainty), but is present as a strongly propelling force in the "unhappy" homosexuals.

Descriptively, this is correct, but the external impression casts no light on the real problem. For the guilt so pronounced in the ten homosexuals described in Chapter Two, and apparently invisible in Mr. A., never belongs *genetically* to homosexuality. Homosexuality, so to speak, is the official name of the "firm"; the real "owner" is psychic masochism. Homosexuals' guilt-feelings are not directly connected with their homosexuality. Even the average, not-too-cynical young person, and certainly any member of the "cool" and "beat" generation, can easily convince himself that rejection of homosexuality by "squares" and philistines is outdated nonsense. "Why should I feel guilty?" he asks.

But if the guilt in homosexuality always belongs to the underlying masochistic scourge and is only secondarily shifted to homosexuality, how can we account for such "happy" neurotics as Mr. A.? Can there be people who, without guilt, violate the most stringent rule of the unconscious, the rule forbidding the pleasures of psychic masochism?

No, such people do not exist. If they appear to exist, it is merely because the investigator failed to follow the externally visible clue—repeated self-damage—to its source, a hidden deposition of guilt.

Let us attempt to scrutinize Mr. A., although we know practically nothing about him. He issued only official communiques in our interview, and refused to give any real information about himself.

His formula was brief and simple: "I am happy and like my way of life." How did it fit the following facts?

First, it was clear that he fully intended to take every possible advantage of his parents' wealth. He did not want to give up the luxuries available as long as he lived at home, and he knew that these luxuries would be secured to him for years, at the nominal cost of fulfilling some minimum college requirements. He considered his parents' notions "silly" and antiquated, and had no illusions about their reaction to a discovery of his "modern" homosexuality. Why, then, did he conduct his telephone conversations with his homosexual boy friends from his own home? Even without the help of an extension, his parents could easily have overheard enough of these talks to make the situation clear. His parents had told me that their suspicions were first aroused when they overheard the boy shouting into the telephone in his room. They assumed that he was being blackmailed, and listened in to subsequent calls so that they could protect him against the supposed blackmailer.

They had no idea, at this time, that their son could be a

homosexual. Gradually, as the facts became more blatant, they had to admit the truth to themselves and to each other. They were by no means, therefore, the "sneaks" their enraged son called them. Their misplaced protectiveness was so sincere that they made tape recordings of these conversations, "to trap the blackmailer."

Second, A. admitted—though only indirectly—to a long succession of boy friends. Promiscuity, therefore, prevailed. If, as A. claimed, homosexuality brought him so much happiness, why the inability to settle on *one* love object?

Third, A. dismissed as "lovers' spats" his running battle of injustice collecting with his boy friends—a battle so violently fought that his parents mistook the separate engagements for threats by extortionists. Could this, too, be accepted as proof of unbroken happiness?

Fourth, A.'s provocative behavior towards me could have been mistaken, by the uninitiated, as an outburst to be expected from a normal person caught in an embarrassing situation. The normal reaction, quite to the contrary, would have been one of "safety first." A. could very well have listened to what I said with equanimity, mentally pronounced it the "nonsense" he thought it was, and left with a polite "Thank you for the information. I will think it over." Instead, he did his best to provoke me, and in his last question begged openly for humiliation. He knew that a psychiatrist does not have moralistic notions about illness. He had read an explicit statement to this effect, but had conveniently repressed his knowledge. This is a typical method of slipping into place behind the eight-ball—which is the vantage point unconsciously sought by all psychic masochists.

*

The popular notion that guilt betrays itself in cries of "mea culpa" and in tearing of the hair is very far from the clinical facts. Most guilt is silent, consciously nearly unperceived and when perceived, unrecognized as guilt. The real betrayer of silent, unconscious guilt is not self-accusation but self-damage.

When, rarely, silent unconscious guilt announces itself to consciousness, it is always fastened to "the wrong reason." This merciful shift has the purpose of saving the victim additional pain. If a heterosexual psychic masochist, for example, accuses himself guiltily of aggression against his poor wife, and blames himself for making her unhappy, his eloquent reproaches still contain a built-in safeguard. They leave intact his self-portrait, in which he appears as the complete he-man, and securely close the door on the intolerable sight of himself as he is, a masochistic weakling.

This "double attachment of guilt" plays a decisive role in the lives of all psychic masochists. Here is a typical example from the analysis of a successful business man in his early forties. He was a cynical and supercilious individual, a heterosexual who had come into treatment because of compulsive infidelity.

During one appointment, he told me: "Yesterday I had intercourse with my wife. During the foreplay I touched her breast. At that moment I remembered, to my surprise, an episode years ago with a French girl. This girl was rather unsatisfactory, but she had beautiful large breasts. She had no objection to my fondling her breasts, but she insisted that the movements be from below upwards, not the other way around. Her reason was some peculiar notion that downward movements could make her breasts pendulous. I saw at once that the memory was an aggression against my wife—why should I think of another girl while I was sexually engaged with my wife?—but this interpretation did me no good; my guilt persisted."

"Before blaming the interpretation," I said, "let's check on whether or not it was correct."

"You check me. I'm paying you for this job."

"Correction, please, as Charlie Chan would say. You are paying for my time, and for the application of my specialized knowledge. Some cooperation on your part is necessary."

"O. K. I'm listening."

"That's nice. To get down to brass tacks: You misunderstood both your interpretation and the hitching post you provided for your guilt. If my memory serves me correctly, one of the reasons your wife insisted on your entering analysis was what she called your way of making 'tactless remarks in public' concerning her breasts. Another reason, she said, was your 'pathological jealousy.' According to her, your main topic of conversation in company was the 'big tits' of other women, from which you would proceed to not-so-veiled allusions to her own comparatively small breasts. Do I remember correctly?"

"Yes. But you also know that these harmless jokes and allusions to breasts would never have pushed me into analysis. I came into treatment because of the guilt I felt in connection with what I've learned to designate as 'compulsive infidelity.' Every time I went on a business trip, I had to have a prostitute sent up to my hotel room—even when I was tired, even when I wasn't in the mood."

"I am familiar with the fact that your official and your real reasons for entering treatment are not identical. This has nothing to do with another fact: your 'breast allusions'—a thoroughly euphemistic way of referring to the tactless remarks you would make in public—were real enough and had a psychological meaning."

"So what?"

"Well, every time you praised the large bosom of another woman, you were indirectly complaining that your wife was unjust to you because she did not satisfy your alleged wish for your much-prized 'twenty-pounders.' "

"Where is the connection with the French girl?"

"She was an injustice-provider, too; wasn't she more concerned with the future shape of her breasts than with your present pleasure?"

"And what do you conclude from all this?"

"The thought of the French girl did not enter your head yesterday as a means of playing one woman off against another but for the purpose of lumping all women together as disappointers. There's no difference between a girl whose breasts are too small to suit you and another one whose breasts are large but who puts an embargo on them. Both are disappointing."

"And my guilt?"

"Your real guilt pertains exclusively to your masochistic elaboration of your infantile conflict. Only secondarily—and fraudulently—is it attached to the lesser intrapsychic crime of pseudo-aggression."

"Why the double attachment?"

"To make life easier."

"How?"

"The masochistic passivity included in your wish to be refused

—what you ironically called the Schmo in you—strikes a false and contradictory note in your concept of yourself as a he-man. The pseudo-aggression does not."

"How can you prove it was fake and not real aggression when I thought of the French girl during intercourse with my wife? Wasn't I playing one woman off against the other?"

"If that had really been your purpose, you would have chosen another example. Didn't you say that the French girl was 'rather unsatisfactory'?"

"That's true. She had wires of some kind instead of pubic hairs. I had to give her up because intercourse did hurt."

"There you are."

"I'm still confused by this maze of possible interpretations. One time it's aggression, another time it's something else. I need a simple, handy formula to fit all occasions."

"I've told you again and again that in your case every interpretation which does not start with psychic masochism is wrong. This basic solution of your early infantile conflict is warded off in different ways—there are few inner wishes, and innumerable defenses. To simplify your interpretations still further, you can exclude 'real' aggression from your list of possible choices. 'Real' aggression is never used as a defense against masochism. Such a defense always consists of spurious or *pseudo*-aggression—'fake aggression,' to you. For instance: When, during intercourse with your wife, you find yourself weighing the reality against the recollection of a satisfactory sex experience with another girl, you are using pseudo-aggression. On the other hand, when you think of an unsatisfactory girl during intercourse with your wife, you are using another weapon from your armory of pseudo-aggressive defenses in order to ward off the identical masochistic conflict. You are saying: 'I'm not masochistic; it's just that all women are disappointing, refusing, and bitchy.' "

"How does all this fit into the interpretations of jealousy and compulsive infidelity?"

"It fits very well. Your ridiculous jealousy—ridiculous because it's indiscriminate and groundless; didn't you recently accuse your wife of having an affair with the mechanic at the garage because she had to wait fifteen minutes for a repair job to be finished before she could get the car?—has as its basis the fantasy of being deprived. The defense here is 'I want exclusive possession.' And your compulsive infidelity while on business trips is based on two pseudo-aggressive defenses as well. The first of these is the fantasy that sex equals the forbidden. The second is this: by having affairs on your trips, even when you are near exhaustion and not in the mood, you are simply proving that your bogey is passivity. You even take genuine physical weariness as a proof of passivity, and you have to counteract this by playing the he-man in sex."

"All these interpretations are too time-consuming. I can't use them."

"How long did it take you to get the thought of the French girl?"

"A split second."

"If you 'digest' the interpretation, it will take you no longer to apply it."

What this patient aptly named "double attachment" of guilt corresponds to the clinically observable fact that neurotics fight their inner battles on foreign territory. Just as an invading army's attempt to devastate the enemy's country concentrates military activity within the victim's boundaries and leaves the invader's land unscathed, the neurotic's choice of this spurious front serves as a defensive device. When the inner torturer, unconscious conscience, accuses the neurotic of masochistic passivity, the accused defends himself by admitting to pseudo-aggression. The ensuing "battle of alibis" is then fought out on foreign territory; the "homeland," psychic masochism, remains outside the sector of attack and persists untouched.

This tactic was clearly perceptible in the patient's inner argument. "All women are disappointing," he claimed; "I am not even demonstrating pseudo-aggression by playing one woman off against another, but am merely stating a fact."

*

The fact that the patient in this example was heterosexual has no significance; what is important is that he was a psychic masochist. Since all homosexuals are psychic masochists, plus, their tactic of defending themselves against inner guilt follows the general rule for masochistic neurotics.

Those homosexuals who cannot live without their pseudo-aggressive alibi—an alibi displayed in their view of themselves as "fighters," "despisers," "flouters" of established and accepted custom—*have "no intention of changing over" to heterosexuality.* And yet these pseudo-happy homosexuals are the most precariously balanced, the most frightened of them all; deprived of their fear-propelled alibi, they are like fish out of water.

The allegedly happy homosexual is not ready for treatment; this does not mean that he is not in need of it. His guilt is deposited in the never-ending, always painful crises produced by homosexuality. These crises are both internal and external. As long as the individual neurotic succeeds in striking an inner ("trade") balance between his unconscious guilt and his self-created and unabsorbed external difficulties, there will be no detectable "surplus" of guilt; therapy can only work with this detectable surplus. Consequently, these people shun the psychiatrist, and announce themselves members of the nonexistent tribe of "happy homosexuals." The analyst, if nobody else, sees that they are merely making a virtue out of an inner inability.

Among the homosexuals who do consult psychiatrists, some display therapeutically usable, others unusable guilt. Guilt is invariably present in homosexuals, whether or not they are aware of it, and proclaim it loudly. Unhappily, the differentiation between usable and unusable guilt cannot be made in a few preliminary interviews. A trial treatment of four to six weeks is indispensable. During this period it is possible to test the patient against six key questions:

1. Can his inner guilt be detached from its spurious point of deposition and "mobilized" for analytic-therapeutic purposes?

2. What is the patient's reaction when, in treatment, he is constantly confronted with his psychic masochism?

3. What is the purely quantitative state of self-damage, as revealed in the patient's past history? (Reticence and shame invariably delay the full story.)

4. Is the patient's ego more or less stable, or fully psychopathic?

5. Was his wish to change a mere fluke, or is there some stability behind it?

6. What external facts, in full detail, are responsible for propelling the patient into the desire to change?

The answers can be clearly indicated, if not fully outlined, during the trial period. It is then possible to tell the patient "yes" or "no." If the case is favorable, he will be advised to continue treatment. The chances of cure for a favorable case are, statistically, 90 per cent. If, for reasons which the psychiatrist will fully explain, the impression created by the patient is unfavorable, he will be told that he can continue treatment at his own risk, or leave.*

* It is amusing to observe how easy it is to misinterpret, or distort, an honest statement. In my book, HOMOSEXUALITY: DISEASE OR WAY OF LIFE? I stated that by the middle of 1956 I had cured one hundred homosexuals, adding, "Thirty other analyses were interrupted either by myself or the patient's leaving" (p. 188). Statistics were promptly deduced from this statement; they were based on the figure 100:30. The vital detail overlooked here was the fact that these figures constituted an aggregate of nearly three decades of experimental work in a field that was once, and is still to a large extent, terra incognita. The experiences of the last few years have enabled me to improve the technique of treatment, and to establish the stringent criteria essential for determining the suitability for treatment of the individual patient. Today it is comparatively rare for a case, judged "favorable," to prove a dud. It is only in the world of cartoons that psychiatrists attempt to play the omniscient and all-knowing.

4

Excerpts From Five Successfully Treated Cases

THE TITLE of this chapter is an exact statement of its contents. The five case histories* to be recounted will not be fictionalized** or pruned into neat climaxes; neither will they be exhaustive, tape-recorder reproductions of every halting step taken towards affective understanding. Of necessity, they will have to be accounts of high points standing out from a long and often dreary period of hammering away at details.

Most people are familiar, at least as far as the words are concerned, with the fact that analysis begins with exploration and then settles into the stage of "working through" in transference*** and resistance.**** What these words mean to them is another

* The cases are chosen to show the great variety of clinical pictures encountered in homosexuality.

** Only names and recognizable circumstances have been veiled, to assure anonymity and protect the patients and their families.

*** Analytic transference denotes unconscious repetition of bygone conflicts, with the chance figure of the physician substituting for a personage out of the infantile past.

**** Resistance designates the static element in the unconscious, the element adverse to alteration of "the neurotic balance."

matter. Regardless of these phrases, it is safe to say that the majority of people think of "cures" through analysis as resulting from a sudden burst of insight, aided and abetted by the analyst, that in the flash of a moment shoves the patient out of darkness of neurosis into the clear bright day of normality. Unfortunately, the form into which these histories of cases must necessarily be cast tends to strengthen this impression. It would be futile to attempt to reproduce the day-by-day progress of an analysis. No reader could have the fortitude to follow the painstaking search for infinitesimal details; nobody, without urgent personal involvement, could maintain his interest through thousands of words describing the difficult process of unearthing and working through the material that confirms the analytic diagnosis. A word-by-word report of one dream interpretation, for example, or one session of free associations, would constitute an entire chapter of a standard book. And it would be an unreadable chapter: Molly Bloom's soliloquy, in *Ulysses,* is a literary tour de force and not a sample of what the analyst hears in his consulting room.

This apologia is not included for the sake of breaking to the reader, gently, the news that these case histories will be less effective, as "slices of life," than chapters in a novel. It has a more serious intention. Understandably, the reader is not automatically on the side of the analyst; as a vicarious participant in these analytic sessions, he often cannot help feeling a reluctant sympathy when the patient is proved wrong, a hesitant wish to champion him when he proffers a plausible rationalization, a puzzled resentment when the analyst (as he often seems to be doing in these resumes) serenely and with assurance mows down his "opposition" and again proves that he "knows best." The fact that the "opposition" is not the patient but the neurosis does not affect the reader's reaction.

There is no way of fighting these misconceptions, except to remind the reader beforehand that in dealing with the unconscious one is handling a high explosive. Despite the reader's distance from the scene, he is not a truly detached spectator. He is swayed, not only by his possible involvement in the situation being depicted, but also by traces and remnants of his childhood rebellion against any authority. And to the patient, the analyst, representing as he does stern reality, mirrors authority. Often people state their reaction accurately as "The analyst is probably right, but I hate the way he chooses to show it." The inability to see the analyst, any analyst, as a sympathetic figure rests on a foundation of unconscious reasons, and therefore cannot be dispelled by logic alone.

Often, too, people complain of the analyst's apparent "hardness" and obliviousness to his patient's unhappiness. These people overlook a vital point: the patient's conscious misery is no more and no less real than the unconscious pleasure he is getting out of his unhappy external situation. The analyst's business is to fight against the patient's desperate desire to be left undisturbedly in possession of the unconscious bargains and defenses that make this inner pleasure possible. If the analyst were to permit himself to be distracted from this purpose by the patient's conscious suffering, he would be aiding and abetting the neurosis, not working to destroy it.

The necessary conciseness of these accounts explains, too, why many of the analyst's remarks sound apodictic, dictatorial, unkind. In a genuine analytic session, this impression would not arise. The tone of voice which cannot be reproduced, would prevent it, to begin with. Then, the remarks which here are recorded as statements would in reality begin as hypotheses, introduce a long search (to which both parties contribute) for confirming or non-confirming material, and finally be repeated as proven facts (or dropped as untenable). These intermediary stages, like the intermediary stages which prove or disprove the analyst's original opinion of the patient's problem, must here be omitted.

Another misconception may also arise from these shortened accounts. Irony and sarcasm are not predominant weapons in analysis; interpretations, even when the patient's resistance must be fought, are both friendly and detached. But often there comes a point when the analyst can with profit to the patient enlist irony in his aid as a weapon against an entrenched neurotic trait. This step invites the patient to identify himself with the analyst's sarcasm, and himself join in the battle against his own unconscious. Often, too, an interpretation that has remained no more than a theory for weeks on end does finally penetrate when presented to the patient in a cutting way.

Mr. L. — "Intellectually I know that I'm a homosexual, but emotionally I refuse to acknowledge it."

Mr. L. was twenty-four and contentedly waiting to inherit a fortune of fifty million dollars when he first came to my office.

"According to your book on homosexuality, I am a homosexual," he said. "But I don't consider myself one."

"If that's the only trouble, why not throw the book away? Who cares about other people's definitions?"

"It isn't so simple. You half-convinced me that I am a homosexual."

"But you must have had your suspicions before reading that damaging book?"

"Sometimes I did, when I was bothered by homosexual fantasies. But I never try to uncover the facts behind my doubts. Let's put it this way: intellectually, I know that I'm a homosexual, but emotionally I refuse to acknowledge it."

"Very convenient."

"I know I'm being irrational."

"What did the book clarify for you?"

"That homosexuality is homosexuality, whether it's executed in reality or fantasy."

"And before you read the book, how did you manage to convince yourself of the contrary?"

"I suppose you'd call my reasoning a rationalization. I explained it this way: I had never had actual bodily contact with a homosexual. Then, I detest the typical and pronounced homosexual. And I believed that I had not yet outgrown my puberal fantasies."

"What type do you prefer in fantasy?"

"A boy between nine and twelve, with a beautiful body, on a beach, naked or in tight trunks. He has to have his hair in a crew cut. He also has to have beautiful feet. With high arches."

"Does the fantasy stop at this point?"

"No. Mutual play with the organs follows."

"And why do you want to change?"

"One can fool oneself for only a limited time. I detest homosexuality. I dread the consequences. Besides, our family is a dynasty in its way, and I have to marry."

"Does your family know anything about your real inclinations?"

"Of course not. My parents would die of shame. Especially my father—who is something of a tyrant."

"There is no reason for them to know. If your inner rejection of homosexuality is as strong as your intellectual objection, this may all be no more than a disagreeable recollection in a few months."

"But my fantasies—with and without masturbation—are, I could say, compelling!"

"That's totally immaterial. The only important question is whether you *unconsciously* want to change."

"I cannot testify to that."

"You were not asked to. Only a trial treatment of a few weeks can answer that question. By the way, have you ever had sexual contact with girls?"

"The way you mean it: no."

We arranged for appointments, to begin in a few months. Reality factors made the delay necessary; the young man was scheduled for a long business trip (he was being groomed to succeed his father as head of the "dynastic" firm) and I did not have appointments available at the moment.

As he was leaving, Mr. L. made an unexpected remark: "Please don't tell my father why I'm really here."

"But why should I see your father in the first place? I told you that there would be only one justification for approaching your father with a merciful white lie: if you could not finance your treatment. You told me, then, that your father gives you more money than you need. We agreed that your family should be spared all depressing information. Why come back to a settled point, and talk as if we had not even mentioned it?"

"I just assumed you would like to get some information about my childhood from my father."

"How could I see your father without your consent? No, that's not a likely explanation. Isn't it more probable that you are casting me in the role of the enemy who plots against you behind your back? And that you want—unconsciously and masochistically—all the trouble you can squeeze out of the situation?"

The young man had nothing to say, but his face showed how he took his first analytic interpretation: with surprise, embarrassment, and sheepishness.

When he came into treatment, some months later, he received —as do all my patients—a brief explanation of the ABC of analysis. He listened quietly, bored a good deal of the time, but occasionally piqued into interjecting a question pertaining to himself. Obviously he "wanted to get into the act" as quickly as possible. I asked him:

"Are you always so intolerant to information imparted, or are you taking this introduction as a sermon? Who preaches to you at home?"

The patient laughed. "Both my parents are given to long discourses."

"Do you know the story of the man who sits in a train, screwing up his face in disgust every few seconds and at the same time making derogatory movements with his hand? The passenger sitting opposite finally asks, 'What are you doing?' The man answers: 'I'm bored and so I'm telling myself jokes. But I've heard them all before.'—Do you think I'm giving you this information to amuse myself?"

"I beg your pardon."

"Your good manners, which I grant you, are not under scrutiny. Your defenses are."

"What's defensive about being impatient?"

"You are *outwardly* impatient with me because of my—you think—long-winded introduction. But what makes you think this *inwardly* constitutes just impatience?"

"What else?"

"Didn't you say that both your parents are given to 'long discourses'? Didn't you also call your father a 'tyrant'? Didn't you also suspect me of intending to see your father behind your back? Doesn't your 'impatient' attitude during your first two appointments show that you think I'm wasting your valuable time, meaning robbing you of your hard-earned money, meaning injuring you?"

"What are you driving at?"

"A duality of factors. First: your tendency to maintain the fiction that your elders make trouble for you, do you dirt, or at least annoy you. Since you're lumping me in with the others, or—if you prefer—had from the very beginning unconsciously tagged me as a provider of nuisances or damage, you cannot (and this introduces the second factor) accept something useful or favorable from me, even if it is only useful information, without getting jittery. Or, as you put it, 'impatient.' The two attitudes are contradictory; you prefer the former."

"Do you mean that to accept useful information presupposes a favorable state of mind?"

"At school, didn't you observe that you learned more from the teachers you liked than from those you didn't like?"

"Yes, of course. But I don't dislike you."

"You misunderstand. I spoke of your having, unconsciously, tagged or typed me. How else do you explain your suspicion that I intended to conspire with your father, behind your back, against you?"

"Let's close this discussion with the mutually agreed-upon observation that I suspect the possibility of a malicious motive even when someone is nice to me. Let's add that this suspicion will have to be analyzed later."

"You are learning the analytic escape-technique fast. O. K. Let's put your suspicions in the psychic icebox to be examined later. In the meantime, please give me a personality sketch of your parents. Tell me how you see them, now, as an adult, and how you used to see them as a child."

Mr. L. suddenly seemed to have a bad taste in his mouth. He was not enthusiastic about either parent in any time-division: past, present, future. His father, when not on one of his innumerable business trips, had been a shouting and tyrannical presence in the house; his mother had always played the *grande dame*. In childhood he had seen little of his mother; she had left him in the hands of a series of "disagreeable governesses." His mother counted for little in his adult life. She was still the *grande dame*, still full of "silly prejudices," and lately a hypochondriac. Hypochondria was beginning to engulf his father as well.

"Tell me more about the disagreeable governesses," I said.

"I remember one in particular. She was a good-looking, high-breasted girl, but sour and unappreciative. Once in my bath—I couldn't have been more than four—I proudly showed her my sex organ. She scolded me severely, and made a disgusted face. She was always impatient with me; she didn't like me and made no bones about it."

"So nobody really appreciated you, and you had to love yourself?"

"Strange that you say that. I am, people tell me, goodlooking. I never thought so myself."

"What was wrong with your hair and feet?"

"First tell me: what gives you that idea?"

"I suspect that the boy of your fantasies is a radiant and improved edition of yourself, before puberty. Didn't you specifically stress the haircut and the beautiful, 'high-arched' feet?"

"I never thought of that! You mean I'm Narcissus admiring himself?"

"Exactly. But not simply Narcissus, an improved edition of Narcissus. Now tell me what you didn't like about your hair and feet."

"The deduction floors me . . . Well, I had flat feet and for years I had to wear high shoes that made me conspicuous, I thought, and certainly ridiculous. And the hair? It was too wavy and there was too much of it, and I was forced to display it."

"Wouldn't you say that you masochistically gave up, very early, the hope of being loved by others? Isn't the reasoning, 'Nobody loves me, therefore I must love myself,' rather defeatist?"

"Yes, of course—if you are right, and the boy in my fantasies is really an improved edition of myself."

"Can you, offhand, suggest another model?"

"No, I can't. But that doesn't prove anything."

"Correct. Do you still remember, from your school days, what a 'working hypothesis' is? Instead of constantly saying 'X' or 'We don't know,' one substitutes a temporary theory to work on. It can always be discarded as soon as the original tentative assumption is proved wrong, or can be supplanted by another assumption that seems more promising."

"I understand your caution, but having read your book I suspect that you don't make use of even a 'working hypothesis' without good reason."

"At the present moment, the Narcissus theory seems the most promising."

Some days later, the patient brought the Narcissus theory up again; it had been preying on his mind:

"You said that I had a defeatist attitude—'Nobody loves me'—that practically amounts to a form of masochistic abdication. Since then I've been thinking about something that happened to me two years ago, in Rome. A young boy, absolutely *not* my type, followed me; I was on my way to my hotel. After a few blocks he came up and spoke to me, promising me the usual 'good time.' I said no; the boy actually disgusted me. I went on, and then I turned back and asked him what made him a male prostitute. Then I noticed that there were two suspicious-looking men; they were watching me very closely. I concluded that these two unsavory-looking characters were blackmailers, and that the boy was the bait they used for trapping wealthy Americans. I was frightened; I got an immediate picture of a scare headline: WEALTHY AMERICAN ARRESTED! I went back to the hotel, fast. I told you, and this is important, that the boy was absolutely *not* my type; he disgusted me. Still, this scene comes up time and again in my masturbation fantasies. Why?"

"Can you provide the obvious answer yourself?"

"No, I cannot. I have some inklings, but I can't even formulate what I mean."

"But look at the connection in which you brought it up. You spoke first of 'masochistic abdication,' admittedly quoting me. Isn't the cue in the word 'masochistic'? Obviously, what attracts you in the scene you evoke so frequently is not the sexual connotation. You said emphatically that the boy rather disgusted you, and that he was definitely not your type. Conclusion: under the disguise of a sexual scene, you live out a masochistic fantasy. You are attracted to the situation of danger, as represented by the two 'unsavory characters.' "

"I don't know whether this is the reason or not. At least, it makes a stab at clarifying something I couldn't explain at all. Is this another 'working hypothesis'?"

"No. It's an interpretation. Nothing tentative about it."

"Are you sure?"

"I am."

"How can you prove it?"

"By asking you to give me more material. I am certain that additional memories will produce a good many clear-cut masochistic incidents."

"You mean real happenings, or fantasies?"

"Both."

"I don't believe so."

"Neither of us is in the prediction business. Let's wait."

The confirmation came quickly. A few days later, the patient remembered a "crazy incident" that took place when he was thirteen. He found a hypodermic syringe in his mother's room. Fascinated by the instrument, he began to use it—on himself. First he merely simulated injections; then, having found a spot on his side that was comparatively insensitive to the point of the needle, he half-filled the syringe with alcohol, and pierced his skin. This recollection brought back a still earlier one. At the age of twelve, during a vacation trip to the Orient, a man invited him to "go for a walk." He refused and ran to his mother. His mother informed the hotel employees, who held the man until the police arrived. The police beat him severely before taking him into custody. For weeks, the boy had relived, again and again, what he imagined the man had felt during his beating.

A third recollection then emerged, haltingly: he had some vague memory of a puberal fantasy in which he was alone with a man on an island; the man would "torture him."

"Now do you believe my interpretation of the incident in Rome?"

"Half-and-half."

"As soon as you inwardly digest the fact that homosexuality has a masochistic basis, originally projected upon woman and later—in a frantic flight—shifted to man, you will not be a homosexual any more. If you want to express masochistic torture-fantasies, why not do it directly? Why hide behind homosexuality?"

"But I don't want to be a masochist either!"

"Nobody is asking you to be. First, we have to separate the deeper masochistic tension from the more superficial homosexual one."

"And where did my masochistic tension come from?"

"It started so early in life that we can only reconstruct it. Even though you were only four at the time, your famous scene with the governess was undoubtedly a later edition of the original, but buried, basis."

"What scene? What are you talking about?"

"Isn't it strange that I should remember your own material better than you do? I am alluding to your penis-exhibitionism, in the bath, before your governess, that 'good-looking, high-breasted, but sour and unappreciative girl.' I hope you recognize your own words. The governess who scolded you severely and made a disgusted face when you proudly showed her your organ. Do I remember correctly, or am I confusing you with another patient?"

Blushing and rather embarrassed, the patient admitted: "You remember correctly. I don't see, though, what you want to prove."

"What I want to prove presupposes some knowledge of theory. To explain it, I need both your indulgence and your permission to 'waste your valuable time.' Promise not to be too impatient?"

A small smile brightened Mr. L.'s serious face, and he motioned me to go ahead.

"You see," I began, "this scene with the governess is only one of many repressed incidents in your childhood. Perhaps it was the culmination and the turning point in what could be called 'exhibitionistic reparation.' That calls for a somewhat long explanation. Everybody hears about the boy's 'penis pride,' but few people know that this is a rather late development, coming after a feeling that to the adult seems fantastic. What comes first is *breast envy*. It doesn't matter whether the infant boy was breast-fed or bottle-fed; in either case he envies the giantess of his nursery because she possesses a mysterious organ—big, long, and capable of producing fluid. Then comes the tragedy of weaning, one of the last tombstones of infantile megalomania. Weaning proves to the boy that he is dependent on someone else; it shows, finally, that he was wrong in his theory that this 'someone' is a part of himself, or a slave obedient to his magical power. The child's way out is *reparation*. He discovers that his own body possesses an organ that he reasons can substitute for the envied breast. It is big, long, and it produces fluid. He does not see all the objective differences between his mother's breast, or the bottle, and his own penis. Anatomical, physiological, histological, functional, chemical differences are of no importance to him. All he cares about is that he has discovered a 'substitute,' and it belongs to him. In fact, he finds that his 'penis-breast' has superior qualities. It produces pleasurable feelings when he manipulates it. Only one detail seems unsatisfactory: its size. Though he knows that the organ is capable of expanding at certain times—even babies have erections—he never seems to be sure that the mysterious expansion will be repeated; his penis exhibitionism proves this. All male children go through a period of penis exhibitionism, shocking their elders by their 'indecency.' Their purpose is not so much direct exhibitionism as some kind of confirmation; they want to prove 'how big' the organ is, as projected upon the size of the breast.

"Now admittedly, this sounds fantastic, when simply stated as a deduction. Let me give you two examples of the material from which this deduction has been drawn.

"In one of my earliest publications, in 1932, I described a case of pseudo-mental debility, where the following scene was recalled. The boy was thrown out of school when he was in the first grade because he masturbated in the presence of the whole class. He was then sent to a country school, where he boarded in a house run by the head mistress of the school. This probably meant that he received some special consideration. When he was six and a half, he watched a gypsy woman nursing her baby. That gave him the idea for a game: he took a long straw, put one end into his penis, and the other into his mouth. He then drank his own urine. Forget the disgusting element for a moment, and think only of the meaning of the game. Obviously, it is an attempt at autarchy, a declaration of independence from the mother.

"In my book, THE SUPEREGO,* I described—among other cases—a recollection that came to the fore in the analysis of a French photographer. He was three and a half, and at the beach with his mother. He came out of their cabin naked; his mother scolded him and told him to cover himself. He obeyed—by draping a towel around his neck.

"There are two sides to the story of the boy's frantic penis exhibitionism. He exhibits to confirm his contention that he couldn't have been deprived of the breast (in weaning), because

* Grune & Stratton, New York, 1952.

he possesses just such a 'breast' on his own body. The other side of the story is the cultural necessity of inhibiting this exhibitionism, a necessity imposed by his mother or her representatives. Both parties involved feel fully justified, although of course their justifications have different motives.

"This leads to one of the real tragedies of childhood. The scoldings, the faces showing disgust or even horror, with which the mother reacts to the exhibitions, at best interfere with the boy's attempt at compensatory (and illusionary) reparation, and sometimes keep him from using the mechanism at all.

"There are a series of possible results. To name but three: One type—a classification of future neurotics—acquires and keeps the 'complex of the small penis.' These people are constantly concerned with the size of their penis, complicating the matter by taking an unusable standard for their yardstick. This standard is the non-erect organ. Since the size of the non-erect penis is no indication of its size in erection, their self-torturing inspections and comparisons are valueless. Besides, the usable length of the vagina in intercourse is two and a half to three inches. The average erect penis is larger than that, which makes everything above three inches a 'luxury.'

"Another type, the normally developing boy, weathers all criticism of his exhibitionism, and solves his problem by mentally reversing the roles played by his mother and himself. As a baby, he had been passively fed by the 'long organ'; now he sees his 'long organ' as the means through which he can become the active feeder. Later, in intercourse, he will push a 'duplicate' of the 'long organ' into the vagina, which he will unconsciously identify with his own baby-mouth. At the same time, he will unconsciously identify sperm with milk. This 'active repetition of a passively endured experience' enables him to rescue his narcissism and re-establish his shaky self-esteem. No wonder the average man calls his wife 'baby!'

"The third solution is that of the homosexual. I have called his solution the pursuit of 'the reduplication of his own defense mechanism.' Although he has found in his own penis a substitute for the disappointing breast—the vanishing breast, if you like—he is so unsure of his trick that he constantly requires to be reassured that 'it works.' His partner's possession of a penis confirms his belief that 'nothing is lost—yet.' Ironically, the penis he so eagerly seeks in his partner is only a substitute for the breast that he so often finds 'disgusting' in real women.

"There is another facet to the boy's penis exhibitionism. He is also using it as a defense against his mother's prohibition of peeping. When his passive wish to peep is thwarted, it changes into its opposite, following an unconscious law, and becomes defiant and active exhibitionism. The formula is something like this: 'Who wants to look at your ugly udder, anyway? I have a beautiful breast-penis myself!' Don't forget that you specifically mentioned that the governess was 'high-breasted.'

"Now you will ask: What does all this have to do with you? Only this: in view of its undoubted precursors, the scene with the governess acquires additional importance."

For the first time, Mr. L. interrupted: "You agree, then, that her objectively rejecting attitude did damage me?"

"I would not say that. I have seen cases in which the boy's penis exhibitionism was checked in the friendliest way, and severe aftereffects developed; I have seen other cases in which the parents interfered brutally and there were no deleterious effects. It all boils down to the child himself: how does he accept the unavoidable? This is what accounts for my suspicion that children who 'cannot take' the constant unavoidable offenses to their megalomania are sure candidates for psychic masochism. Don't forget that the psychic masochist rescues some vestiges of megalomania under self-damaging conditions. By unconsciously provoking the kick, he gives himself the unconscious satisfaction of being able to say: 'This fool thinks he's kicking me, but actually I, through my initial provocation, *made* him kick me!' "

"And what determines the ability to 'take it?' "

"Probably the biologically conditioned amount of megalomania, which is different for every child."

"A very disquieting conclusion."

"Did you ever hear the French saying, 'The most beautiful Parisienne cannot give more than she has'? That's the present state of my knowledge. Ask me again in a few hundred years."

The topic of compensatory penis exhibitionism occupied us through many subsequent appointments. I pointed out additional facts: The patient had casually mentioned, once, that certain sandals worn by men and especially by boys at the beach had some sexual attraction for him. What he really meant was that these sandals attracted him by prominently displaying the big toe, which he symbolically saw as a penis equivalent. The flat feet from which he had suffered in childhood came into the attraction also. His flat feet had made the symbolism personally inapplicable, since they left him "nothing to brag about." It was not by chance that he had endowed his improved self-portrait—the boy of his fantasies—with "beautiful, high-arched feet."

At this point the patient—still with perfect politeness—revealed the strength of his unconscious resistance by making an openly defiant, rejecting remark. "You have finally achieved a result: I am totally confused."

"Why do you blame me for the complexity of the psychic apparatus? If you just want to be angry, enjoy yourself—but you should know that you are again playing the masochistic injustice-collecting game in the transference (meaning, using innocent outsiders for the repetition of infantile conflicts), and assigning to me the part of torturer and to yourself that of innocent victim. If it's not that you want to indulge your anger, perhaps you have stumbled on one of the famous 'contradictions' that every patient discovers in the course of his analysis. Let's see whether what you call your confusion (why not say disbelief and suspicion?) can be straightened out."

"I really have lost the thread; I don't understand. On the one hand you claim that I created my improved Narcissus-type in order to be loved and love. On the other hand, as the Roman blackmail episode shows, you claim that I derive my real pleasure from my masochistic enjoyment of danger. Which is which?"

"There is a contradiction between your two types of homosexual fantasies, but it is a contradiction you implanted yourself, and it is spurious. Every homosexual declares that he wants 'love.' Yet he conducts his love affairs in such a manner that masochism comes out on top."

"As simple as that?"

"What do you call 'simple'? The fact that the human mind is capable of piling one defense on top of another in what seems to be an endless tower has occupied the attention of thousands of analysts, all over the world, for the past sixty years. Is this what you call 'simple'?"

"I didn't mean to be offensive."

"You are invited to be as skeptical as you wish—provided you also cast a skeptical eye on your own skepticism. By the way, this is a good opening for attacking your hyper-suspicion. At your suggestion, we once put this in the psychic icebox. Let's take it out of the deep freeze."

"Why? So that you can have another argument against me?"

"Do you really believe that the purpose of this analysis is to attack you? Isn't your statement another grab at masochistic enjoyment, this time by way of falsifying facts?"

"O. K. You have the floor."

"My deduction is short and—you will like this—simple. By being hyper-suspicious, by being unable to distinguish between friend and enemy, you constantly put yourself behind the eight-ball, and make yourself into an innocent victim, unjustly attacked. Don't you see that by imputing to everyone, everywhere, under all circumstances, sinister designs, you are still fighting your unfinished infantile battle of suspecting all your educators of underhanded tricks?"

"Are you suggesting that I ought to be naive? Wealthy people have to be suspicious."

"Yes. But they don't have to issue a blanket indictment against all of humanity. Is naivete the only alternative? Why not discriminate?"

"Why should anyone do anything for me without expecting a return?"

"Human kindness does exist, or, if you prefer, some people are sometimes not interested in damaging others. Neurotic malice exists, too, of course, but it is—neurotic."

"The distinction is slim."

"I don't think so. Take your own attitude as an example. Every time I try to fix your attention on some new facet of your problem—'new' meaning an aspect not yet discussed here—you behave as though an attack had been launched against you personally. Do you think this attitude justified?"

"Do you claim you are contributing to my happiness?"

"Definitely yes, if you take the long-range viewpoint."

"I see that I'm in for a new disclosure."

"My condolences to your dying neurosis. Why you should defend that beast is less logical. Well, this is what I want to bring up: Remember the episode of the syringe you found in your mother's room?"

"What about it?"

"Do you also remember how you used it?"

"Of course."

"Would you agree that you must have had some masochistic-sadistic fantasies about the sex act at that time?"

"I don't see that."

"Why did you fill the symbolic syringe with a fluid, and apply it—in spite of the pain—passively *against* yourself? Why didn't you experiment on, say, a cat or a dog, playing the *active* part yourself?"

"I don't know."

"Both possibilities did exist."

"That's true. I never thought of that."

"What would you conclude from this selectivity?"

"Do you want me to say 'feminine identification'?"

"I want you to think, not to play the parrot with half-digested phrases. No, it wasn't feminine identification at all. That was your mother's syringe you found; therefore you were acting as her representative. Your game meant: 'Mother inflicts pain—and that's sex.' Is it surprising that you should run away from that 'torturing monster'?"

There was no answer.

"And do you also remember a fantasy you had in puberty, of yourself imprisoned on an island and tortured by some man?"

"Yes."

"There you have another part of the riddle that troubled you to the point of 'confusion.' In your flight from the 'monster,' woman, you run away to man, at first maintaining your masochistic torture fantasies. Then, as defense, you create the romantic boy-Narcissus fantasy."

"Let me think this over."

A few days later, Mr. L. said, in a matter-of-fact way: "Your theory is that every time I have a homosexual fantasy, I really mean a masochistic one."

"Correct."

"Since I have two types of homosexual fantasy, the romantic and the more obviously masochistic, can I pick any one I wish?"

"I doubt that. Which you choose probably depends on the state of your inner fear of the masochistic danger. I would guess that the romantic fantasy is the stronger alibi."

"A perfect alibi?"

"A very imperfect alibi. You still, alibi or not, run away from both dangers, woman and man; you still work on the reparation level; you still cling to the defeatist conclusion, 'nobody loves me.' I have always doubted the theory that the 'narcissistic type' in homosexuality simply expresses high-pitched narcissism. It seems to me that the narcissistic type begins as a terribly beaten-down and masochistic child who, in his despair, secondarily rescues himself by retreating to the only refuge he knows, his narcissism. In other words, narcissism is not the propelling factor, but a defensive island of safety, to which the child goes when everything else has failed."

"Once more, nothing to be proud of."

"Let's face it: undigested fears and narcissistic reparations are not exactly heroic. By the way, your romantic fantasy of the boy on the beach contans two 'reparation payments' worth mentioning, aside from the elements already discussed. One of these is the crewcut. This is not just a protest against your own curly and superabundant hair, as you assumed. It is also an attempt to repair and overcome the tragic—to the child—fact that he has no genital hair. It is possible, too, that some Samson-Delilah fantasies are involved, in an acceptance of castration executed by a woman. Second, you prefer the boy in your fantasy to be naked on a beach, or wearing very little. In other words, the boy exhibits defiantly; you tried to exhibit and were slapped down. Again, an attempt at reparation."

"What is real about it all? What isn't fake?"

"If you call reparative defenses fake, nothing is real."

"What am I so afraid of?"

"Of woman's power to damage—meaning, of woman as the executive organ of your own innermost wishes."

"How can you prove that I'm afraid of women?"

"Well, you are not exactly a woman chaser, are you? And what about the cave dreams you have had repeatedly in the last few weeks? They are all uncanny, all full of danger. I told you—although we haven't yet uncovered any recollections to back this up—that most likely castration fantasies are involved: if woman herself is castrated, she may revenge herself by castrating man."

These dreams, finally, gave the patient what he had been looking for since the beginning of analysis: a partial and pseudo-justification for his resistance to the analytic process. No recollections of vaginal inspections in childhood emerged, nor was much material on peeping elicited. He harped on these "missing links" incessantly, until I told him:

"According to Freud, recollections and reconstructions have the identical dynamic effect. Of course we prefer recollections, if only because they are less vulnerable to attack by unbelievers in analysis. Why don't you substitute reality for the reconstruction?"

"Meaning?"

"Look for the girl."

"So early in the game?"

"Five and a half months of analysis are not 'too early.' "

After some time, Mr. L. began an affair with a young girl who professed to love him. He made it clear that marriage was not his intention; she claimed that she was not interested in marriage either. Mr. L. was potent with her, though he declared himself irritated by her "stupidity." After we had worked out his "irritation on principle," which proved to cover fear, he admitted that he was enjoying his sexual experiences, and the affair itself. I then reminded him of his bitter question: "Do you claim that you are contributing to my happiness?" His only reply was a laugh. To the patient's great surprise, even his homosexual fantasies disappeared.

* * *

Mr. M., the man who believed that his trouble was not his homosexuality, but his wife's discovery of it.

Mr. M., aged thirty-four and the owner of an engineering firm, had this to say:

"I am desperate, I need help desperately. Please help me!"

"What's your problem?"

"I've been married for five years. I have two beautiful children and a wife who puts up with a great deal of nonsense . . ."

"Consisting of?"

"My homosexuality. I have always been one. When I met my wife I was elated; I never thought a woman could arouse me. I was potent, and everything went well."

"Were you in love with her, or did you marry her for an alibi?"

Mr. M. gave me a suspicious look, and said, slowly: "You know how it is. I really believed that my troubles would be over as soon as I got married."

"And what happened?"

"Not long afterwards, my potency collapsed. It wasn't sudden, but I gradually got less interested, there was less incentive, I had more homosexual fantasies. I started to slip back. And I had been so sure I was cured!"

"Marriage cannot cure homosexuality."

"I found that out the hard way."

"Did your wife know anything about your homosexual past?"

"Of course not."

"But does she know now?"

"That's the whole trouble."

"If I understand you correctly, your trouble isn't your homosexuality, but your wife's knowledge of it."

"Do you know that Rimbaud said, 'Morality is weakness of the brain'?"

"I also know that Rimbaud was a homosexual himself, and that Verlaine nearly killed him because of homosexual jealousy. He lived the life of a tramp, adventurer and recluse on three continents, ending up as an African trader, and dying at thirty-seven of the results of syphilis. He was an important symbolic poet, but he did all his work between his eleventh and nineteenth years. After that, he was probably psychotic. I doubt whether he carries much weight as an authority on morals."

"Oh, boy, did I put my foot in it! Cross Rimbaud from the record!"

"Do you often 'put your foot in it' when you open your mouth? Is this how your wife found out about your homosexuality?"

Mr. M. gave me a second suspicious glance, this time indistinguishable from a dirty look, and asked: "Did Mrs. M. telephone to you?"

"I have never heard from her."

"Then how in hell do you know?"

"I know one thing for sure: you are, and you have said you are, a homosexual. And in my book every homosexual is a psychic masochist to the nth degree. I have seen too many allegedly bisexual husbands confessing the painful truth to their wives to be unprepared for this irrational step."

"Why should a fool of a husband confess?"

"Psychic masochism includes the tendency to play for ever-increasing stakes in the game of making trouble for oneself. How can a bisexual make sure that his marriage will make trouble for him? By confessing. That's exactly what so many of them do. It's not always a direct confession. More often they unconsciously set the stage for the big scene by arousing their wives' suspicion. Potency troubles are one way. Another way is 'forgetting' to destroy incriminating letters, or engaging in indiscreet telephone calls when they supposedly don't know their wives are listening, or letting themselves be discovered in a questionable situation with another man. Then the wife starts her inquisition, and finds the suspect very willing—unconsciously, of course—to confess. How was it in your case?"

Mr. M., in subdued tones, told his sorry tale: he had been homosexually involved with a man who turned out to be an extortionist. He confided in his lawyer, hoping that legal advice would help him to reach a "compromise" with the extortionist. His lawyer telephoned to him to discuss the case, and he spoke unguardedly, knowing that his wife was not at home. But his wife returned while he was on the telephone (allegedly, he heard nothing) and listened to some revealing remarks. Afterwards, she "made a terrible stink," pleading with him to tell her "only the truth" and promising that "everything, whatever it is, will be forgotten."

"Of course she didn't keep her promise?" I asked.

" 'Of course' is right. All hell is loose, and I don't have a moment's peace. When she isn't hysterical she is overbearing. 'You dirty pansy' is all I hear."

"Did you really believe she would forget it?"

"So help me, I did. In retrospect I call myself a naive idiot, but there it is."

"Who gave you the idea of consulting me?"

"Is this important?"

"Of course it is. It's one thing if your wife read a review of my book and forced you to telephone to me, and quite another if you yourself want to change."

"I still don't believe that my wife didn't call you."

"Sorry. She didn't. I take it I guessed correctly, and she sent you here?"

"If it's really a guess, it's a good one."

"Do *you* want to change?"

"To be honest, I don't know. One thing is clear: the fix I'm in now is intolerable. I have a choice between being a slave to a bitchy wife, or getting a divorce. Of course she says 'Over my dead body' to any mention of divorce, and then threatens to do the divorcing herself and make it really dirty. I couldn't afford that. On the other hand, why should I pay a premium for her bitchiness by becoming a good, lovey-dovey husband, and giving up all my homosexual fun?"

"The trouble is that analysis can help you only if you *inwardly* want to change. Analysis on order doesn't work."

"Don't give me up so easily. When you figured out how I got here, you made one mistake. The lady didn't just read a review. She bought your book. She forced it down my throat. Now, I think you're dead wrong about homosexuals, but this business about self-damaging tendencies did impress me. It made me ask myself why I really confessed, and why I got mixed up with an extortionist in the first place. My conclusion was that you may have something there."

"In other words, you want to eliminate your self-damage, but not your homosexuality. Cannot be done, because homosexuality thrives on self-damage."

"Would you accept me as a patient under these conditions?"

"At your risk, without promising you anything, and for a trial treatment—yes."

Rather elated at having bought for so modest a price an interval of domestic peace, Mr. M. prepared to leave. A thought occurred to him, and he said in a sardonic manner: "You know, we forgot to take another possibility into consideration."

"What was that?"

"Perhaps I really may change because of the treatment. Then I could get rid of my bitchy wife, and marry a nice one. That would be something!"

"Your idea of getting revenge on your wife is something to look into. Don't you think you did her an injustice to begin with, by marrying her for the sake of an alibi?"

A shrug of the shoulders, and a resigned "What the hell" was the answer.

*

Mr. M.'s analysis began unfavorably. He did not want to change; he was in analysis to make the best of an impossible domestic situation. It is true that what he had read of masochism in my book had "impressed" and frightened him; what he hoped analysis would do was help him outsmart his wife, who had forced him into treatment, by freeing him from the tendency to self-damage. As for the connection between psychic masochism and homosexuality, he frankly stated that he "did not believe one word of it." A streak of megalomania also colored his attitude towards the analysis: he had "put one over on me," he thought, by persuading me to take him on as a patient even though he did not meet the standards set forth for treatment in my book.

Mr. M.'s satisfaction over his two alleged triumphs—over his wife, potentially, and over me, simply by becoming my patient—was intriguing. He took each triumph, before the event, as a *fait accompli,* sweeping aside the obvious uncertainty that he would be cured of psychic masochism so that he could tell himself he was outsmarting his wife, and conveniently forgetting that I had agreed only to take him on for a trial treatment of several weeks. What he could not know was that I had formed the impression, though without putting it into words, that he was more nearly ready to give up his homosexuality than he realized.

Three months intervened before I had time to begin his trial treatment. This interval was all Mr. M. had hoped for. His wife continued to reproach him as "a dirty pansy," but he had a perfect, unanswerable rejoinder: "Go on like this and I'll drop the analysis." She would not go on.

The first three appointments were taken up by an exposition of the aims of analysis. Mr. M. listened very carefully, as a lawyer listens to an opposing attorney's argument. I asked him, at one point, "Why are you listening so carefully? Is this the way you register information, or are you gathering material for a rebuttal?"

"Why, doctor, you have a dirty—or at least suspicious—mind!"

"You shouldn't be talking about 'a suspicious mind.' No less than three times, in our first appointment, you gave me that famous suspicious-dirty look that meant 'Aha, you've been plotting with my wife!' Three times, you accused me of conspiring with her. True or fantasy?"

"I'm still not convinced that you didn't."

"I'm going to tell you something that—I hope—will convince you. We analysts don't lie to our patients in general, and specifically not about family contacts. The reason is not devotion to truth, but experience: we have learned that we cannot trust anyone. Suppose, in spite of my denial, I actually had gone behind your back and talked to your wife. What assurance would I have that her neurosis would not prompt her to tell you about it?"

"I'm glad to hear that you consider her a neurotic."

"She married you, didn't she? Why didn't her 'instinct' warn her about what she was getting into?"

"Not too flattering, doctor. Thanks for nothing."

"Well, as a husband—department, emotions—you aren't exactly a success."

"Let's skip it."

Once the introduction was complete, I asked Mr. M. for a short history of his nursery past. He was prepared for "analytic indiscretions" and answered promptly:

"Nothing, but nothing, in my uneventful childhood pointed in the direction of my future troubles. Father: a shy though friendly, quiet man, a postal inspector in a small, upstate New York town. He spent most of his free time in the basement of our mortgaged house, playing with his inventions—all very minor. His idea of a great inventor wasn't Edison, but the man who got the idea of the square clothespin. None of his experiments ever came to anything."

"Did your mother object?"

"She was pleasant enough. No, she was condescending with

a sort of ironic kindness. She was the one who wore the pants; she decided everything."

"I asked you whether she objected to your father's hobby."

"Before I answer, I would like to know why you are stressing the point."

"This is the fourth example of your hyper-suspicion . . . There are no hidden strings attached to the question. Your father was a tinkerer, and obviously an amateur. You became a mechanical engineer, a professional. Superficially, it seems as though you identified with your father, and then outdid him. On the other hand, your mother treated him with ironic condescension. That didn't give you a very imposing ideal to look up to and identify with. I suspect, therefore, that behind this pseudo-identification with your father lies a more deeply repressed aggression of some kind, directed against your mother. If she had objected to your father's hobby—a game that consumed time and money and brought no results—then your identification with your father's only interest would appear in a different light. It would mean rebellion against your mother. Satisfied?"

"Is this the way you construct theories?"

"If that's irony, I don't see the point. Yes, that's the way tentative assumptions are built up in analysis. I know from other cases that homosexuality means unsolved, unconscious conflict with the image of the mother. I know that you are a homosexual and therefore—unless you are the exception never before encountered—you must have harbored that very conflict. On the other hand, you apparently identified with your stepped-on father. Why should you find it strange for me to be following this trend of thought, and trying to link the known material with what is still unknown? Please note that I did not give you an interpretation; all I did was ask for specific information. Please answer the question."

"It seems my fate to confirm your hunches and guesses. O. K. You win. Mother did object, and I mean forcefully. From time to time she would go into hysterics about it: he never spent any time with his family, she would tell him in no uncertain terms, he spent every available cent on tools, raw material, and so on. That isn't all. I did well in high school; I was captain of the football team and in general what they call these days 'big wheel on campus.' Full of confidence, I told her I wanted to study mechanical engineering. She threw up her hands in desperation, and said, 'I hope you don't become like your father!' Now I'll ask your favorite question: Satisfied?"

"In a minor way, yes. Aren't *you* pleased when you've made a correct guess?"

"And when will I score by satisfying you in a major way?"

"When you are cured."

"I asked for that one. Skip it."

"One of these days we will take up your frequent use of that phrase, 'skip it.' In the meantime, tell me this: Didn't you arouse talk, in high school and college, because you didn't have girl friends?"

"Who told you that I didn't?"

"If my memory serves me correctly, in our preliminary interview you told me of your reaction when you met your wife: 'I was so elated that I could be aroused by a woman,' you said. Is it far-fetched to assume that this was a new experience for you? Or do you suspect that I am in contact with some of the girls you disappointed in high school?"

"Can't overdo it. Aren't you a suspicious person yourself?"

"Of course—when it makes sense to be. But not because distrust is a principle, as it seems to be with you. What about your constant suspicions here?"

"First prove that you are being open and above-board with me."

"I certainly am. Since you are the accuser, it's up to you to present the indictment."

"Look, I'm no dope. The fact is that after I told you that I'm not sure whether I'm interested in changing my homosexuality, you should have sent me away. That statement meant that I don't come up to the standards you yourself set up for treating homosexuality. You printed them in your book. Instead, you took me as a patient. Could it be the money, I asked myself, but I couldn't be satisfied with that answer after you told me I would have to wait two or three months before you could give me any time. If not money, what was it? I told you that I was impressed with your pet idea of 'unconscious self-damage.' Could that have flattered you enough to make you break your rule? I excluded that possibility, too; you must be bored to death talking about psychic masochism. How am I doing?"

"Very well, so far. Let's hear the sinister aim you finally uncovered."

"I came to the conclusion that you are an inveterate experimenter—or is it 'experimentalist'? After all, your whole idea of curing homosexuals, when your esteemed colleagues offered nothing but a shrug of the shoulders, was just an experiment—an experiment that came off successfully, if you are telling the truth. I simply asked myself: What does this son of a gun hope to find in me? First I couldn't figure that one out. I reread your book again, this time looking for a single clue—a case like mine. I found it, in an unexpected place. In describing the case of a Lesbian—amusingly enough, your heading reads 'Example of an unchangeable case'—who did not want to change her homosexuality, you wrote that characterologically she *did* change. Here was your challenge, your opportunity for experimentation! And this was a long time ago; the date you put on it in the book is 1942. Since then you must have been tempted to try it again with your 'vastly improved experience' (your phrase) to help. This makes it clear that you are not playing fair with me. Consequently, my suspicions are justified."

"I am going to divide my answer into two parts: your suspicions in general, and your specific suspicion of specific motive in taking you on as a patient. The first part of the answer is easy. You mixed up your chronology. You gave me the three dirty-suspicious looks *before* we discussed whether or not I would take you on as a patient. Is this correct?"

"Well, perhaps."

"Therefore the statement that you are pathologically suspicious stands."

"Now let's see how you manage to squirm out of the main indictment."

"You misinterpreted the case history that gave you your 'clue.' If you reread the passages, again, you will discover that I considered this Lesbian a therapeutic failure, and said so in so many words. Her characterological changes were minor; she always came back with 'injustices.' You also stressed the fact that it has been more than sixteen years since that analysis. Today, I would not have continued her analysis beyond a certain point. When I became sure that she really did *not* want to change, I would have ended it. As these things are done today, she would not have survived the trial period.

"There is another item that you knew, but conveniently forgot about. You asked me: 'Would you accept me as a patient under these conditions?' I answered: 'At your risk, without promising you anything, and for a trial treatment—yes.' You see, your whole deduction collapses because it is based on the erroneous assumption that I accepted you as a patient for prolonged treatment. I did not. You are here on probation, for four to six weeks. After that, we'll see."

"You haven't said anything about your interest in experimentation," said Mr. M., waving the only flag he had left.

"There is nothing to experiment with in a situation that has already been clarified. It is impossible, therapeutically speaking, to isolate an individual's masochism and leave his homosexuality intact. Masochism itself is the basis of homosexuality. I have already told you this. If that isolation were possible, many otherwise inaccessible homosexuals would welcome therapy. They would want to have the self-damage removed and the homosexuality left untouched. Freud had something to say on this point, though in another connection; he was speaking of the patient's preferences and selectivity in regard to the symptoms he wants to change in treatment. Freud said that although a man can father a child, even the strongest man would falter if he were given the task of producing only the right arm of a child."

"There must be a trick to this, somewhere."

"Of course, a trick! The irony of the situation lies somewhere else: you have not figured out my real motive."

"Here it comes!"

"Certainly, but you should have figured it out, and you didn't. That's not a criticism of your intelligence, but evidence of your neurotic pessimism."

"I'm curious."

"If one has as many dealings with homosexuals as I do in this office, one acquires something like a finger-tip knowledge of them. This 'feel' tells you intuitively how to judge the individual homosexual's real psychic situation. This extra tentacle, if you will let me call it that, told me that you are inwardly much more ready to change than you consciously know, and consciously declare."

"Don't kid me!"

"Facts. I took a chance on you to test my intuition, not to experiment. Why didn't that positive possibility occur to you? My answer: you were stopped by your neurotic pessimism."

"I'll be damned!"

"I can prove the point from another angle. Didn't you tell me that your father was always conducting experiments that never came off? Isn't it possible that you inwardly identify experimentation with failure? This makes your theory that I accepted you as a patient in order to experiment on you into a pessimistic prognosis a priori. You will have to grant that some experiments are successful."

The patient fell into a gloomy silence, and maintained it for the few minutes that remained before his appointment ended. His expression, typical of patients when a cherished theory collapses and something intervenes to cut the disappointing discussion short, was that of a fighter saved by the bell.

Mr. M. arrived for his next appointment in a "brilliant mood," and announced that I had given him "a new lease on life."

"Your enthusiasm seems fishy to me. Who told you that all intuitive ideas are correct? Sometimes they are, sometimes they are not."

"The old technique again. Back I go into the slough of despond!"

"*Old* technique? Whose old technique? What are you repeating in the transference?"

"It was my mother's technique, of course. She played cat and mouse with me, too, first getting me all puffed up with pride, then smashing me down!"

"How did she do that?"

"Whenever she gave me something with her right hand, she took it away with her left."

"For instance?"

"When I was five she bought me a new suit, and I was very proud of myself. Immediately she pounced, and told me that conceited boys, especially in new clothes, are disgusting. Then, in high school, when they made me captain of the football team, she started out by saying she was proud of me, and then gave me a lecture on how physical accomplishments mean so much less than mental. These are just two examples; it went on all the time."

"Why did you take it so tragically? Many mothers go in for these educational afterthoughts, and many children take it in their stride. Isn't it more likely that you selectively retained and magnified the negative connotations?"

"Why do you want to absolve my mother?"

"Because reality is only raw material. What the child does with his individual reality is his, and exclusively his, business."

"That's convenient for mothers."

"Facts, again. Parents just don't have the power to create lifelong neurosis in their children."

"I still believe that my mother's dissatisfaction with my father colored her relationship to their only child."

"Shifting responsibility from the inside to the outside is typical for every neurotic. He wants to hold on to his 'basic fallacy.' "

"What's that?"

"The mistaken idea that someone else is responsible."

"Then what the hell is responsible?"

"An unfavorable elaboration of the neurotic's own unconscious ego."

"Yeah, I know. 'Reality is just raw material.' Don't say I'm making fun of you, because I am."

"You are entitled to some fun."

A short time later, the patient produced a piece of evidence that "really threw him." In his words:

"I remembered something—a painful incident—that confirmed what you said, and frightened me out of my wits. You caught me on the experimentation business; you said that for me experimentation equaled failure, in line with my mother's attitude to my father's inventions and experiments. A few years ago I had a partner, a real screwball, but a man with new ideas. He proposed that we develop a new kind of machine, at our own risk. I turned the idea down cold, and insisted that we break up the partnership. I have a horror of anything that isn't 'practical.' It turned out that I was dead wrong. My screwball ex-partner got a backer, started producing his machine, and sold his invention to one of the really big manufacturers for half a million bucks.

On top of it all, he's getting his money in ten yearly installments, which reduced the tax bite to the minimum. It occurred to me yesterday that I threw away a quarter of a million dollars because of a souvenir from childhood: 'Don't experiment.' Boy, oh boy!"

"You see, neurosis eats into business life, too."

"What do you mean, neurosis? Didn't my mother actually implant this precept in me by letting me witness her attitude towards my father?"

"And who asked you to accept this precept?"

"Aren't you underestimating a child's susceptibility?"

"And do you still believe that children are brought by the stork? Or in your case was it the doctor, in his black bag?"

"I am confused."

"I don't see why you should be. You accepted your mother's ideas about the futility of experimentation, not because she pronounced them, but because they fitted into your masochistic, pseudo-aggressive grievance against her. You saw in her, first, the frightening giantess, then the killjoy, and finally the excuse for avoiding risks, and therefore the chance of scoring a big success."

"But my partner's idea could have driven us into bankruptcy."

"Very possibly. But as I see it you didn't reject his idea on its merits or demerits, but on principle."

"That's true. The whole project was distasteful to me from the start."

"There you are."

"If you are right about all this, then masochism is really dangerous!"

"That's like the story of the young soldier in his first battle, up against a real enemy, with real bullets, for the first time. 'A guy can be killed here!' he exclaims. Is the effect of masochism news to you?"

A few days later, in another appointment, Mr. M. reverted to his ironic tone. "According to you," he said, "I spend all my energy putting my mother in the wrong. If that's true, how could I have built up a sizable and quite profitable business?"

"Showing that your mother was wrong was the defensive contribution made by your neurotic corner. But the healthy part of you also contributes to your life. If a neurotic were all neurosis, without undiseased sectors in his personality, he could not exist outside of Skid Row."

"Skip it!"

"Who used those words?"

This question set off a typical resistance situation: for a reason that could not be logically perceived or explained, the patient became furious. "Who the hell are you," he yelled, "to reduce me to a plagiarizing automaton? Why couldn't I have a few phrases of my own? Is this asking too much?"

"Who used those words?"

"Why do you insist that I'm a plagiarist?"

"Every time you hear something you consider disagreeable, you use that phrase."

"I am sick and tired of providing confirmations for your fancy guesses!"

"You forget that 'fancy guesses,' when backed up by confirming evidence, become—facts. And the more correct facts we unearth, the more probable your cure."

"O. K. Father used to use it when mother bawled him out."

"In other words, whenever you use that phrase you are identifying with the father reproached by the mother. Is this, or is this not, masochism?"

This discussion took place at the end of the fourth week of treatment. The patient came to his next appointment penitent and apologetic. "Before you say it, I will," he began. "I got into that rage and threw my fit just to provoke you. I must have known that this is the time—after four weeks—when you decide whether or not to discontinue treatment. Being a masochist, I want defeat, and therefore I provoked you."

"All correct, except for your phraseology. You did not provoke me, you only tried hard."

"You aren't angry?"

"Why should I be? To you, I am a movie screen on which you project past feelings, guilt, anger, masochistic provocation, and what not. That's transference. Personally, I don't come into this at all."

"You will not throw me out?"

"On the contrary, I was just about to say that I consider your prognosis excellent, and suggest that you continue."

"But so far we haven't said a word about homosexuality."

"You are quite mistaken. Every time we discussed your masochistic acts, we were talking about your homosexuality."

"How? When?"

"My experience shows that homosexuality means running away, in deadly fear, from the 'dangerous,' 'bad,' 'damaging' mother image. At the same time, the homosexual is masochistically attached to this same image. I use the term 'mother image' because a child's perception of his mother is not identical with her real attitude."

"I am absolutely amazed."

"Experience also proves that disassociating the masochistic tension, preceding the sexual tension, from the sexual tension proper, kills homosexuality."

"That's unbelievable."

"Wait and see. In the meantime, fill me in on your early sexual experiences."

"This time I am going to correct *you.* You should have said 'fantasies.' "

"I stand half-corrected—fantasies, for your information, are experiences, too."

"O. K. Sex always seemed to me to be something mysterious. I didn't believe the dirty stories I heard from other boys; I thought they were all lies. Of course I masturbated, with terrific guilt. In adolescence, I rescued myself by overdoing sports. I actually got to the top in football because I thought that exhausting myself would keep off the sexual devil. I avoided intimacies with girls, though I did go out with them a good deal. That meant petting, of course, and I played the hero about it, but I didn't get anything out of it, really, and that frightened me. I never put my somewhat dubious sex to a real test. Then, in my freshman year at college, I had my first homosexual experience. My roommate seduced me, if it's accurate to put it that way. What is true is that he worked me up to it by disparaging women. Obviously, that fitted into my fear of women very well. It's easier to disparage than to admit irrational fears. That seems to be standard homosexual technique, by the way. I was rather amused to read almost an identical—what can I call it, persuasion scene?

—in a recent novel, *The Immortal*, by Walter Ross.* I have it with me. The hero is an actor, representing the beat generation. He seems to have been modeled after a foolish, reckless fellow who killed himself racing his car. What interested me was the way the hero's first homosexual 'contact' broke him into homosexuality."

Mr. M. found the right page, and before reading from it, explained: "This is the seducer describing—to his psychiatrist, by the way—his first time he tried to put the idea of homosexuality into the hero's head." He then read aloud:

> "I was careful not to rush things," he (the seducer) said. "It was obvious that Johnny had not learned to feel about me, or about any man, as I felt about him. He was what we called a 'tenderfoot.' "
>
> "A what?" (The psychiatrist is speaking.)
>
> "A tenderfoot. It's an American expression that comes from the cowboys. It means someone new, someone who doesn't know the ropes," he said.
>
> "I understand," I said. "I shan't interrupt again."
>
> "Meanwhile, back at the apartment," he said, "I continued talking to Johnny, recognizing that the way to his heart was through his mind, first, and through his ambitions, second. The conversation took a more intimate turn when I asked him about his emotional life. He said he didn't know any girls in New York. I remarked that it should be easy for a handsome young man like himself to meet girls.
>
> " 'But I don't have any money to take them out,' he said.
>
> "I said that any girl worth her salt wouldn't care about such things. 'There are too few good-looking young men around with your interests and your sensitivity,' I said.
>
> "He said, 'Do you know any—I don't mean some dog—who would want to go out with someone who can't take them to dinner, or even to a movie?' he asked.
>
> "I smiled and said I wasn't speaking factually, only theoretically. 'Really,' I said, 'I suppose you're right. Girls are so materialistic. All they seem to want is a good provider to get

* Simon & Schuster, New York, 1958. The following quotation, and that on p. 153 *ff*, are reprinted with permission of the publisher.

married to. It's only with another man that you can have a disinterested relationship.'

"He hadn't said anything of the kind, of course. I was putting the thought in his mind by attributing it to him. But he accepted the idea as his own. It was probably the first important step in seducing him."

Mr. M. closed the book and said nothing. I asked: "And what sexual objects did you prefer after your 'seduction'?"

"Always boys in their late teens or early twenties. They always seduced me, meaning they sought me out."

"Why?"

"Today I suspect that it wasn't a matter of feminine passivity on my part, but just a need to shift responsibility."

"And what about your wife?"

"I met her at a time when this passivity—always being chased by stupid boys, and always for only one evening—was beginning to disgust me. My sex life was all one-night-stands: none of my boy friends wanted love or appreciation or anything but sexual release. My wife showed from the first that she was interested in me. She took the initiative in a gentle way, and that was new and exciting. Somehow, I wasn't afraid of her; she made me understand that I was wanted without danger."

"In short, in the beginning she was 'nice'?"

"Definitely."

"And yet you lost interest in her."

"Why did I?"

"Because she was nice."

"Nuts!"

"Look at what happened. When you confessed, you turned her into what you call 'a bitch,' though she is probably no more than an outraged girl whose illusions have collapsed."

"You mean, I provoked her till she became a bitch?"

"Precisely."

"That's fantastic."

"Look at the record."

"I'll admit this much: before my confession, I did think she was nice, not critical of me—in fact, admiring."

"And still you lost your sexual interest in her before your confession and her sudden change into 'a bitch.' "

"That's true."

"Conclusion?"

"You would say that I looked for and created the unfavorable, critical situation, and made her into a duplicate of my critical mother. And made myself into the target for her criticisms."

"And what would you say?"

"I'm confused."

"You can do better than that."

"What, for instance?"

"You could understand that you have again acted according to the formula I told you about in our first appointment, when you asked me why 'a fool husband should confess.' I told you then that psychic masochism includes the tendency to play for ever-increasing and always more dangerous stakes in the trouble game. The formula fits this situation, too. Your mother did not know of your homosexuality; she could not attack you on that score. Your wife does know about it—because you told her. It's clear that you increased the stakes, in order to increase your troubles. Q. E. D.?"

"Am I such an idiot or such a severe masochist?"

"The latter, if that's any comfort."

Months of working through, going over and over the same explanations, endless repetitions of the clarified material followed. After seven months Mr. M. was discharged as cured. Since then he has paid me occasional "social visits" (his own terminology). On one recent visit, he remarked: "I still can't figure out how and when health descended on me, and I still marvel at it." I suggested: "Just marvel and stay healthy."

His marriage settled down into a successful relationship; Mrs. M., whom I met after his cure, turned out to be—when not provoked—a really nice person.

* * *

Mr. Y.: "I enjoy homosexuality, but it makes me uncomfortable to be one. Don't ask me why, because I don't know."

My first contact with Mr. Y. was on the telephone; I heard a deep and ponderous male voice asking for an appointment. Word followed word majestically, at a measured—not to say halting—pace. The voice did not identify itself; when I asked for a name I was told: "There are reasons; I would rather not mention my name. Will it do to call me 'Mr. Y.'?" An appointment was arranged.

Mr. Y.'s appearance was as solemn as his voice; he looked as if he could have been the model for the joke about undertakers that ends with the punch line: "You just do the dying; we'll do the rest." He was tall, rather heavy, a man who might have been anywhere from forty-five to sixty. His clothes were as black as men's clothes can be. His face had deep lines, especially around the mouth; it was dominated by suspicious eyes. His expression could have indicated depression, disgust, a sardonic or bitter mood, or merely hypocrisy. Pursuing my thought about the undertaker, I decided that the imitation was too exact to be a professional uniform, and that Mr. Y. was probably a Wall Street lawyer. But the undertaker-impression was so powerful that I concluded: "Nobody, not even a miser, would like to bargain with this fellow about the price of his own funeral."

These thoughts passed through my mind during the few seconds it took to usher Mr. Y. from the waiting room into the appointment room. They are reproduced to transmit an impression; these random thoughts bring out the effect he made much more clearly than a detailed description could.

Mr. Y. seated himself and said, in his slow, rather irritating manner: "I would like to start with a compliment: I have read some of your books and I must say you have a lawyer's mind."

"Coming—I presume—from a lawyer, this seems a compliment indeed."

"Not only from a lawyer, but from a lawyer who comes of generations of lawyers. You understand that I do not wish to divulge my name and address. Is this acceptable?"

"Yes, provided that you make no changes in the actual facts you tell me, aside from the question of your identity."

"There would be no point in doing that. I also want to stipulate that, should I be seen in or near your office by someone who knows us both, my presence would be described as a professional call, to discuss a client of mine who is a half-psychiatric case."

"It is unlikely that our circles touch, but that condition is acceptable."

"One never can tell: you treated and cured a young man of my acquaintance. He was the first to tell me about you."

"I have no idea of whom you mean, but I can deduce from this statement your reason for consulting me."

"Really?"

"Well, such confidences presuppose an intimate situation. You did not say 'a young man whose family I know.'"

"Do I look it?"

"No. Nobody can detect a homosexual who doesn't want to be detected."

"In any case, your deduction makes my presence easier to explain. I enjoy homosexuality, but I do not feel comfortable about being a homosexual. Don't ask me why, because I do not know. I abhor loose ends and unsolved questions. That is why I am here."

"Please clarify your aims. Do you want to find out *why* you feel uncomfortable about being a homosexual, or do you want to *change*?"

"A good question. I must reserve my opinion."

"You can do that, for a few weeks. Some day you will have to come out with a considered opinion."

"I shall take the question under advisement."

"Please take this under advisement as well: you have partially prejudiced yourself in favor of the 'why.'"

"What led you to that conclusion?"

"Your choice of a pseudonym. The standard symbol for the unknown is X; was there any reason for you to be original? None, except for the possibility that to you 'Y' stood for w-h-y."

"That is interesting. What else can you deduce from the letter 'Y'?"

"Your predilection for young men. Isn't 'Y' for 'young' or 'youth' one of our more familiar abbreviations, as in YMCA, YMHA, CYO, and so on? And didn't you just mention a *young* homosexual who told you about me?"

"Perhaps every lawyer should have psychiatric training. I am on the Board of my alma mater, one of the more distinguished Eastern universities. I may see to it."

"Is your alma mater also the source of your recruits?"

"You are good at guessing. Yes. But, taking the great reservoir into consideration, scarcity is no danger."

"Is your problem of 'feeling uncomfortable' a new acquisition, or has it always been present?"

"Always. In the last few years it has intensified."

"For any special reason?"

"No. A certain exclusiveness provides adequate protection against the danger of detection, blackmail, exposure. A naive apprentice might have moral scruples; I have none. At forty-three, I am too old to ponder over biological inadequacies. I stand with both feet in real life; I am not concerned with what the stupid plebs call normal or abnormal. I have no religious qualms about the 'abomination' that homosexuality allegedly represents. Nevertheless, I am uncomfortable. I want to get at the root of my uneasiness."

"Is there a Mrs. Y.?"

"Of course, and two grown sons. Externally, everything is in excellent order. Unlikely as it sounds, nothing except my own feelings is pressing me into this inquiry."

"Still, there is this guilt."

"Why guilt? I have described the situation exactly: I feel uncomfortable."

"Experience proves that behind such a feeling there is always guilt, hidden somewhere."

"If so, let us dig for it."

The "digging" began with a "brief," carefully thought out by the lawyer and delivered orally at a dignified, leisurely pace:

"The direction of my life was determined before I was conceived. I was to be a corporation lawyer, and to enter the firm which for generations had borne my family name. I was to uphold the family honor, marry, produce at least an heir, and commit no nuisances. Old families produce representatives dedicated to their duty; my parents were dedicated to theirs. Whether my mother thought—as Tristram Shandy's mother did—of the need to wind the clock while she was being impregnated I cannot of course know, but I consider it a distinct possibility. In my childhood, 'duty' was the first commandment. As was expected of me, I was the 'Yes, sir' type of boy. Inwardly, I surmise, I rebelled mildly. The home atmosphere was emotionally cold. Life seemed gray. In puberty, I once complained to my father. He looked at me piercingly, shrugged his shoulders, and said: 'You will find that life is not a bed of roses.' I was determined to disprove his theory, and at school spent a good deal of time running after pretty girls. My mother interfered; she told me coldly that in our station in life more discrimination was indicated, and she named some acceptable candidates for my attentions. I thought her candidates dull, ugly, boring. When I was nineteen I became secretly engaged to a girl who, I realized later, was a warm-hearted scatterbrain. My mother found out, rejected the girl as 'flighty' and 'beneath me,' and broke it up. I did not understand, and was sullen and angry.

"While at college, I started a homosexual affair with a boy whose background was like mine. The affair came to nothing because it was impossible to live peacefully with him. He was jealous, and made scenes constantly. We separated; I decided that I preferred shortlived, transitory affairs. I have followed that rule ever since. It has saved me trouble, but has also deprived me of emotional pleasures.

"After I passed the Bar examination, I followed my mother's advice and married. She chose the girl: high-born, high-strung, and with a remarkable knack of proving herself indifferent to everything I cared about. Early in our marriage I lost all emotional interest in her; she complained but resigned herself. She submerged herself in our two sons. They became our sole topic of conversation. I learned never to talk to her about my business or my interest in civic affairs. We live in the country, but I keep a small apartment in town to stay in after a late conference. This gives me a bachelor's freedom, and I take full advantage of it. As I told you, everything has worked out satisfactorily, on the surface.

"I also told you that I am on the Board of my alma mater. The flow of students means a constant flow of eligible young men. No entanglements, no rumors, no danger.

"My parents died ten years ago, within a few months of each other. I am the head of our large firm; I brought in new and important clients. As lawyers go, I am a good one. Admittedly, any idiot would have been successful, given my start. Still, I can say that I have done well.

"Why I am not happy, I cannot tell. I have money, position, luxury, and a host of young friends who understand me. What I told you about 'feeling uncomfortable' in my homosexual pursuits is the exact truth. There is no logic in it. But here it is—make the most of it."

I asked him: "Am I mistaken, or do I detect a *leitmotif* of anti-woman feeling in your brief? Your mother was cold; she prevented you from having a liaison with a warm-hearted girl, suggested and put over a marriage to a woman with the knack of being uninterested in everything that interests you. All anti-woman. Please correct me if I am wrong."

"I was not aware that I had put that special emphasis into my account, but your summary seems correct."

"So you rescued yourself to young men who 'understand' you. And in spite of that, you admit that you are not happy."

"That, too, is correct."

"Possible conclusion: *You don't want to be happy in the first place. Or your technique of finding substitute-happiness does not work.*"

"The first possibility seems to me to be a fantasy; the second an enigma."

"Let's follow lead No. 1. You mentioned that your mother objected to your secret engagement, and broke it up. How did she break it up? Why did you permit her to?"

"I told you that I was a 'Yes, sir' boy"

"On the other hand, you made an attempt to disprove your father's theory about earthly misery, and—this is decisive—shortly after your secret engagement was broken you began a homosexual affair. Is this, too, proof of being a 'Yes, ma'am' boy?"

"You drive a hard bargain!"

"Please explain the contradiction."

"I cannot."

"Then we must conclude that you did not want that climate of love, understanding and companionship from 'the warm-hearted girl' in the first place. Obviously you were after something else; you were building up a case against your mother."

"Your logic is irrefutable, but everything on the emotional side tells me that you are wrong."

"Are feelings admissible in court, when all the evidence points in the other direction?"

"We are not in court."

"We are, but not a court of justice. We are arguing before your own cruel inner court of conscience."

"Are you seriously claiming that for some people happiness consists of unhappiness?"

"Precisely. We call such people psychic masochists."

"I have read about psychic masochism in your books; I found myself shaking my head throughout your explanations."

"A time-honored gesture, without any standing in court."

"May I object by pointing out that I must have had the wish for emotional warmth in me: that is exactly what I look for in my young friends, at least *inter alia.*"

"If your emotional thirst were real and not pseudo (it cannot be real, because it is defensive), you would have found happiness in homosexuality. You didn't, and that's conclusive."

"Do you have other evidence?"

"At your service. You knew of your parents' social prejudices, and of your mother's hyper-prejudices. You must have known they would never consent to a marriage with a girl they considered beneath your station, as 'the warm-hearted girl' was. Another hint that you were building a case, not a future."

"You disturb me deeply."

"It is the weight of the evidence that is disturbing you. Please think this over."

Mr. Y. did not succeed in uncovering any contradictory evidence. Admitting his failure, he added, acidly, "When a situation like this arises down town I call in the brightest of my bright young men. That is inadvisable here; I have to rely on you."

"May I add another confirmation of my conclusion that your secret engagement was meant to build up a case against your mother? Your mother had rejected the girl because she was 'beneath' you. A short time afterwards, you began a homosexual affair with a boy who had a background like your own. Is this correct; did you say that?"

"Yes."

"Well, if this isn't masochistically tinged irony against your mother, what is it? Didn't your action say, 'You want me to stay in the upper crust; all right, I will!' "

"I see the hidden irony, but why do you call it 'masochistically tinged'?"

"Because homosexuality always spells trouble. By the way, I said 'tinged.' In your mouth, it sounds like 'tainted.' "

"You can be proud of yourself; you have silenced a lawyer."

"I don't think I have. After the initial shock, you will find some arguments."

"I would like to take up your *second* lead. You said that either I didn't want conventional happiness in the first place, or that the substitute-happiness I tried to get from homosexuality did not work. Can you, please, enlarge on the second point?"

"You were defeated before you began your rescue attempt. Homosexuality is a synthetic product, built on an unconscious flight from the mother-image. Because it is synthetic, it cannot produce happiness. You yourself found that more or less permanent homosexual relationships don't work; you complained of your partner's pathological jealousy. That is only one of the manisfestations of constant injustice collecting, and injustice collecting is the true basis of homosexuality. You solved this problem by limiting yourself to short affairs, or occasional sexual meetings. But you saw the drawback; you yourself said it was a way of avoiding conflict, but a way that deprived you of emotional pleasure. The inescapable conclusion is that your whole life has been directed by the pleasure-in-displeasure pattern. The only exceptions have been a few futile attempts at reparation."

"And my 'feeling uncomfortable' in homosexuality?"

"That is guilt, because of the masochistic devil you tried—but failed—to exorcise in homosexuality. That guilt has nothing to do with homosexuality *per se*; it is just *shifted* to homosexuality. We call it 'return of the repressed.' Freud found an illustration of that tendency in a drawing by Felicien Rops. The drawing shows a saint who rescues himself by prayer from a plague of sexual fantasies. He looks up, and instead of the Savior sees a beautiful, voluptuous woman on the Cross."

"The whole story seems too pat to me."

"I predicted that the lawyer would not be silenced without a fight."

"Again I say: Let me think it over."

Mr. Y. kept our discussion to a subject other than homosexuality during our next appointment. He was appalled at the extent to which he had aged during the last few years, he said. "I am only forty-three, and I look much older. No reason for that. My diagnostician finds nothing wrong with me. Is there a psychological cause here, too?"

I told Mr. Y. of a study I had published some years earlier: "The 'Old Man Act' of the Middle-Aged Man." The study described the type of man who avoids one familiar pitfall of middle age—the tendency to make oneself ridiculous by acting and dressing like a youngster—but makes exactly the opposite error: he takes on the appearance and manner of a person much older than himself. The wife of one such man complained that he had prematurely "pulled the old-man act."

These people do not slow down with middle age; they surrender. They accept the penalties and attributes of decrepitude without objective justification. While their exact contemporaries still appear to be in their vigorous forties, their hearty fifties or their well-preserved early sixties, these men seem to be fully eligible for old-age pensions.

In my recent book, THE REVOLT OF THE MIDDLE-AGED MAN,* I described a transitory phase typical for middle-aged men: they go through a period of "second emotional adolescence" in which they attempt to start life anew. They concoct grandiose plans to divorce their wives, remarry (the second wife will be young, of course), and "enjoy life," whatever that may mean. Other middle-aged men resolve the identical inner upheaval by retiring to hypochondria and waiting for the ultimate blow to fall. The blow can be coronary thrombosis, a stroke, cancer, or any other disease they have read about.

The middle-aged man who "pulls the old-man act" does not fit into either of these categories. He is resigned to wearing the ball and chain, which is the way he thinks of marriage. He is equally resigned to the other circumstances of his life, and does not plan to change them. He merely gives up. His characteristic air becomes that of bankruptcy, exhaustion, resignation or depression.

* Hill and Wang, New York, 1954.

He is neither a hypochondriac nor a rebel. He lives a life of half-hibernation, without hope of spring. He looks feeble and haggard, and he stoops; his posture emphasizes the grayness of his hair. His memory is not what it was. Two drinks after dinner leave him drowsy, and he falls asleep at nine o'clock. His sex life has withered. He has no hobbies; nothing interests him; he is not even bitter. He performs his duties in a distracted and mechanical way, like a zombie, although diagnosticians cannot find any special pathology. The over-all impression he makes is that of a man waiting for the undertaker.

These men generally come into treatment because their wives insist upon it. In analyzing them, one finds a rather typical situation: their "old-man act" is a preventive unconscious technique of evading the reproaches of the inner conscience. Their alibi runs: "I'm old; I have one foot in the grave; I've suffered enough. Why kick a man when he's down?" External actions and attitudes dramatize this plea.

Nearly three hundred and fifty years ago, Francis Bacon observed: "Men of age object too much, consult too long, adventure too little, repent too soon, and seldom drive business home to the full period, but content themselves with a mediocrity of success." Inwardly, these premature "old men" do not derive contentment from their "mediocrity of success." This very mediocrity is the basis of the reproaches leveled against them by the inner conscience. Maliciously, the inner torturer recounts the hopes that have failed to materialize, the promises—made to themselves—that remained unfulfilled, the aims that have not been achieved. To escape the need to search for a remedy—and to renew his efforts in general, the victim produces his alibi old-age act for the benefit of his inner conscience. It is superfluous to mention that the entire process is unconscious.

One does these rather tragic figures an injustice by accusing them, as their wives consistently do, of being conscious fakers, and of "lacking initiative." One impatient wife said of her husband: "He acts the schoolboy playing hookey, pretending to be sick." When asked what illness her husband allegedly simulated, the lady was at a loss to name one.

A remarkable byproduct of this neurotic disturbance is the acceleration of the aging process, as far as external appearance is concerned. Equally remarkable is the fact that this process is partially reversible. To the extent to which it has been psychologically induced, it can be therapeutically repaired, provided that psychiatric treatment attacks and works through the masochistically instituted and dramatized inner alibi, directed at the unconscious conscience.

In treating a series of cases, I told Mr. Y., I gathered the impression that three inner conditions prevail in individuals using the old-man act as an inner defense.

First, they are neither very successful nor very unsuccessful people; typically, theirs is a middle-of-the-road success. When middle age makes them realize that the door is about to close, they become panicky. They reject rebellion and hypochondria, and as their way out choose to be submissive and to dramatize their aging.

Second, these are people in whom exhibitionism has previously been pronounced. Though their achievements have been moderate, they have had to shine within their small spheres of influence. This exhibitionism, though defensive (it covered more deeply repressed masochistic vicissitudes), served them well. No longer able to maintain their pace, they now shift into *negative* exhibitionism, displaying their unenviable physical decay.

Third, these are people in whom the masochistic component has always been pronounced. Now they take refuge in the argument that their pitiable condition calls for special consideration. Dramatizing their decay, they beg the inner tormenter to spare them.

"The cases I treated were all heterosexuals," I added, "but the problem undoubtedly applies to homosexuals as well."

"What do I want to prove?"

"You are pleading with your inner conscience: 'I am old; leave me in peace.' To prove the point, you exaggerate your physiological aging process."

"Fantastic!"

"There may also be an element of shifted guilt involved. Didn't your father tell you that life was no bed of roses? Posthumously, you may want to prove he was right."

"You are insufferable!"

"Is this a term you used to your mother?"

Mr. Y. stared in astonishment, obviously searching his memory, and said nothing.

Real life is not always too obliging to neurotics who believe that they have solved their problems by outsmarting neurosis. Mr. Y. came to his next appointment deeply disturbed: fate had played him "the dirtiest of all dirty tricks."

"My nineteen-year-old son came to me and confessed that he is homosexual. He is desperately unhappy. I gave him your book. He's reading it, and will consult you."

"Now you are accusing yourself, and telling yourself that 'the sins of the fathers,' etcetera."

"You will admit it looks that way."

"Appearances are deceptive at best; when you are dealing with unconscious processes, watch them even more carefully. This will give you a good opportunity to test your psychic masochism. It is not necessary to make a tragedy out of something that can be cured in a few months."

"Do you really believe that I am not responsible?"

"Well, your father certainly wasn't a homosexual, and the results were identical."

"That's true."

"Since this is the case, why do you accuse yourself? It is another case of a boy running away from the distorted image he himself created of his mother. Of course, there might be reason for you to reproach yourself because yours was not a good marriage; in a good marriage your wife might not have hovered over the boy as she did. But where would that argument lead you? Once more to your mother, who seemingly forced you into a misalliance. And you need not stop there. You could bring up your grandmother, and your great-grandmother. In short, the environment, and the personal responsibility of the people in it, cannot explain neurosis.*"

"But I can't just shake off my feeling of responsibility. Look at the possible consequences: he may meet one of my own boy friends. There could be—you might call it—incest! If this weren't a tragedy, you might say it was a farce!"

* Some parts of this particular discussion (shortened here) are included in Chapter Ten.

"The irony exists, of course. But as far as your guilt is concerned, it would be as justified for you to accuse yourself of having caused Pearl Harbor."

"You aren't saying that just to console me?"

"So far, you haven't accused me of hyper-delicacy."

This crisis brought out an interesting shift in Mr. Y.'s attitude. The crisis itself was dealt with promptly. The boy came into analysis with an excellent prognosis; he desperately wanted to change. A few days after his son entered treatment, Mr. Y. embarked on a process of synthetic reparation. "You know," he remarked, "the boy has no stamina. I didn't run to *my* father!"

"I wouldn't say that stamina entered into this at all. Your son acted much more reasonably than you did. He wanted to be helped, and asked for help where he could expect it. What's wrong with that?"

"Now you are going to turn my own words against me, and claim that it was masochistic of me not to consult my father about my homosexuality!"

"Precisely. But—at the time it 'hit' you there was no cure for homosexuality."

"Then it was not masochistic of me!"

"It was. You didn't know there was no cure."

I had the impression that whole generations of well-mannered ancestors were holding Mr. Y. back from a barrage of obscenity.

To turn Mr. Y.'s mood away from his senseless self-accusations, I suggested analyzing two sets of facts: his overweight and his "undertaker look."

"Why do you overeat?" I asked him. "And why your chronic funereal facial expression?"

Mr. Y. was so deeply wounded by my criticism of his facial expression that he ignored the matter of overeating. "I never heard such nonsense!" he said. His words, for once, followed one another in quick succession. "Is being serious a crime?"

"Isn't this your father, again, declaring that life is no bed of roses?"

"Seriousness and funereal expressions are not identical."

"Sorry. May I be blunt?"

"You have been already."

"Do you want facts, or do you want to skip over facts?"

"Go ahead, damn you!"

As tactfully as I could, I described the initial impression Mr. Y. had made on me.

"Are you serious?" he asked. "Do I really make you think of an undertaker?"

"You did when I first saw you."

"Can you suggest a reason? Why should I have that expression on my face?"

"The same guilt—guilt arising from psychic masochism and secondarily shifted to homosexuality."

"Another technique of appeasing conscience?"

"Yes."

Clearly, this day's session, with its revelation of an external pose he had not consciously chosen, was the strongest shock Mr. Y. had sustained in treatment. He recovered his poise with his usual "Let me think it over."

During the next few days Mr. Y. moved in a thick cloud of gloom. Abruptly, then, he shook off his depression and announced —with a smile!—that he had decided "to act" a younger man.

"That wouldn't do," I told him. "I suggest that instead of *acting* a younger man you become one."

"You drive a hard bargain."

"You have used that phrase before. Please straighten yourself out on this: you, not I, will profit by the 'hard bargain'."

Mr. Y. thought this over and burst into unexpected laughter. "I am really behaving like an ass," he conceded.

"I wouldn't say that. But it is ironic that neurotic people who are in treatment often act as though contentment in life were an analytic come-on, to be avoided at all costs."

Mr. Y. now permitted me to analyze his overeating. I gave him a brief account of the unconscious tributaries to this problem, starting with the attitude of the very young child towards his food. Food means milk to the infant: a bland, tepid fluid. It also means "mother"; in the course of the inevitable rebellion against infantile passivity and dependence all people, normal and neurotic, learn to "prefer" other foods to what mother had to offer. The adult, therefore, expects his diet to be one of variety. He chooses the sweet, the sour, the thick, the thin, the spiced, in careful combinations and successions; he rejects with scorn the tepid and the neutral. The entire science of gourmanderie is at bottom built out of pseudo-aggression against the mother.

The neurotic twist often given to this simple and unimportant rebellion reveals its underlying pseudo-aggressiveness. One wealthy young man had for years limited his diet to one dish: tuna fish salad. "It is nourishing and inexpensive," he explained. But his entire life had also been unconsciously devoted to proving that "bad mother starves me."

Another man, after having been a food faddist for years, settled into a routine. For three days he subsisted on black coffee ("I'm not hungry," he would declare) while he waited for "a real appetite." At the end of the third day, when he was "really hungry," he would dine like Henry VIII and discover that his food "did not agree" with him. He would then go back to black coffee for another three days. He, too, unconsciously acted out the drama of "bad mother starves helpless child."

A young girl from a wealthy Western family, living in New York on an allowance so that she could study music, received her checks on the first and fifteenth of every month. Two days after her check arrived, she would discover that she had spent virtually every cent of it. She would then live on a slim diet of cottage cheese and milk until the next check appeared. In this simple way, she "proved" how unjust her family (her mother, actually) was being to her.

People with exquisite culinary taste often represent the opposite extreme. Especially in the case of the man who is a "marvelous cook" and cooks his own food, this is an attempt to prove autarchy, and complete independence of the mother.

These examples show how far the refinement of masochistic pseudo-aggression can go. The common or garden variety of unconscious pseudo-aggression is the individual who merely overeats. Here, too, the thesis is "bad mother starves me," but overeaters fight against the danger preventively by "eating like pigs." Small details betray their underlying fear: they cannot wait to be served, but snatch tidbits from salad bowl and meat platter.

Mr. Y.'s analysis continued for many months before he changed into something approaching a human being. Externally, the alteration was marked: he looked as if he had lost twenty pounds and twenty years. He abandoned his homosexuality and discovered a new world: woman. I asked him whether he was unaware of the possibility of getting into trouble with women, too. He smiled (one of his new acquisitions) and answered: "I'm an old hand at avoiding trouble." Time helped him here; in a comparatively short while he abandoned his promiscuous phase. In any case, the transformation of "the undertaker" into a living and feeling person was a spectacle that astonished even myself.

Mr. N.: "I am a homosexual. I have no intention of changing. But I would like to know from experience what a 'normal guy' feels."

Mr. N. was a man of forty-eight who looked his age and more. He introduced himself with the sentences quoted above. Although I generally take statements made by neurotics in my stride, the novelty of this approach stopped me for a moment. "Why?" I asked him, with real curiosity as well as professional interest.

"New experiences."

"Like taking a trip to a country you have never visited?"

"Why not?"

"There are passport difficulties."

"I have no subversive record."

"Tell me this first: Are you teasing me? Or are you really naive?"

"Look, I pride myself on being a cynical guy—no illusions—who can pay for what he wants. The government takes seventy per cent of what I make. I am curious about normal sex. What's so strange about my request? After all, I pay only thirty cents on the dollar. That makes your extortionist's fee, whatever it is, a bargain."

"Very cute, but you are still talking as if you were a blind man comparing colors."

"Why?"

"Because you began with a series of faulty assumptions. First of all, you want to dance at two weddings at the same time. An impossible proposition. Second, you believe that homosexuality and heterosexuality are interchangeable; apparently you have swallowed the popular misconception of bisexuality. For your information, the supposed bisexual is a homosexual with some mechanical potency retained—until further notice. Third, you underestimate the work done by psychoanalysis. Psychiatric treatment changes the individual radically, or else—if applied to an unsuitable subject—does not work at all. Obviously, neither of these possibilities is to your liking. Fourth, the experiment you suggest has all the earmarks of a business transaction arranged by a psychological ignoramus. You apparently believe that anything can be bought at cut rates—thirty cents on the dollar. It was a moderate pleasure to make your acquaintance. Goodbye."

Mr. N. was not prepared to have his approach taken seriously. The middle-aged roue had wanted to buy some fun; my rebuff was a shock.

"Wait a minute!" he said, eagerly. "Not so fast! Don't go serious on me! I just made you a harmless proposition, and you throw the book at me! Where is your sense of humor? You're talking like a high priest who saw someone commit sacrilege. I didn't intend to piss at your holy Mecca."

"What else do you want?"

"Some fun. What good is money, except for buying what you want to have?"

"Correct. Unfortunately, some things cannot be bought. Moreover, I don't believe that you are such a happy homosexual in the first place. If, in spite of my invitation to leave, you intend to continue this conversation, be prepared for a few disagreeable surprises. You can still go, if you don't want to hear them."

"I'll stick it out."

"You impress me as a fading, aging homosexual who pretends to be happy, although he is forced to admit that his so-called exploits are yielding diminishing returns. I know from other cases the tragedy of the homosexual who has reached middle age. The young boys don't come around any more; they have to be bought. Some homosexuals cannot accept having only prostitutes as partners. That leaves only the possibility of another middle-aged homosexual as partner: an unacceptable solution because homosexuality includes both an accent on youth and a form of naive banter encountered only among the very young. My conclusion: you are nearly through as a homosexual. Backed by your large capital or your large income, you come here and play the big shot, pretending that you are the buyer when actually you are a miserable supplicant begging for some crumbs of sex. How do you like my assumptions?"

"I could spit in your face—or agree with you. Which would you prefer?"

"Your cynicism is almost played out, too. Do you know what a cynic is? A scared boy, draped in iconoclasm, looking for allies. If he is caught, he protests: 'Why do you take me so seriously? I was only kidding!' Well, do you still want to spit in my face, or have you decided to agree with me?"

"Why are you so angry with me?"

"Your attitude reminds me of a saying of Samuel Butler's: 'I don't mind lies, but I hate inaccuracy.' I am not angry with you. The anger you apparently see is your own fantasy. What I did was to put you in your place after you took unreasonable and unwarranted liberties with me. Impudence has no place in medical problems. If you are sick, say so."

"What do you mean by 'sick'?"

"Fading homosexuality in a middle-aged man without mental resources is a bitter lot. What do you have as a substitute?"

"Who gave you the right to sit in judgment?"

"Isn't it amusing when a cynic becomes indignant? Doesn't cynicism protect you from indignation? If, as you cynics claim, everything has a price and every human being is a malodorous misfit, why be surprised?"

"I surrender! O. K., I was playing the big shot. Let me tell you my troubles."

"That's better."

"My wish to get some heterosexual fun is really based on what you called 'waning and fading' homosexual pleasures. You're right: homosexuality is for youngsters. When you're middle-aged, you're out. What am I supposed to do? What's so wrong with wanting to switch to the opposite sex?"

"What do you expect?"

"Maybe I could find somebody in the other camp who would care for me a little bit."

Mr. N. became a rather pathetic figure as soon as he stopped playing the big shot. He told his miserable and pitiful story; it confirmed my assumptions. He even expressed his "admiration" for the speed with which I had seen through his pose. Obviously, having failed with the cynical approach, he was trying flattery. I told him so, and got this indignant answer:

"Cynicism doesn't work, humbling myself doesn't work; what approach would you suggest?"

"Simple statements of fact."

"O. K. The simple facts are that I never foresaw my present situation. Homosexuality is failing me. If you want the exact facts, my partners are failing me. What you said about the tragedy of the middle-aged homosexual is quite true. Of course I could buy those young stinkers, but I can't bring myself to it. Call it pride, illusions, inability to abdicate—there it is, I can't bring myself to pay. Believe me, I have a case against homosexuals, too."

"But how does this make you a candidate for heterosexuality?"

"What else is there—animal contacts?"

We both laughed, though Mr. N.'s laughter was bitter. Finally, he said: "Can you do something for me?"

"I have no idea."

"But you described a case like mine in your book: that middle-aged man who longed for 'those twelve glorious penicillin days'—meaning the time when the young friend who had deserted him came back unexpectedly. He was so involved he didn't care that the boy wanted only his money in the first place, and came back only because he had an anal infection and needed someone to pay his medical bills. And still that fellow became a heterosexual after treatment. Why can't that miracle be duplicated—or wasn't that the true story?"

"Provocation, again. You remind me of the story of the two enemies whose mutual friends finally persuade them to shake hands on New Year's Day. They do so, and the first man says: 'Well, for the coming year I wish you all the happiness you wish me.' And the second man answers: 'Are you beginning all over again?' "

Mr. N.'s pretensions, luckily, included the possession of a sense of humor, and he laughed heartily—either to please me, or because he was genuinely amused. After the laugh came a pause, and then a sober question: "What are my chances?"

"I would say: decimal point, several zeros, and then a reluctant 'one.' "

"Is it worth trying?"

"That's up to you."

"Let's try it. But please don't pull that trick of yours and make me wait months for my first appointment. Even if it isn't a trick, don't make me wait. I am in a bad state. If you can't do better, at least see me once a week till you have more time."

"It isn't a trick; I have no time. But your case does call for special measures. I don't work on Saturdays; I can see you on Saturday mornings."

"Why are you so accommodating?"

"I am curious."

Mr. N., I discovered, had a particular reason for coming to me rather than to another analyst. He was distantly acquainted with two of my former patients, both cured homosexuals. Before he learned of their analyses, he had approached one of them with an invitation; to his surprise, he found the man adamant in his refusal to enter a relationship on a homosexual basis. This was his first intimation of the fact that homosexuality can "really" be cured by analysis. Before this firsthand experience, he had read one of my books on homosexuality, but had dismissed it as "eyewash," "fakery" and "publicity." Shortly after this encounter, he approached the second ex-patient and met with the same outright refusal. This impressed him enormously; he began to doubt his negative judgment of the theories and examples he had read in my book. Doubt fought against anger: to his resentment, both ex-patients had "rather condescendingly" recommended that he enter analysis.

These refusals added two more unpleasant experiences to an already staggering total of rejections by homosexual prospects. Mr. N. felt that he was "too old for them." He tried a male prostitute, only to react with a disgust so profound that "it floored him."

In his desperation, he concocted the idea of switching to heterosexuality. "You see," he explained, "my choice is between homosexual whores and decent, heterosexual women. Why should my prospects be so poor?"

"Because logic does not regulate the unconscious. Logically, you have every reason to change. Neither of us knows—yet—what is going on in your unconscious. By the way, in enumerating your reality choices you forgot to mention another alternative: you could always retire into fantasy."

"You mean, masturbation?"

"Yes. Provided your chances in reality *are* totally nonexistent. I doubt that, too. There are so many recruits . . ."

"Yes, there are. But all the young ones are quick-change artists. After a short time they find someone their own age, and they leave. The pleasure is shortlived; the misery longlived. The game isn't worth the candle. As to masturbation, I detest it."

"I did not recommend either of these solutions. I simply stated that you still have homosexual choices."

"*Some* choices!"

"Since I see you so infrequently, I am not going to ask you to begin with your life history. That would take up several appointments. Instead, while we are on this interim schedule, let's take up two traits of yours. You displayed both clearly in your preliminary interview. First, your cynicism; second, your trick of provocation, and your inability to live in peace with anybody."

"I understand what you mean by cynicism, though I don't see what it has to do with my visits here. I definitely don't see what makes you say I can't live in peace with anyone."

"I'm thinking of your parting shot at our first meeting. I told you that I would make an exception in your case, and see you once a week on Saturday, when I do not work. You had insisted on being seen immediately, without a waiting period. Do you remember what you said then?"

"Vaguely."

"I shall refresh your memory. Rather ironically, you asked, 'Why are you so accommodating?' That meant that I was damned if I did, and damned if I didn't. If I had told you that there was no way out, and you would have to wait or else consult a colleague whom I would recommend, you would have called me a coward playing a trick on you, and you would have been offended. When I told you that I would arrange to see you once a week, you deprecated the concession and reacted with irony. How can one live in peace with you?"

"Do you want to deduce that I'm a very aggressive fellow?"

"Exactly the opposite. I want to suggest that under the disguise of attacking, you try to make sure you will get a kick in the pants."

"You told me, at that same interview, that you insist on civil language. It is difficult to keep one's temper in the face of an unjustified accusation."

"May I enter two corrections? My stipulation about civil language referred to the introductory session, only. As soon as you entered treatment—even on this interim basis—that rule was necessarily suspended. In your resistance, you may—and will—open all the dams holding back all the obscenity, abuse, profanity at your command. Second correction: Why do you classify an observation—right or wrong—as an 'accusation'? In this room nobody accuses you of anything. We'll have to find out what prompts you to classify observations as 'accusations.'"

"You are a spoilsport and a killjoy! When I know that you don't mind being abused, where's my fun?"

"Translate: I want to make people angry, and since angry people retaliate, I want a kick in the pants."

"The first part of that sentence clicks, but not the second. You forget that in my position—I am the president of a large corporation and the majority stockholder—I can afford to be abusive; I don't have to watch out for consequences."

"Did you ever hear the truism: 'Few people can help us, but almost everyone can damage us'?"

"I don't give a damn! Let them!"

"Confessions of a masochist. Nobody can defy the entire world with impunity. I have some homework for you. Search your memory, and check on whether you haven't been damaged by people you abused, or made enemies of."

"I'll do that. What else?"

"Explain, to me, the advantages of having provoked me mercilessly throughout our first appointment. I assume that you did not create this attitude for my special benefit; it can be taken as typical. You wanted something from me; in fact, you wanted it badly. How did you go about getting it? You were abusive; you treated me contemptuously; told me that you could afford to pay my 'extortionist's fee' because of your tax bracket—thirty cents on the dollar, remember?—put on an act about wanting to try heterosexuality just out of curiosity, to be sure who's better off, and so on. I called you to order, and you retired behind the not-so-good excuse that you were just kidding. You called me pompous. You said you had no intention of 'pissing on my holy Mecca.' When this did not help either, and most of the fake story you told me was shown up, you changed your tactics again. To use a few convenient cliches, you ate humble pie, came down off your high horse, cut a not very heroic figure. Tell me (or figure it out, as homework) whether a different approach would not have been, in its end effects, more propitious."

"The only mistake I made was in underestimating your independence. I should have looked up your income tax returns before coming here. I didn't know that a psychoanalyst can afford to talk that way to a wealthy customer. On the other hand, I should have been forewarned, but I took a statement of fact for a wisecrack. After all, I *had* heard that the only place where the customer is always wrong is in the psychiatrist's office."

The next Saturday Mr. N. made no reference to his "homework." Instead, he brought up the problem of cynicism.

"You said something like this—a cynic is a little boy dressed up as an iconoclast. May I contradict you? I always assumed that cynicism is the superior way of coping with the nonsense that surrounds us. My authority is Ambrose Bierce; in *The Devil's Dictionary* he defined the cynic as 'a blackguard whose faulty vision sees things as they are, not as they ought to be.' "

"The answer to that well-written sentence is another equally well-written one: Oscar Wilde's 'A cynic is a man who knows the price of everything and the value of nothing.' "

"But Wilde was a cynic himself!"

"Exactly. But that doesn't exclude the possibility of moments of self-appraisal. Let's see what happened to our two literary authorities, both cynics themselves. Your Ambrose Bierce, after a life of self-created trouble, vanished of his own will somewhere in Mexico. Nobody knows what happened to him, but the probability is that bandits killed him. Oscar Wilde, having invited his own downfall by bringing his hopeless, really suicidal suit against the Marquis of Queensberry, the father of one of his homosexual cronies, went to jail, became a bankrupt, and spent the remaining few years of his life penniless in exile in Paris. Cynicism doesn't seem to be a guarantee against masochism."

"What is cynicism, in your opinion?"

"To begin with surface impressions, a cynic is a man playing a calculated role. He wants the world to think of him as someone with an eye that pierces through all disguises, an authority who can tell you the inside story, no matter what the subject is. Allegedly, he knows the real, concealed truth about what everybody else accepts at face value and takes for granted; he is the one who can see through accepted institutions, morals, cherished opinion; this inside story is that all these institutions and beliefs are rotten to the core."

I went on to explain the unconscious basis of cynicism. The cynic's inner problem consists of masochistically tinged ambivalence; he must contend with his possession of contradictory feelings which simultaneously pull him towards *and* away from a single figure in his childhood world. He defends himself against the charge of psychic masochism, leveled by his unconscious conscience, by stressing false aggression; this forms the basis of his attacks on accepted customs and institutions. To strengthen this defense, he looks for allies in the outer world. This is a typical move, but the cynic enlists his allies by using a unique method. His irreverent and often disturbing opinions, openly expressed, carry with them an unspoken invitation: "Stop pretending that it shocks you to hear me say these things! Admit that you agree with every word!" The invitation would be meaningless if there were no hidden ambivalence in the listener; often enough there is, and the cynic uses the listener's momentary approval as unconscious proof that he is a spokesman for the many rather than a solitary sinner.

At the same time, the act that he puts on satisfies his conscious need for reassurance. Whether he has persuaded his audience into covert agreement with him or not, he has managed to sell himself successfully as an "aggressive," active, daring wit.

His anxious campaign for defense and reassurance leaves him no time to question his own point of view, to ask himself why he possesses (figuratively speaking) infra-red vision, and therefore sees clearly only the dark side of human nature. If he could actually see through appearances, he would penetrate to his own inner realities, and realize that he is not a free agent but an instrument manipulated by the inner need to fight back against the unconscious torturer, conscience. He would penetrate, also, to the real attitude of his environment, and realize that it rejects him or never takes him seriously. Unconsciously, however, he does sense this last drawback; unconsciously, he derives masochistic satisfaction from it.

The next time I saw Mr. N. he complained, gloomily, that everything thus far done in his analysis seemed intended to "undermine his morale."

"Do you think I'm doing this on purpose, or accidentally?" I asked.

"You wouldn't like the answer I have in mind."

"Try me."

"Well, I think you're still offended at my—as you would say—supercilious behavior in the beginning, and you're paying me back."

"Not very original; very wrong. My job is to look into every corner that might hide a store of masochistic passivity. That means examining provocative behavior, cynicism, homosexuality. These are all cut from the same cloth. How can personal malice, or an attempt to pay you back, be involved?"

"I didn't consult you to look for nonexistent passivity stored in corners of my personality. I gave you the job of making a goddam normal out of me!"

"The enthusiasm for normality seems on the wane, too."

"If the road is too tough . . ."

"You can quit any time. But before you do, better ask yourself this simple question: is the passivity really nonexistent?"

"What does homosexuality have to do with passivity?"

"Homosexuality is the high point of passive fear. That fear propels its victim into a frantic flight from woman, the alleged torturer."

"But the flight—if it is one—can be very active."

"You are confusing aims with the execution of aims. One can be very active in pursuing a passive aim. For example, you executed your initial provocations with vigor. But they still had a passive aim: you wanted to be thrown out."

"I can't see it. I *am* active and energetic. You should see me in my office. I can't see myself as a passive (he paused to search for a word)—a passive washout."

"You are active and energetic in your office, you say. And in your homosexual activities?"

"Don't get personal!"

"You don't realize how funny that remark is. Analysis is based on 'getting personal.' If you don't want that, how can you be treated?"

"I took it for granted that selected chapters would be enough. Do you really insist on knowing the whole mess?"

"This is an example of involuntary humor. Let's find a parallel and see what you think of it. A woman finds a suspicious lump in her breast. She makes an appointment with a gynecologist. When she gets to his office she refuses to undress. 'Don't get personal,' she tells him. 'Don't forget that I'm a lady.' "

"O. K. You've had your fun at my expense. Where do we go from here?"

"Either to the homework you didn't report on—whether or not you were damaged by some of the people you have offended—or to a scrutiny of the details of your sexual practices. Take your choice."

"You are really a stinker, hiding hypocritically behind analytic necessities!"

"Do you know this story? In 1814 Napoleon threatened Fouché, his secretary of state, with execution, shouting: 'I should put you before a firing squad!' Fouché simply said: 'I am not of Your Majesty's opinion.' Modify that answer, and it fits here."

"I just said that to test whether you really are the good sport you say you are."

"I hope I passed the test."

"I suppose you have a pretty good idea, by now, of why I'm making such a fuss about passivity."

"I have."

"Say it."

"I already have, in following up your statement about activity in business, and asking whether that applied to sex, too."

"No secrets?"

"Freud once said that self-betrayal oozes out of man's every pore."

"O. K. My favorite game in homosexuality was this: I used to make biting remarks, taunt the other fellow and keep at it until he got so angry that he beat me up. You don't have to say it: this was active execution of a passive aim."

"This was to be expected. Skillful provocateurs—and you are certainly king there—always want a beating."

"Do you seriously claim you suspected that detail?"

"I do. When you asked me if I thought you were aggressive, I told you that, under the disguise of attacking, you are hoping for a kick in the pants. I could have used an equally familiar phrase, and said 'a kick in the teeth.' The switch was deliberate. What's more, I used those words at a time when both of us were trying to be very polite."

"I wondered about your choice of words."

"Well, it was a hint. The ironic touch came when I stormed your 'passivity corners,' and you became indignant. What was the purpose of this camouflage?"

"Remember the lady with the lump in her breast?"

"I do."

'Now I can also tell you why I was so skeptical about your book. You keep laying down the law about 'psychic masochism' being the basis of homosexuality. That lets me out, I thought; I'm a 'perverted masochist.' "

" 'Fantastic' isn't a strong enough word to express my reaction. Don't you understand that psychic masochism is an attenuation, a watering down of the *severer* illness, perversion masochism? That originally all psychic masochism starts with the actual wish to be tortured, beaten, mistreated?"

"I didn't know that."

"According to you, a penny is bigger than a thousand-dollar bill. By the way, you are not the only one with the Aristophanian idea that perversion masochism is a less serious disease than psychic masochism. Recently I saw a minister who began a homosexual affair with a parishioner, and consoled himself—after reading my book—with the idea that he is 'only' a perverted masochist; beatings were the substratum of his affair with his parishioner. And here is another example. One of my ex-patients, a well-known musician, was trying to persuade a friend of his, an actress of some importance, to go into analysis because of psychic masochism. She stopped wailing about the husband who had deserted her long enough to disagree, and to tell a story that she thought proved she was not the possessor of 'inexhaustible mental masochism.' She had once had a shortlived affair with a man who bit her hard on the breast. She was furious, and threw him out. During her sleepless nights, it was this recollection that repeatedly came back to her as so-called consolation. This convinced her that she was not a psychic masochist, but *only* a perverted masochist."

"The way you tell these stories, it sounds funny."

"Of course tragedies are hidden behind these superficially ridiculous situations. Would you deny that the wish to be beaten on the buttocks is rather infantile?"

"No, I wouldn't."

"And don't you see how, during our short acquaintance, you have again and again tried to maneuver me into the role of cruel torturer, busy 'undermining your morale'? If you show this tendency so strongly in the transference, your whole emotional life must be dominated by the same aim."

"But if I tell you all about my childhood and my past, you'll see that I had the most permissive, don't-lay-a-finger-on-the-child bringing-up imaginable. Figure that out!"

"No mystery here. Beating wishes are by no means direct repetitions of experiences in the nursery."

"What are they?"

"Modifications and attenuations of something too deeply buried in the unconscious to be consciously expressed. They are the successors to much worse tortures imputed to the masters of the nursery."

"What can be worse?"

"The whole septet of baby fears: the fear of being starved, devoured, poisoned, choked, chopped to pieces, drained, castrated."

I explained the "septet" in detail; it was a slightly shortened version of the explanation already given in Chapter One. I ended: "The beating actually desired represents an admission of the lesser intrapsychic crime."

At this time, another patient left the city on an extended business trip, and I was able to see Mr. N. regularly three times a week. The analysis could now proceed along more orthodox lines, and we began by taking up Mr. N.'s life history.

"My parents were more than twenty years ahead of their time," he told me. "Most children were still seen and not heard in the years before the first World War, but I was brought up according to the method that became known in the Thirties as 'progressive' or 'permissive' education. My mother's upbringing had been cruelly strict; she had sworn a solemn oath to treat her own children differently. I was the oldest; in fact, I was the only child until I was eight. When my sister and brother finally appeared on the scene, the age differences were so great that there was no chance of 'sibling rivalry.' You could almost say there were no 'siblings.' To all practical purposes, I did as I pleased. My mother never punished; my father fell in with her ideas. I wasn't even scolded or lectured to. When I behaved badly, I was called into 'conferences' where my mother would explain—using adult logic, of course—why my behavior was impractical or undesirable."

"May I interrupt? Here's your reason for calling an observation a reproach; you remember you did that during one of our early appointments, when I was talking about your initial provocations."

"But they never reproached me at home!"

"It seems that you had to work hard to get your beatings at home; they weren't part of the program. The generations brought up in the era of 'progressive education' faced the same problem. Extreme permissiveness thwarted children's masochism, and they had to pile provocation on provocation until they finally made their mothers desperate enough to resort to punishment. Then their poor parents tore their hair, horrified at the thought that they had spoiled the child's whole future life."

"Do you think the old technique of 'do as you're told or I'll smack you' was any better?"

"No, I don't. Both techniques, both extremes, were bad. Finding the happy medium is the nearly hopeless task of education. But these failures show that any type of education can have only a limited effect on the child. The decisive factor in the triad: biology, environment, and the elaboration of the two performed by the child's unconscious ego, seems to be the reaction of the ego."

"In that case, you can say that the elaboration performed by my ego turned me into an intolerable brat. We had more and more conferences, and they lasted longer and longer. Whenever I was with my parents, I would catch them exchanging exasperated looks. Then, finally, we had a big scene—provoked, of course, by me. I stole a few dimes from my mother's purse. This was too much even for her: she smacked me. You see, you could have used the phrase, 'kick in the teeth.'"

"And your reaction?"

"I was highly indignant, and for a little while quite good. It seems that at the age of seven—that's how old I was at the time—I had already learned how to hit below the belt. Every time I showed up Mother's educational methods, she was deeply hurt. Of course I knew the other kids were beaten, and even severely beaten. I don't remember envying them, but maybe I did. My favorite homosexual game makes me wonder."

"I don't think you've given a precise picture of your mother. Yes, you said she was frantically against punishing children, because of her own experiences. But what kind of person was she? Stern or mild?"

"Why do you use the word 'stern'?"

"I am simply asking for information. The word 'stern' came to mind because of experiences with such women in analysis. I have found that beneath the layer of 'mildness on principle' lies a strong temptation to repeat their own infantile experiences with their children as substitutes for themselves. The 'solemn oath' they swore, pledging that they would not emulate their parents, prevents them from doing so. The result is a peculiar attitude, one of frozen sternness. Their words and actions are mild, but their attitude is forbidding."

"You are describing my mother perfectly! I had exactly that feeling with her. I also freely admit that I never really liked her; I believe I must have been scared of her—without reason."

"That fear undoubtedly existed; its results can be seen from another angle. You developed into quite a hypocrite—no offense meant—if you follow my deduction. Look at your fantastic, hypocritical denial of a few weeks ago, when you refused to admit your passivity, and became highly indignant about my suggestion, just as if you and passivity were not even nodding acquaintances. Now, experience proves that hypocrites come out of families where lip-service is held to be more important than inner acceptance of the family rules. In other words, they come from authoritarian families. You describe your home life as the exact opposite. Conclusion: You must have viewed your mother, unconsciously, as an authoritarian, and therefore feared her."

"I must agree—looking at the results. Very strange!"

"By the way, you hardly mentioned your father. What about him?"

"A rather friendly nonentity, parroting Mother. His educational principles can be summed up by his favorite phrase: 'Do what your mother *suggested*!' You see they were afraid to 'tell' me anything; they would only 'suggest'!"

"What were your first sexual experiences as a child?"

"Sex wasn't mentioned at home. I learned the facts of life from boys my own age; I was rather surprised."

"What were your earlier misconceptions?"

"I have no idea."

"But you know that you were surprised at the facts?"

"Definitely, yes."

"Did you have any notions about your parents' sex relations?"

"I don't remember having any."

"Did you consider your mother a kind person?"

"Kind? Wait, I remember something. I was watching, once, while she was busy in the kitchen. She was preparing some dish, and she was cutting up raw meat—maybe a chicken or a fish. She must have caught a peculiar look on my face, because she said, 'It is necessary.' Strange that this memory should come back as an answer to your question."

"Well, that kind of experience is remembered in the same way by many children; it is typical for them to take it as 'proof' that their mother (and all other women, too) is capable of 'any cruelty.' Unconsciously, these children identify with the allegedly victimized animal. Here you have some rather late aborigines of the septet of baby fears. And it is exactly the terror that the supposedly cruel mother inspires in the child of this type that pushes the future homosexual away from the dangerous female sex into the arms of men."

"On the other hand," I continued, "these remnants of fears that are probably pre-verbal, and therefore cannot be remembered in words, explain why the masochistically imbued fears of a later date, fears that are in themselves formidable, are executed in a relatively harmless way, through beating fantasies and beating realities. The inner conscience's accusation, for example, might charge that an evisceration wish exists. This is denied by demonstrating that a comparatively harmless wish to be beaten does exist. This has enough similarity to the accusation to be plausible, but it certainly does not endanger life, and in addition it echoes either an actual educational method or a disciplinary threat. This also explains why so few perverted masochists come into analysis. The ones who do ask for treatment are usually heterosexuals pushed into a corner by a potency disturbance."

I illustrated this point by telling Mr. N. of an experience I had had years ago in Vienna. A man strutted into my office on a Wednesday. He was an imitation Napoleon in his late thirties, with a brusque and self-satisfied manner. He came directly to his point: he had an acute conflict that had to be solved by Saturday. His treatment was to be completed in three days that remained; under no conditions would he enter analysis. He described himself as "a contented perverse masochist," completely impotent with women but sexually satisfied with his routine of being beaten by prostitutes. His emergency had been thrust on him by a peculiar feeling of *noblesse oblige*: a "high-class" girl, unaware of the reasons for his sexual diffidence, had interpreted it as shyness and decided to help him out by making the advances herself. This explained why Saturday loomed over him so ominously: on Saturday evening he was expected to be on hand for a "dinner and bed" party.

The man repeated his requirements: Never, but never, would he consent to being analyzed; all he cared about was being made potent by Saturday, and for Saturday. What was my advice?

I told him that since he suffered from perversion masochism, which on the average cannot be cured in less than three years of analysis, had come to me only three days before his crucial deadline, and did not want to enter analysis in the first place, the only advice I could give him was not to keep his date on Saturday.

At this the man became furious. "You are an ignoramus!" he shouted. I ironically accepted his verdict, on condition that he give me his reason for reaching it. "The reason is obvious!" the man bellowed. "You do not recommend hormonal injections."

Now, any success achieved by this method rests entirely on suggestion, and suggestion could not possibly have any effect in so severe a case of potency disturbance as this man's. I explained this to him, and then asked why he had consulted an analyst at all, if he rejected analysis "on principle." He could have gone, instead, to an enemy of analysis, from whom it would have been logical to expect a recommendation of hormonal treatment, or approval if the patient had made such a suggestion. His reply, again, was shouted: "That's none of your business! What do I owe you for your worthless advice?"

I named my fee. The man threw the bills on the floor and with an air of triumph asked: "What will you do now?" I told him: after he left I would pick up the money, quoting to myself what Talleyrand had said when Napoleon had upbraided him in the presence of the Court: "What a pity that so great a man had so poor an education." The man left without saying another word.

From a rational standpoint, this man had made a fool of himself in our interview. Obviously a well-informed individual, he could not have failed to learn that analysts do not recommend hormonal injections for potency disturbances such as his. If he had naively made himself believe in the efficacy of such injections, why had he not consulted someone who specialized in that treatment? Why, if he so violently rejected analysis, had he not consulted an enemy of analysis? At that time—about twenty-five years ago—he would have had no difficulty in finding one. His conduct could be explained in only one way: he did not want to change his sexual habits, not even for three days; he did want to collect an alibi to prove that if he had not been the victim of an unwarranted "injustice," he could have obliged that hopeful girl. And he had cleverly seen to it that I had to do him an "injustice."

Mr. N. smiled politely at this example and then recurred to the information I had given him on the genesis of the masochistic perversion. He asked: "Do you mean that sexually I'm still a baby wanting to be treated in ways that match the septet of baby fears?"

"Yes."

"And my turning to homosexuality was the way I protected myself against the mother who was capable of such cruelties?"

"Again, yes."

"This is completely idiotic. Wait—you don't know what I mean. Why am I surprised? I read this; I heard it from you; what's new about it?"

"You seem to be experiencing one of the high points in every analysis (meaning every successful analysis): the moment when something *intellectually* understood sinks in *emotionally*. The two kinds of understanding are independent of each other. Your surprise is quite appropriate for the *emotional* system; in that system, it is news."

"You mean this is a good sign?"

"Definitely."

"That's unbelievable," he said. "That's unbelievable," he said again.

This phrase became his theme song, dominating many subsequent appointments. "Understanding 'masochism,' in the newly-acquired sense," became his favorite topic. After some weeks he surprised me with the flat statement that he was "through with homosexuality," and could not be tempted even by his favorite types. I had my doubts.

I said: "Let's see. If that's true, you must be ready to face the facts that forced you into the fantasy of heterosexuality, in theory. You were curious about what a 'normal guy' feels, you told me. We uncovered one pretty obvious explanation for this: the idea came to you when the supply of young homosexuals became scarce. We won't go into that again. Let's work on the real, *unconscious* reason for your sudden interest in heterosexuality."

"I smell a rat. Don't spoil my mood!"

"What was the phrase your mother used? 'It is necessary.' Any suggestions?"

"I told you my reason: I thought perhaps a woman could give me *some* love."

"Why be naive? Since when did *you* want love? All your thousands of homosexual contacts were beating experiences, or attempts to provoke your partner into beating you."

"So what?"

"It's only logical to conclude that you wanted the same experiences with a woman, but under heightened conditions of danger. Didn't you originally run away from women because they were too dangerous?"

At this Mr. N. became uncontrollably furious. He called me every unpleasant name he knew; his repertory, I can attest, was extensive. I let his fury run its course, and took advantage of a pause for breath to ask:

"Aren't you suspicious of your own fury?"

That did it. Mr. N. sobered up, and asked: "You really believe my idea of switching was just an unconscious scheme for increasing the masochistic stakes?"

"Yes, I do."

"Why?"

"Neurosis is a progressive, not a self-limiting disease."

At this time I had to attend a medical meeting in Chicago; treatment was interrupted for a few days. When I saw Mr. N. again, he wore—with an ease that seemed habitual, though I knew it was not—a new manner: he was jovial, cordial, receptive, unprovocative.

"What happened to you?" I asked.

"I'm preparing myself for the stronger sex, woman. Aren't suitors, even wolves disguised as suitors, supposed to be charming?"

"Are you acting out a comedy, or did a change really come over you, and is this your rationalization?"

"Half and half."

"Accent on the former or latter half?"

"Believe it or not, there has been a change!"

"I don't want to pour cold water on your enthusiasm, but do you know that you need a few lessons in the anatomy of the female genitalia? I bet you are completely uninformed."

Mr. N. started to laugh; this seemed to him a wonderful joke. "Sexual enlightenment at the age of forty-eight and one-half! Well, why not?" he said.

The next few months, Mr. N. repeatedly announced, had "the quality of a fairy tale." There were ups and downs, slight disappointments, great enthusiasm, comical episodes, before he reached his goal of normal sex. He changed to a degree that I had never believed possible. Even his rate of recovery was astonishing; he was in treatment for only seven months. He made good his claim to be "a good heterosexual winner"; when using the phrase he always stressed the word "heterosexual," as if pointing to a badge of honor. I had told him that his chances of cure were infinitesimal; still he had "won." A remarkable zest for living characterized the new Mr. N. "I was always a good winner," he told me triumphantly. "Don't ask me about losing—that's not in my dictionary."

"Hadn't you better add 'any more'?"

"Add it," Mr. N. agreed, with a munificent gesture. "Today I'm in a giveaway mood."

Mr. O.: "I am a classical example of what you call 'the statistically induced homosexual.'"

Mr. O. was twenty-six, married, and a father. He and his wife had three children; a fourth was expected. His parents were wealthy, and his job was in the family business. The phrase he used to explain his presence in my office, "the statistically induced homosexual," is one that I coined, and used for the first time in a lecture delivered at the fourth meeting of the Academy of Psychosomatic Medicine, in October, 1956. I used it again in my book, HOMOSEXUALITY: DISEASE OR WAY OF LIFE? This was what I said when I first introduced this concept:

> After the appearance of Kinsey's Volume I (1948), a new type of homosexual appeared. I have suggested for this type the name "statistically induced homosexual." Although Kinsey's fantastically exaggerated claims regarding the prevalence of homosexuality received only rare mentions in the press, his figure of 37 per cent was slyly put to use by the older, more experienced homosexual, who would ask a wavering youngster: "Who are you to argue with one-third of the male population? Do you know how many tens of millions are involved? So many good Americans can't be wrong!" Of course, the argument did not produce new recruits among true homosexuals (they needed no arguments), but it was quite effective with some borderline cases of post-adolescents in their late teens or early twenties, in whom the decision to be a homosexual had been hanging in the balance. Only a certain percentage of these temporary borderline cases are true homosexuals. Many are not. Their pseudo-modernity and misplaced experimentation, growing out of the erroneous belief that homosexuality is "scientifically" approved and "normal," have the unhappy result of burdening them with damaging guilt and self-doubt. These burdens remain even after reversion to heterosexuality. The tragic and

pitiful spectacle of these "statistically induced homosexuals" is due entirely to the failure to disseminate medical facts.

"Why didn't you publish your book earlier?" Mr. O. asked sadly. "I could have been saved the shock of my life—a homosexual experience. I can say honestly that I was taken in by the Kinsey statistics. If every third man you meet on the street has had homosexual experiences, obviously I couldn't be an exception. When I first heard these statistics, in college, I had no suspicion that Kinsey had padded his high incidence curves by including puberal play. I didn't know, either, that Kinsey's statistics were unreliable to begin with, because of the way he had selected—or been selected by—his volunteers.

"My college roommate used the Kinsey statistics as his argument. I fought him off for a long time; finally, when I was nineteen, I gave in. The affair went on until I was twenty-one. If you want to know what that period of my life was like: it was misery concentrated, guilt heightened, depression the order of the day. My idiotic bringing-up might have been responsible; in our house there was a taboo on anything even remotely smacking of sex.

"And on top of everything else, my roommate was promiscuous, and I was jealous. I suffered hellishly, which wasn't in the code; he kept reminding me, ironically, that 'modern' people aren't jealous. Those two years— But when I was twenty-one I met a girl from a neighboring college, and we got married. I've been happy. But the recollection of those two years haunts me—three children or not. I can't get rid of my doubts . . ."

"About what?" I asked.

"About whether or not I am really a homosexual. I start every sex act fearing failure. What this Kinsey did to me!"

"Let's not exaggerate. I certainly agree—and was the first to point out—that Kinsey did damage by providing confirmed homosexuals with a seemingly irrefutable argument to use when they are 'on the prowl' and looking for new recruits. But the argument is irrefutable only to a person who worships statistics. A statistic, of course, means nothing unless it has been properly computed on a representative sample and properly interpreted afterwards, but this doesn't matter to the naive people who insist that 'figures can't lie.' On the other hand, you remember how Jimmy Walker defeated a proposed censorship law when he was serving in Albany: he said, 'No girl was ever ruined by a book.' In other words, Kinsey or no Kinsey, the problem lies in *you*."

"I agree. But without the Kinsey statistics, I wouldn't have been such a pushover!"

"That's possible. But here is the more significant fact: This is an event in your past, but it is still alive in you, and a burden. Under more favorable inner conditions you would have relegated it to the storehouse of disagreeable memories; you would have 'forgotten' it. Especially since your sex life is now, and has been for years, quite normal."

"Do you believe that analysis can free me from those—as you believe—senseless apprehensions and fears?"

"I certainly do."

"Where do we start?"

"At your tendency to torture yourself."

"I can show you, right this minute, how twisted my thinking is. I figured that out—the torture tendency—on the basis of your book. 'Don't torture yourself with these fears, you masochist!' I told myself. And then I felt sure I was lost: you also wrote that masochism is the basis of homosexuality. It's a vicious circle!"

"No, it's a closed circle of self-torture. One could say that you misused my book, too, though for a different purpose than Kinsey's. It is true that 'masochism-plus' is the basis of homosexuality. But it's also true that masochism alone does not make a homosexual. You conveniently overlooked the fact that psychic masochism is a *universal* phenomenon, found in heterosexuals and homosexuals. Finding out that you are a psychic masochist doesn't warrant the conclusion that you are a homosexual. That conclusion can appear only when the 'plus' is discernible: the shift of the executive power to torture and harm from woman, representing mother, to man."

"That's wonderful! If masochistic propensities alone can't prove homosexuality, then that disposes of my greatest fear."

"Intellectually, it may. But emotionally, the story reads differently. If it did not, one discussion with a specialist could break up the pattern of self-torture. Analysis is not that easy. Change comes only after the lengthy emotional experience of 'working through' in transference and resistance. But I am very optimistic about your chances."

Apparently, Mr. O. was an avid psychic masochist who, having found a hitching post for his homeless self-torture, was by no means willing to surrender his negative psychic possessions without a struggle. First, he put all the blame on Kinsey, ignoring the undoubted fact that without some traces of a welcoming attitude in himself, no arguments backed up by Kinsey or anyone else could have persuaded him into a homosexual affair. Then he went through a period of torturing jealousy with his homosexual roommate. Once more, a convenient hitching post for masochistic torture. Why had he continued the affair for two long years? As a defense, he had then married; he had been potent and "happy." Why had he continued to brood over his homosexual past, instead of dismissing it? He had then read my book, misapplied the information found in it, and again misused the situation for the purpose of self-torture. Why did "examination fright" attack him before every sex act? All this added up to uncontrovertible evidence: he was a faithful adherent of the "trouble game."

Mr. O. had no hesitation about discussing his early history; unfortunately, his words provided neither enlightenment nor clues. He described his parents as "quiet, rather reserved people who traveled a good deal, enjoying their wealth." They had treated their only child with kindness and consideration, never trying to impose their ideas or aspirations on him. They took it for granted—and so did he—that he would eventually go to work for the family business. He never doubted that circumstances had mapped out a secure future for him, and he saw no objection to this peaceful prospect.

"Nice, orderly, well-mannered, quiet." No clear or genuine picture of the family emerged from the patient's string of polite phrases. He spiced his narration with only one criticism, and even this had been a single comment made during our first interview, when he remarked that any reference to sex had been taboo in his home, and that in this respect his had been an "idiotic bringing up." But when I asked him to elaborate on this point, he immediately retired into excuses. He had not meant it as it sounded, he explained; it had merely happened that the "serious" domestic atmosphere had not been conducive to any mention of sex.

All questions drew blanks. Mr. O. did not remember his dreams; attempting free associations produced long stretches of silence, interrupted by self-reproach for his failure to bring out any material to work on. These accusations, and occasional attacks of the jitters, when he would again paint his past sins and his expectations for the future in the darkest possible colors, were the only breaks in his general mood of subdued seriousness.

I asked him, finally: "What is the matter with your sense of humor? Do you never smile, laugh, feel any gaiety?"

"I can't help being a serious person."

"Did you say serious or depressed?"

"Serious."

"Why are you?"

"It's a family trait."

"What does that mean?"

"Everybody in the family is serious."

"But you said that your parents traveled a good deal, and enjoyed their money."

"In a quiet way, they did."

"And what do you enjoy?"

"Freedom from guilt."

"That's negative. What do you enjoy in a positive way?"

"I have to admit, not much."

"Why?"

"In the last few years I've been so preoccupied with my various fears; they didn't leave me much time to enjoy anything."

"That isn't accurately put. Since you created your bogey yourself, you must have enjoyed your fears."

"I assure you I haven't consciously enjoyed them. On the contrary."

"What kind of fellow were you before the incident at college?"

"A quiet, friendly, well-mannered boy."

"Never difficult?"

"That isn't done in our family."

"Do you appreciate jokes? But don't tell me: that isn't done in your family!"

"I appreciate some jokes."

"Please tell me the best joke you ever heard."

"Are you serious?"

"Very serious."

"I know you have published a book on the psychology of laughter. Are you still exploring the subject?"

"No. I want to apply the results of my studies to you."

"You really want me to tell you my favorite joke?"

"Yes."

"Well, if you insist. It goes something like this: A young ostrich comes home. His whole family is standing there with their heads in the sand. The young one asks: 'Is anyone home'?"

"Not bad. How does this apply to you?"

"There's no connection."

"Do you really believe that our favorite jokes just happen to be our favorites?"

"Yes."

"You are mistaken. Take this favorite joke of yours. It shows that you consider your family unwilling to face facts; they play ostrich. When did you first hear the joke?"

"In high school."

"And you still remember it, after ten or twelve years?"

"I should remember it; I've told it often enough."

"And you really believe it has no connection with you?"

"None at all."

"I've asked you several times why you aren't a little more alive. Several times you've answered with a pat phrase: 'That isn't done in our family.' Do you think that only a listener with absolute pitch could detect a note of accusation in that statement of fact?"

"Really?"

"Really. I believe that you are acting out—unconsciously, to be sure—a mechanism called 'the negative magic gesture.' That refers to something very tangible: an unconscious dramatization of how one did *not* want to be treated in childhood. The dramatization always includes an ironic exaggeration as well as a masochistic accusation. In your case, I believe that your extreme seriousness is an ironic way of reducing your parents' quiet, subdued manner to absurdity. The bitter accusation—'See what you did to me!'—comes through at the same time."

The patient did not answer.

"Well, say something. Or are you one of the individuals the French astronomer Flammarion alluded to when he said that some people would not commit themselves even to the statement that castor oil is a laxative?"

Mr. O. achieved a tentative smile. "It's not that I don't dare to commit myself," explained. "I'm just thinking."

"Tell me the results when you are ready."

There was silence.

"Did you ever hear of 'thinking aloud'?" I asked.

"You will laugh, but I have to say it isn't done in our family."

"Can you make an exception, and break the family tradition? After all, you have violated the unwritten code before, when you had your homosexual affair."

"Just rub it in!"

"You finally did come alive! Now I'm the enemy! Are you offended?"

"No, but you have a very blunt way of expressing yourself."

"How about adopting it for the duration?"

"I will think it over."

The young man did think it over, and concluded that he didn't understand himself: "The family tradition and the way I was brought up really consists of one rule: be reticent, don't let your feelings show, keep a stiff upper lip. I fell into step without any trouble; it seemed natural to act that way. But I acted quite differently on two occasions. During my homosexual affair, I showed violent jealousy; I felt it a good deal more often than I showed it, of course. And when that was over, when I began to fear that I could never recover from the damage, I was nearly hysterical, though again I covered up and suffered in silence. I may seem to others to be lifeless, but these examples show that I'm not. I don't understand myself."

"Why not assume that underneath the quiet, apparently unperturbed surface, is a hidden volcano, and that the volcano erupts inwardly?"

For the first time, I saw Mr. O. laugh.

"A volcano!" he repeated. "You don't know how that sounds to me. You should tell this to my wife; I mean, I wish you could, if it were possible, and if I didn't want to keep my analysis a secret."

"Does your wife complain about your reticence, too?"

"Yes. She seems to accept the fact that I'm not exactly demonstrative about my emotions. But from time to time she reproaches me for my coldness."

"You didn't mention that. All you said was that you are happy with her."

"I am; it's gratitude-happiness, if such a word exists."

"But are you affectionate, tender?"

"In actions, yes. Not in words."

"Not such a good policy, is it?"

"I agree."

"Why not simply accept the fact that you are carrying over grievances from your childhood—a lot of grievances? You cover up your inward tears with outward detachment and a pretense of equanimity."

"But what is true and what is pseudo?"

"Your masochistic propensities, your 'inward tears,' are the end result of your individual infantile conflict. The stiff-upper-lip attitude is a secondary defense."

"Then what I told you about not being able to understand myself doesn't make sense."

"You will have to learn to think in multi-dimensional terms."

Mr. O. eagerly accepted the idea of a "new dimension" within himself; he had only one regret: "Why didn't I figure that out myself?"

"Because you would have spared yourself inner anguish by perceiving these parallel and multiple layers within your mind. And the anguish was exactly what you wanted."

Very gradually, Mr. O. became conscious of evidence of his "inner volcano." He recalled that in early childhood, at about the age of six, he had been quite critical of the "dead house" in which he and his parents lived. The memory astonished him into exclaiming: "So I was 'alive' then!"

"Who taught you the stiff-upper-lip attitude?" I asked.

"No one. But some atmospheres drag you down . . . It was like that at home."

"In short, instead of rebelling against this atmosphere, you used two very damaging defenses. You repressed your feelings, which led to your use of the negative magic gesture, and you defied your parents' teachings by taking up pseudo-homosexuality."

"It seems so—if you say so."

"Just observe the ambiguity, ambivalence and hidden irony in that remark!"

For the second time, Mr. O. laughed; for the first time, he laughed at himself.

"Well, there is hope for you," I said. "Perhaps we can defrost you."

This question arose: When Mr. O. displayed violent jealousy of his homosexual partner, during his college affair, had this been part and parcel of his general masochistic technique, or had he been repeating (for masochistic purposes) some episode from his childhood? I assumed that his jealousy had actually represented a repetition which could be traced back to his parents' frequent trips. I asked him: "Who took care of you when your parents were absent?"

"Usually I went to camp; sometimes I stayed home with my governess."

"Did you resent that?"

"No."

"I don't believe that your conscious recollections are precise."

"I can only tell you what I know."

"Well, we shall see."

Some time later, the patient said: "You know, you always laugh at me for having the soul of an accountant. You are wrong."

"What's that? I never used that phrase! What are you projecting on me? Or is this your estimate of yourself?"

"You call me 'detached.' That's the same as saying 'the soul of an accountant.' "

"I disagree. Please continue."

"I was about to say I always had a flair for figures and statistics. They always fascinated and impressed me. But this is ironic: *After* I became the victim of Kinsey's statistics somebody published a book called *How To Lie With Statistics*. That book made me furious. The irony of this just struck me. Why should I get into a fury because of a book that debunked statistics?"

"I remember the book; I happen to have it." I got the book and the patient read the following excerpt:

You, I trust, are not a snob, and I certainly am not in the real-estate business. But let's say that you are and I am and that you are looking for property to buy along a road that is not far from the California valley in which I live.

Having sized you up, I take pains to tell you that the average income in this neighborhood is some $15,000 a year. Maybe that clinches your interest in living here; anyway, you buy and that handsome figure sticks in your mind. More than likely, since we have agreed that for the purposes of the moment you are a bit of a snob, you toss it in casually when telling your friends about where you live.

A year or so later we meet again. As a member of some tax-payers' committee I am circulating a petition to keep the tax rate down or assessments down or bus fare down. My plea is that we cannot afford the increase: After all, the average income in this neighborhood is only $3,500 a year . . . Am I lying now, or was I lying last year?

You can't pin it on me either time. That is the essential beauty of doing your lying with statistics. Both these figures are legitimate averages, legally arrived at . . . My trick was to use a different kind of average each time, the word average having a very loose meaning . . .

The $15,000 figure I used when I wanted a big one is a *mean*, the arithmetic average of all the families in the neighborhood. You get it by adding up all the incomes and dividing it by the number there are. The smaller figure is a *median*, and so it tells you that half the families in question have more than $3,500 a year, and half have less. I might also have used the *mode*, which is the most frequently met-with figure in a series. If in this neighborhood there are more families with incomes of $5,000 a year than with any other amount, $5,000 a year is the *modal* income.

In this case, as usually is true with income figures, an unqualified "average" is virtually meaningless (pp. 27 ff.).

"That's it," said Mr. O. "And now I remember who wrote it—Darrell Huff.* I don't know if I ever mentioned this: I'm good

* W. W. Norton & Company, 1954. Quoted with permission of the publisher.

at figures—I reorganized the bookkeeping department of our firm . . ."

"Well?"

"Well, I'm just surprised at the contradiction. The victim of statistics loves statistics and figures. What's the answer?"

"An irrational infantile element that you are using and perhaps misusing."

"But what?"

"Only your recollections—so far, still repressed—can answer that."

It was not long before the pertinent recollection came to the surface. The boy had never accompanied his parents on their trips. When he was eight, he threw a temper tantrum when he found out that he was again to spend his summer in camp while his parents traveled. He wanted to go with them; his parents explained why he could not, quoting statistics which proved that a large percentage of the boys in his age group went to camp when their parents could afford to send them. In this way, the statistical average was made into an accepted argument. Years later, Mr. O. unconsciously turned the same "statistical average" against his parents when he reasoned: "If the statistical average is decisive, Kinsey's statistical argument is irrefutable."

I told the patient: "You see that I was justified in suspecting that you bitterly resented not being taken on those trips. Of course, the 'diabolical joke' you played on your parents was masochistic. I once described a case in which a four-year-old was taught the alphabet by his father, a professor of technical engineering. The father constantly complained that the boy wasn't 'thorough enough' in his studies. Twenty years later, when the boy came into treatment, he was a student of technical engineering who had been refusing, for two years, to take his final exams. His procrastination infuriated his father. 'Take that idiotic examination,' the father kept urging. 'I'm not thoroughly prepared—yet,' the son always answered. This was unconscious irony. He was using the same old stick—thoroughness—to beat his father with. And you did exactly the same thing, using statistics. In both cases, the unconscious irony was highly masochistic. Both the other patient and you were damaging yourselves more than your parents."

Uncovering Mr. O.'s "statistical irony" marked the dividing line between the preliminaries and the real work of his analysis. Months of "working through" his masochistic and anachronistic tendency followed.

In time, Mr. O. changed remarkably. His fear of homosexuality disappeared. His college episode became meaningless. Most remarkable, he "came alive." His astonished wife once asked him, "Have you been taking vitamins behind my back?" In her opinion, this was the only "reasonable" explanation possible. As an old German proverb has it, "You never can tell what makes you fat."

5

Duration of Treatment

THE MOST DARING EXPERIMENTS spring from the exigencies of reality. Two unchangeable factors in many patients—limited means and/or residence at a distance from New York City—led me to attempt to fix the minimum requirement, in terms of time and appointments, for the effective analytical treatment of homosexuality.

Experiences with these patients have produced the following conclusions:

The *optimum* situation calls for three appointments a week over a period of four months (which includes the trial treatment), after which the patient sees the analyst twice a week for another four months. This comes to eight months and approximately eighty to eighty-five appointments.

The *minimum of the minimum* falls to two appointments a week over a period of eight months. In some (by no means all) cases the minimum aggregate of approximately sixty-four appointments proved insufficient, and three appointments a week had to be scheduled during the first four months.

Certain additional measures must be taken in order for this drastically curtailed treatment to become effective.

1. Whether the patient comes into treatment "with great confidence" or burdened by "severest doubts," he invariably and immediately—as part of the analytic transference—projects the image of the "bad, cruel and draining" mother on to the psychiatrist. This tendency was illustrated in the case of Mr. L. (see Chapter Four); this patient displayed his unconscious identification of the analyst with the "cruel" mother during our very first interview, when he took it for granted that I intended to damage him by discussing his problem with his father behind his back. Similarly, Mr. M. (in the same chapter) "figured out" that I had malicious reasons for accepting him as a patient: I took him on, he reasoned, only in order to "experiment" with him, and certain childhood experiences had made experimentation synonymous with failure in his inner vocabulary. And Mr. D. (see Chapter Two) took it for granted that I, being a "dangerous fellow," meant to confuse him with verbal casuistry. Mr. G. (see Chapter Two) leaped immediately to the conclusion that I did not want to cure his potency troubles because I was propelled by malicious missionary zeal for the heterosexual status quo.

Projection cannot be avoided; this situation, compounded by the patient's ignorance of psychological facts and therefore necessarily handled on an interim basis, can always be counted on as the first knotty tangle encountered in treatment. But in these deeply regressed cases, the classical analytic procedure makes it more difficult to smooth out the separate threads making up the tangle. The procedure calls for the patient to produce "free associations," but these neurotics misunderstand this sound rule, interpreting it as a process in which they are being "drained."

Asking any injustice collector to "give"—even when the gift is an intangible, like words—immediately activates his main defense mechanism. His entire inner life revolves around the constant effort to disprove by means of fake aggression the accusation, leveled by inner conscience, that he unconsciously loves and seeks refusal, rejection and defeat. Always on the alert for an external situation that will serve to dramatize his standard alibi of pseudo-aggression, he unconsciously perceives the request for free associations as an attack and an invasion, and replies to it with a pseudo-aggressive refusal of words. What strengthens his alibi, here, is another classic routine: the analyst remains silent, thus himself allegedly "refusing" words and involuntarily inviting identification with the cruel, cold, "refusing" mother of infancy.

My experience has shown* that only a complete reversal of approach can clear up this dilemma. Instead of allowing the patient to see a parallel between cold, denying mother and silent, "draining" analyst, the analyst must present a picture of "generous, giving mother" by talking for long periods during the beginning of analysis. This invites the patient to adopt a different inner defense: the contention that he would, if given the opportunity, return kindness for kindness and generosity for generosity. This alibi, though secondary to the alibi of fake aggression, is also standard in the arsenal of the injustice collector, who is always attesting his wish to be kindly treated. By giving words himself, instead of demanding them from the patient, the analyst encourages an inner attitude in the patient that counteracts his otherwise inevitable anger, suspicion and more or less hidden hostility. In later stages of the analysis, of course, this defense must also be dissected and resolved.

2. It is essential to be selective about the material presented; the patient must be *constantly* confronted with his psychic masochism, whenever and wherever it shows up.

3. The homosexual's pseudo-aggression must not be confused with "real" aggression. The patient's provocative technique must be shown for what it is: a means of achieving the unconsciously desired "kick in the teeth."

4. The analyst must consistently stress the fact that what consciously appears to the patient as "*homosexual tension*" is actually "*masochistic tension.*" *This separation of the superficial from the deeper layer kills homosexuality.*

5. The analyst must be clear in his aims: curing homosexuality

* This experience applies to *all* masochistically regressed cases ("oral regression"), and originally had nothing to do with homosexuality. It was first observed by myself on a case of pseudo-mental deficiency (see *Int. Zeitschrift fuer Psychoanalyse*, XVIII:528-538, 1932); it was elaborated on in THE BASIC NEUROSIS, 1949. Since homosexuals are psychic masochists — plus, the advocated technical innovation applies to them, too.

means destruction of a deep-seated masochistic neurosis, and not "adaptation" to it. This presupposes the analyst's conviction that homosexuality is a severe illness and not "a way of life." It also means that the analyst must be *inwardly* capable of constantly singling out (as opposed to constantly overlooking) the masochistic component in the patient.

6. The analyst must remain *inwardly* unaffected by the homosexual patient's repeated attempts to force him into the role of "forbidding" authority. These patients needle the analyst endlessly in the hope of receiving an "order" to abstain from homosexuality. The analyst, however, imposes no restriction, unless it can be called a restriction to utter the obvious warning that analysis cannot be conducted in prison—the domicile which the patient unconsciously desires.

Two specific complicating factors should be mentioned. These arise in some (not all) cases, prolonging the treatment of some homosexuals beyond the typical limit of eight months and approximately eighty appointments. The first of these is premature ejaculation during first experiences of intercourse with women; the second consists of too-extensive inroads of masochistic traits into the total personality.

PREMATURE EJACULATION

Whether in homo- or heterosexuals, premature ejaculation always represents a defense against masochistic attachment to the giantess of the nursery. The defense takes the form of pseudo-aggression: to lend credence to his unconscious assertion that he does not want to be refused by the mother, the prematurist actively refuses pleasure to the mother-substitute, the woman who is his sexual partner. The infantile aim makes use of an equally infantile symbolism. The prematurist, in external reality, is refusing his partner pleasure because of the brevity of his intercourse; in inner reality, he is refusing her "milk" (which he equates unconsciously with sperm) by "spilling it before it can reach the mouth." In the same infantile symbolism, the vagina represents the mouth, and the penis the breast. The aggressive intent is as clear in an intercourse of four to six thrusts, as against the typical sixty or more, as it is when ejaculation takes place before penetration.

These unconsciously engineered disappointments are like the Barmecide's feast in the Arabian Nights, where the table is spread with luxuries, the guest invited to partake—and the food removed before the hungry guest can do more than reach for the delicacies.

In my opinion, the deepest layer in this neurotic symptom consists of the masochistic wish to be refused. The over-all defense, when the masochist is accused by inner conscience of harboring this wish, takes the standard form of pseudo-aggression, in this situation becoming refusal. When, in its turn, pseudo-aggression is vetoed by the inner conscience, the prematurist puts forward an amended unconscious defense: "But I don't refuse; I give *immediately*." The amendment may stand up, temporarily, as an inner alibi; the fact that the woman is denied pleasure remains unchanged.

There is a curious interlocking of identifications in the inner drama of prematurity. The prematurist's partner represents the poor, "starved" baby who he was himself in his fantasy. At the same time, he also represents the cruel, refusing mother—whose rejection of him he still unconsciously and masochistically enjoys. The guilt and depression that arise in him after the act pertain to the masochistic pleasure he derived through his unconscious identification with "the baby." He shifts his guilt from masochism to false aggression in two ways: he himself has been the "active" rejecting "mother" who denied his partner pleasure; he himself reproaches himself for his cruelty to his partner.

Prematurity in intercourse with women provides the partly-changed homosexual with a new depository for his pseudo-aggression. The same masochistic hatred of the mother that was at the root of his homosexuality now activates him in his prematurity. The new symptom must be worked through and perceived as just another unconscious delaying action which must be eliminated so that the patient can continue towards his cure.

MASOCHISTIC INVASION OF THE TOTAL PERSONALITY

Since the homosexual neurosis is masochistic in itself, masochism cannot but invade the other sectors of the neurotic's life. This can easily be seen in the encounters with homosexuals (both in treatment, and in preliminary interviews) already described in this book. Mr. B., in Chapter Two, deliberately courted exposure by applying for a teaching job in a public school, where investigations of his background were certain to uncover his police record, instead of staying on the faculty of a private school, where he was safe from exposure. Mr. F. (also in Chapter Two) virtually invited a dishonorable discharge from the armed forces; coming as he did from a small town, this would have meant advertising his homosexuality to everyone he knew in the area in which he expected to spend the rest of his life. In the same chapter is the case of Mr. I., who deliberately risked his excellent job by attempting to seduce the boss's son.

Mr. M., in Chapter Four, made use of a frequently encountered masochistic gambit. Having protected himself socially by marrying, he jeopardized his valued status by "unguardedly" permitting his wife to discover, not only his homosexuality, but the fact that he was being blackmailed by an extortionist. As already mentioned, the alleged "bisexual" almost invariably confesses his homosexuality—either directly or indirectly—to his wife.

These examples show that the masochistic substratum of homosexuality can seldom, if ever, remain contained within the perversion. The homosexual can always satisfy his appetite for self-damage by using his disapproved sexual habits as a handle. Though this is his preferred, it is by no means his only means of accomplishing self-damage.

The problem of quantitative masochistic involvement is decisive here. Sometimes, though homosexuality has already collapsed in a specific case, a few more months of treatment are indicated, "just to be sure."

Experience has convinced me that the end of an analysis should never be fixed, in advance, on a specific date. This applies to analyses of homosexuals, too. After the usual eight months of treatment have elapsed, and the patient is no longer a homosexual, therapy should be continued at the rate of one visit per month—as long as the patient wishes to come.

The analyst's curtain line, when the analysis is over, seems to be of some practical significance. I usually tell my patients: "For all practical purposes, you are through with your homosexuality. The same cannot be said about your psychic masochism—nobody is through with that until the grave solves the problem. Psychic masochism is universal; I cannot make you healthier than a healthy person. But remember this: you are better equipped than the man on the street to fight the remnants of your psychic masochism. He considers himself healthy; you know what you have to guard against. Use that weapon. Nobody can guarantee you 'freedom from masochism' in your future life. But it is possible to guarantee that nothing will happen to you that can't be straightened out in a few appointments with your analyst. Be especially careful of the old tricks—it may happen that you find yourself with a fleeting homosexual fantasy when another 'great injustice' comes your way, especially from a woman. You may have provoked the 'injustice,' or you may have misused a genuine situation. If that happens, don't take it for granted that you are backsliding. Just fight your masochism. Don't express it in the discredited form of the homosexual 'rescue station.' You will see that the formula—'Fight remnants of masochism!'—works like magic, *after* analysis."

6

The "Confessional Mood" of Some Homosexuals

LEGAL AND SOCIAL NECESSITIES, imposed by an environment biased against homosexuality, make every homosexual into a conspirator leading a double life. The need to keep homosexual attitudes secret is so obvious, the advantages of prudence so patent, that one automatically assumes that no homosexual declares himself voluntarily to an outsider.

Once more, the facts have nothing to do with logic. Confessions are the rule rather than the exception. The confessions are sometimes bald and outright, sometimes hinted, sometimes staged by innuendo, but they are almost invariably forthcoming. If we were not equipped, today, with the knowledge that the unconscious harbors self-damaging tendencies, we would have to conclude that the confessing homosexual is also a moron. This is of course not the case.

Confession is good for the soul, declares the familiar cliche, but nobody has ever asserted that advertising one's secrets is a credit to one's common sense. People do rather casually assume that some kind of catharsis from guilt is achieved in the process. Confessions in general represent an inner story too complex to be summed up by references to popular beliefs, but the confessions of the homosexual are of a special kind, with limited significance. These confessions have a single motivation: the purpose is to get the homosexual into deeper water. No abreaction of guilt is achieved. The homosexual merely cashes in a masochistic I.O.U., paying usurious interest for the accommodation. The irony here is the fact that the I.O.U. is paid by—and paid to—the same person.

Mr. M., whom we encountered in Chapter Four, claimed that he confessed his homosexuality to his wife because she promised to be sympathetic in his trouble, and to "forget whatever it may be"; he was deeply indignant when his naivete was rewarded with constant scenes. He asked me, "Why does a fool of a husband confess?" I answered:

> "Psychic masochism includes the tendency to play for ever-increasing stakes in the game of making trouble for oneself. How a can a bisexual make sure that his marriage will make trouble for him? By confessing. That's exactly what many of them do. It's not always a direct confession. More often they unconsciously set the stage for the big scene by arousing their wives' suspicion. Potency troubles are one way. Another way is 'forgetting' to destroy incriminating letters, or engaging in indiscreet telephone calls when they supposedly don't know their wives are listening, or letting themselves be discovered in a questionable situation with another man. Then the wife starts her inquisition, and finds the suspect very willing—unconsciously, of course—to confess."

Mr. I., the psychopathic homosexual (described in Chapter Two) who wanted to misuse a fake analysis to retrieve lost ground and recapture his position as assistant to the president of a large firm, confessed his homosexuality to his puritanical boss even though he could have denied the charge. His boss had no concrete evidence, and stated he was acting on the basis of hearsay. Mr. I. found a rationalization to cover his eagerness to "tell all"; he said, "I am a fighter for full equality." My rejoinder was: "You are deluding yourself. You are a fighter for the inalienable right to damage yourself."

Mr. A. (see Chapter One), the young man who kept one appointment with me only "to do his silly parents a favor," was found out because he used his home telephone for his jealous scenes with his boy friends. He did this although he knew perfectly well that there were many telephone extensions in his parents' palatial home. When it was pointed out to him that he had unconsciously invited the disclosure of his homosexuality, he denied the obvious, and launched into a furious denunciation of those "sneaks," his parents.

And so on, in an endless procession.*

Those who doubt the predominance of psychic masochism in homosexuals are invited to scrutinize the following cases:

Mr. P. is a young man of thirty who had been brought up in a strongly religious atmosphere. He is at present in treatment with me for homosexuality. He is married, and his wife knows he is a homosexual: he confessed it to her the morning after their wedding night.

"Was there any reason to do that?" I asked him. "Were you impotent?"

"No. Everything went very well."

"Why did you confess? Did you believe it would increase her happiness?"

"In our religious denomination we have a precept: 'Confess thy sins to thy neighbors.' "

"Can you mention a religious precept stipulating that one has the duty to make someone else unhappy by an unsolicited confession?"

"I don't think so. At least, nothing comes to mind."

"Why, then, do you adduce a religious precept to justify this pseudo-aggression—pseudo, because your wife must have paid you back with interest—?"

"That's true. She did."

"Why do you bring this mockery of religion into the discussion?

* Other examples illustrating how young people "inform" their parents of their homosexuality by means of diaries, hints, and so on are mentioned in Chapter Ten.

Why did your religious training, and your abiding by it—as you claim to do—not prevent homosexuality in the first place? Doesn't the Old Testament call homosexuality an abomination?"

"That's true."

"And didn't you tell me that your parents were all for your marriage because a psychiatrist in your home town told you, and your parents, that marriage was your only salvation? (He was wrong, of course.) Did you tell this to your wife, too?"

"I did."

"You told your wife that you married her for therapeutic reasons and not for love. Then why are you surprised that she shows, as you put it, 'a certain antagonism' towards you and your mother?"

This time there was no answer.

Mr. Q., a first-rate scientist in his field, was half-forced into treatment by his wife. I asked him how she had learned about his homosexuality.

"Through a peculiarity of mine," he replied.

"What is this peculiarity?"

"To make my homosexual masturbation fantasies more vivid, I used to write them down during the act. Afterwards, I would destroy them. One day I was careless. I threw the description into the waste-paper basket without tearing it up first. My wife found it."

"And then you confessed?"

"Not immediately."

"But you finally did confess?"

"Yes."

"Wouldn't you say that you asked for trouble by writing these peculiar leaves of a diary?"

"You probably call it masochism to have written them."

"And you, what would you call it?"

"I'd say I'm a stupid ass."

"Are you pleading extenuating circumstances—moronity?"

There was no answer. I continued: "Did it ever occur to you that a diary, in any form, is unconsciously written in order to be read by someone?"

"I did not know that."

Homosexuals claim that some government departments and some large private firms (in their overseas divisions) maintain special sections for the purpose of investigating the sex lives of employees. These investigations are the preliminary to disciplinary action against employees whose conduct is disapproved; homosexuality is considered an offense meriting dismissal.

The official theory behind this policy maintains that the concern is not with sexual morality but with reliability, and that homosexuals, when threatened with exposure, would be apt to buy themselves off by divulging secrets. It is difficult to disagree with this theory; that abuses are possible is undeniable.

I have seen a few people who lost their jobs in this way and, post facto, wished to enter treatment. Those I saw had without exception been discharged on the basis of their own confessions. The details of the accused's behavior are better not discussed: most of them are fantastic, some are ludicrous. It is sufficient to say that the behavior of these people, before they were suspected, was thoroughly self-incriminating. They were, as is typical for the psychic masochist, their own worst enemies.

A special niche in the confession corner is occupied by the bisexuals whose wives have caught them in an "embarrassing" situation with another man in the marital bed.

"How was I to know she would walk in?" asked Mr. R. "She's never home so early in the afternoon."

"You are a man of means. Why couldn't you have arranged for a rendezvous somewhere else?"

"My house is my home!"

"Wives have different opinions about the use of the marital bed. Seriously, are you just acting this naive indignation, or are you indignant because you were naively caught in flagrante?"

"Why is that bitch kicking up such a row? She has everything!"

"Including an air-tight case against you. Do you know what a good lawyer could do with this material?"

"I'll have to buy her off."

"It will be expensive."

"Sure. The bitch will hold out for every red cent."

"I'm afraid it will be every green dollar. According to your wife, there are hundreds of thousands of them."

"Do you think I could appease her?"

"How?"

"By telling her that many men are ambidextrous."

"What you call 'ambidextrous' is objectively neurosis, but also—socially—a basis for ostracism. 'Bisexuality' counts as homosexuality, popularly as well as scientifically. Unfortunately for you, your wife knows that. She also seems to know the cash value of keeping your secret."

"Do you get the impression she would keep her mouth shut if I went into treatment?"

"You know her better than I do. Will she?"

"I guess not. But why did she run to you instead of going right to her lawyer?"

"If your assumption is correct, and nothing can change her mind, she is strengthening her case. It's better for her to begin by acting the concerned wife. She could find herself telling her story to a well-informed judge, someone who knows that homosexuality is considered a disease."

"Somebody must have smartened up that dope who calls herself my loving wife. Maybe she already has a lawyer, and he put her up to it."

"Do you have any intention of changing?"

"Why should I?"

"That's up to you."

"I guess I'll have to pay."

"In any case, it was a costly mistake."

The indignation of some of these trapped homosexuals—trapped by themselves—is sometimes tragicomic. Equally tragicomic are the excuses they give. An outstanding example was Mr. R.'s indignant "My house is my home!" I have seen this odd indignation in a series of cases; I do not believe it can be explained by applying the simple rule that wrongdoers automatically react with indignation when caught. In two analyzed cases, I have observed that this indignation revealed a complex intrapsychic basis. The inner reasoning here ran: "Isn't homosexuality preferable and more 'moral' than the deeper need—masochistic satisfaction? That bitch of a woman is doing it again—she's forcing me out of my 'moral' defense!"

The anger of the trapped bisexual sometimes leads to strongly aggressive measures against the woman-"detective." As a literary example, I am quoting the recent novel, *The Immortal,* handed to me by Mr. M. (see Chapter Four). (According to reports received from wives of bisexuals, this is a close and realistic description of the typical confrontation scene.) The hero of this novel, caught by his girl friend, behaves as follows:

> To start at the beginning (the girl friend writes in her diary), my plane was delayed on takeoff at Chicago. We got to Newark (LaGuardia was fogged in) at 3:30 A.M. By the time they brought us some limousines, it was after 4:00. I finally reached home close to five o'clock.
>
> Johnny was there.
>
> The apartment showed the accumulated effect of two weeks of his existence. Dirty glasses were all over the place. The ash trays were overflowing, with butts and ashes, and the air was heavy with stale, burned tobacco. Clothes—pants, shirts, shoes, underwear—were scattered around, mixed with crumpled newspapers and magazines.
>
> I closed the door quietly and went into the bedroom. I could hear breathing. I put down my bag and, as my eyes got used to the gloom, I could make out two bodies on the bed. There was enough light from the street lamp outside the window to see that one was Johnny and the other seemed to be another man. Both were naked, and the man had one arm around Johnny.
>
> I didn't know what to do. My only instinct was to leave, to get out. I started out the door when Johnny must have heard my heel on the floor.
>
> "Who's there?" he said, and sat up.
>
> "Never mind," I said. "I'm going."
>
> "Wait," he said. "Wait."
>
> The other man stirred and said "Sally?" It was the voice of Harry Costello.
>
> Johnny came over and took my arm. "What happened? Why are you back?" he asked.
>
> "Nothing," I said.

"Harry's here," he said. "He stayed over. We were talking, and it got late—"

I said, "Give him my regards," and walked out.

I suppose I had grown used to the idea that Johnny might sleep around. Even so, finding him in bed with a girl would have been shocking. But with Harry? It was a fact that I couldn't accept.

I managed to find my way over to Times Square and registered at the Astor. I tumbled into bed in an air-conditioned bedroom and actually slept.

When I awoke, my first thought was that I had dreamed the thing. But as I came to, I realized that I hadn't.

I decided not to go home right away. Instead I called up to see if the place was vacant. There was no answer—it was about one o'clock—so I thought it might be safe to go over.

When I reached the apartment, Johnny was waiting for me. "I didn't answer the phone; I thought it was you," he said.

I said, "I don't want to talk to you."

"Why?" he asked.

"Get out," I said.

"What did I do?" he asked.

"Get your things and get out," I said. I turned to go out the door, but he caught my arm and dragged me back. He is very strong.

"You listen to me," he said.

"Let me go," I said, but he wouldn't.

"You've got it wrong," he said. "It's not what you think."

"What I saw," I said.

"So he stayed over," Johnny said. "We'd been working together, it was late, his family's out of town."

"Just two lonely boys comforting each other," I said.

He looked me straight in the eye, a thing he rarely did. "I'm not a faggot," he said.

"I didn't say you were."

"What else?"

"A whore. A male whore."

"Why, you dirty bitch," he said. "You moralizing, dirty bitch."

I said, "I do feel dirty—dirty all over for ever having known you."

"And stupid, too," he said.

"Get out," I told him.

"How could I have wasted so much time with a dame as stupid as you?" he asked. "A dame who thinks there's something holy about screwing a man. Then when he climbs into the hay with somebody else, that's immoral. Man, you've got that deep-down sickness I just don't dig."

"Please get out," I whispered.

He slapped me twice across the face, hard, with his palm.

"That'll teach you to sleep with the help," he said, and went into the bedroom.

I fell down and I couldn't move. I must have stayed on the floor for close to half an hour.

I could hear Johnny moving around in the bedroom. Then I heard his heels on the floor and he was standing over me with his suitcase in his hand.

He said, "I'm going to the Coast with Harry. And when you see me on the screen, you'll have the satisfaction of knowing you didn't help. You don't know how. Nobody does. They all claim they want to help, but all they want to do is take. Nobody ever gave me nothing. They all wanted to take. You've had yours."

Then he grinned. "But I've got something for you," he said, and he spat on the floor.

I heard the door open and close and then I heard the sound of his motorcycle. He raced the engine, then shoved it into gear and blasted off with a stream of backfires. From the way the sound receded, I could tell he was going pretty fast. I could hear the backfires all the way down the street. They stopped again when the light changed and he kept right on going across town.

Sometimes the very choice of partner in a homosexual relationship reflects the unconscious principle of seeking trouble and avoiding success. I have seen many cases in which the loved object was a heterosexual who never knew or even glimpsed the other man's inner torture. The most grotesque case of impossible choice I can recall was that of a Hungarian Nazi, still suffused with racial Hitlerism, in love with a Negro who rejected him.

Homosexual embroilments with the law, with blackmailers or with gossips, are by no means the result of accident in most cases. If a young man approaches a vice squad detective in the rest room of a large hotel, and is arrested—and then, a short time afterwards, approaches another vice squad detective in the same room of the same hotel, his pleas of accident, coincidence or bad luck cannot be very convincing. If a man is *repeatedly* robbed, and beaten up by newly-acquired "friends" in Central Park at night; if another man continues to frequent a bar declared "off limit" in his circles, one cannot but become dubious about the amount of "chance" involved in their mishaps. In these three cases, as it happened, further information entirely eliminated the possibility of "accident." The first patient had been warned by his friends that the hotel in question was being closely supervised; the second had been warned by fellow homosexuals that the Park was not safe after dark "any more"; the third explained his continued use of the doubtful bar by saying that he was "no coward"; he would not "run away."

Repeatedly, homosexuals disregard obvious dangers in a seemingly cavalier fashion.

Mr. S., an ex-student of theology, brought his career to an abrupt end by accosting a city detective in the men's room of the City Hall of a town of one hundred thousand. His arrest was followed by serious difficulties. He resigned from the Seminary he had been attending.

"What made you pick City Hall?" I asked him.

"It was a nice place."

"I understand that in smaller towns the City Hall usually houses the Police Department, too. Is this true?"

"I wouldn't know. In the city where I was arrested, this actually was the case."

"Wouldn't you be more likely to run into a policeman in his own building than somewhere else?"

"Regular policemen and detectives may use all possible urinals."

"I asked you if the probabilities aren't greater in their own building."

"I wouldn't know. No statistics available."

In rare cases, one can give the homosexual the benefit of the doubt and concede that inexperience is responsible for downright "silly" difficulties. More frequently than not, this facile excuse has no justification. It certainly cannot be used when the victim of self-created trouble is a routinier of long experience. And such "veterans" constitute the majority of homosexual trouble-seekers and trouble-finders.

7

The Homosexual Claim that "Normal" Homosexuals Exist

THERE ARE TWO homosexual magazines being published in the United States today, both of them from the West Coast. *Mattachine Review* originates in San Francisco, and *One* in Los Angeles. Both found HOMOSEXUALITY: DISEASE OR WAY OF LIFE? worthy of comment; *Mattachine Review* devoted its entire issue for May, 1957, to a symposium entitled "The Bergler Issue." As could only have been expected from professional homosexuals, the four who took part in the symposium, using pseudonyms, joined the editorial writer—who also remained anonymous—in panning the book heartily. Their comments were characterized by a free flow of abuse and by unmitigated anger. The burden of their story was that homosexuality is not a trouble-maker: Bergler is.

Disregarding the abuse, this issue of the magazine contained one sentence worth reproducing:

> One may observe that Dr. Bergler seems to have been almost unbelievably unlucky in the homosexuals he has known. One may also observe that there are sufficient sick and psychopathic homosexuals to make superficially plausible the argument that all homosexuals are sick and psychopathic. But how does Dr. Bergler know? (Page 22.)

In other words, I missed the normal homosexuals.

The other homosexual review, *One,* came up with a cleverer dodge. Granting that all the points I made in the book under scrutiny hold true for psychic masochists, the notice claimed that only *neurotic* homosexuals fall into that category. Once more, I had missed the "normals":

> If, in reading this book, the homosexual can see through the disguise of the title into what Dr. Bergler is actually talking about, it can be of considerable value. Judged by the book, the title would better read, "Masochism—Disease or Way of Life," since according to Dr. Bergler masochism is the basis of homosexuality . . . Of real value to readers is Dr. Bergler's list of undesirable character traits, stemming from unconscious masochistic tendencies, to which both homosexuals and heterosexuals are frequently prone.

This point about the "normal homosexual" may seem plausible to many people. The crucial question here is: *does the normal homosexual exist?*

This very question was put to me rather belligerently by Mr. John Wingate during an unrehearsed television interview on *Nightbeat* more than a year ago. Here is a transcript of the entire program:

Wingate: Dr. Bergler. Good evening and welcome to *Nightbeat.*

Bergler: Good evening.

Wingate: I would like to start directly with the title of your book here, HOMOSEXUALITY: DISEASE OR WAY OF LIFE? In your opinion, what is the answer? Is the homosexual diseased or is it for him or her a way of life?

Bergler: The homosexual believes it is a way of life. In objective reality, he is a diseased person. He just won't admit to that.

Wingate: How is he diseased? In what way?

Bergler: He is diseased in his personality. The main trouble in homosexuality is a personality distortion. The sexual problem is put into the center only by the person who is involved. In other words, if you meet a homosexual and look at him under the analytic microscope, you find a peculiar distortion of the personality which consists of the fact that basically this person is what we call an injustice collector.

Wingate: Now, in just a moment we will go to that term and another term you have used. I would like first to clear up this. Many people say they can spot a homosexual without any difficulty whatsoever. They emphasize the fact that the effeminate characteristics of a man usually point to homosexuality. Doctor, what about that as a rule of thumb for identifying homosexuals?

Bergler: It is impossible to identify a homosexual if he does not want to be identified. In other words, it is a popular misconception that the male homosexual is always an effeminate man. Even common sense tells us that this is impossible. Why? Because every passive homosexual who imitates a woman is paired with an active one. I once had a patient who was an interior decorator. She is now dead; consequently no medical secret is given away in speaking of her. This woman was in a profession riddled with homosexuals. Consequently she was convinced that she could smell out a homosexual ten miles away.

Wingate: What do you mean, "riddled with homosexuality"?

Bergler: There are many homosexuals employed in this specific industry. Well, I denied her contention. Then an amusing incident happened. She would frequently meet my next patient in the elevator. He was a goodlooking, very virile appearing man. One day, during her appointment, she mentioned him, and said, very indignantly, "Why don't I meet people like that in my social circles?" I could not tell her that he was homosexual. You see, this woman who believed that she could tell a homosexual by appearance was completely mistaken when confronted with a type that did not fit into the category which she believed was the only one in homosexuality.

Wingate: All right. If the effeminate man or masculine woman is not typical of homosexuality, then what is homosexual behavior as you see it?

Bergler: Typical homosexual behavior has nothing to do with the small minority that belongs in these two groups: namely, men who pronounce feminine attitudes and women, active masculine attitudes. Externally a homosexual looks like anybody else. There is no typical homosexual behavior.

Wingate: What about the internal attitudes of a homosexual, in your mind, as you see it?

Bergler: First is the matter I mentioned previously, the peculiar attitude of injustice collecting. Injustice collecting is the popular term for a very complicated psychological phenomenon. The tongue-breaking scientific term is "psychic masochism." That means there are people who constantly construct or misuse situations in which they are badly treated, humiliated, rejected. To express the idea in a metaphorical manner: Imagine a man who has the peculiar hobby of constantly putting his head into the mouth of a lion. Afterwards, he waits. What will happen? Will the lion yawn and push out his head, or will he bite off the head? Obviously, a situation a normal person would never get himself into.

Wingate: Now, Dr. Bergler, are you saying these are internal attitudes confined to homosexuals alone?

Bergler: No. I do not say that. I say every homosexual is an injustice collector. Not every injustice collector is a homosexual. A homosexual is an injustice collector—plus. And now comes the problem: what constitutes this plus? Speaking about male homosexuals for the moment, this plus consists of the fact that the homosexual is not a rejecter of women but a fugitive from women. He is in deadly fear of women. Instead of admitting this fear, he rejects women. Since there are only two sexes, he can run away only to the second sex. He runs from the woman to the man. Secondarily, he elevates this alibi or rescue station to the position of a sexual attraction. The decisive point is that a fear element is involved; it is fear that forces the homosexual to run to "another continent."

Wingate: Now, Dr. Bergler, you have made the statement that the affairs, the relationships between homosexual men, are a matter of what you call five-minute or quickie relationships. What do you mean by that?

Bergler: Well, take the typical heterosexual relationship as an example, as a yardstick of comparison. There are heterosexuals who act as the homosexuals do, but they are a small minority; they are the type generally designated as the "wolf." The wolf is a person who is always disappointed by the woman. In inner reality, he is always afraid that his potency disturbance will become apparent. Using a preventive technique, he discards the woman before this can occur. In homosexuals, the routine is the same, but homosexuals are not so much afraid of a potency disturbance as of being completely bored. The typical homosexual relationship—the typical one—is a five-minute contact in a dark corner in a park, in a Turkish bath, in a comfort station. These people don't know each other. This is a quick—

Wingate: In a comfort station?

Bergler: Comfort station, yes. Why are you so surprised? Perhaps we understand different things for the words "comfort station."

Wingate: Yes. What about homosexuals who live together? Do you call that what you refer to as a quickie relationship?

Bergler: No. This is the smallest minority. Experience shows that these people cannot stay together for a long time because the personality difficulty comes to the fore. If you take bad heterosexual relationships as a comparison: If somebody asked you to name the worst marriage you know, of course, like everyone else, you would be able to name a specific relationship between two people. Take this example, multiply it by ten thousand, and you have an approximate idea of what typically goes on in a homosexual relationship of comparatively long standing. The conflicts of jealousy, the conflicts of constant injustice collecting—one constantly pointing out that the other guy did him an injustice in this way and in that—leads to this: If you ask someone who has been a homosexual for a long time (meaning someone who started, let's say, at seventeen or eighteen and is now thirty) why he doesn't live with a friend, why he doesn't have some stable relationships, the answer is "It cannot be done." Why? Because of personality structure.

Wingate: All right, Dr. Bergler. Let's turn to what is called a bisexual. One often hears stories of the well-adjusted bisexual, the man who marries, has children, perhaps, a happy home life and a successful job. In addition, the same man continues to maintain homosexual relationships with other men. Would you say the bisexual is what you would call sick?

Bergler: The nice picture you paint doesn't correspond to reality but to fantasy, a widespread fantasy. First of all, the popular word, bisexual, is a misnomer. There are no bisexuals in this sense. Bisexuals are people who are basically homosexuals, but who retain some mechanical potency with heterosexuals. They use this mechanical potency for the purpose of a social alibi. They marry. In the beginning, they have a relatively good marriage. There are very few conflicts. Why? Because there is a good deal of gratitude for the woman who in this way gives them the social alibi of appearing normal. After some time, two things happen. The good marriage deteriorates into an injustice-collecting marriage, and the potency of the man, previously mechanical, collapses. Bisexuals are not people who can do it both ways, or invented the amazing technique of dancing at two weddings at the same time. This is impossible. Consequently, the whole story of the bisexual is a fantasy.

Wingate: Are you ever accused of being dogmatic? You say this is impossible, there is no such thing as a bisexual. I mean, these are black and white definitions. I mean, do they go just down the line like that?

Bergler: They go just down the line like that.

Wingate: Are you being absolutely correct about each statement?

Bergler: Wait a minute. One could, of course, introduce every statement which I have made with the following announcements: This has been my experience in thirty years, with so and so many hundreds of homosexuals, through whom—since the turnover of partners is so enormously great in some homosexuals—in treatment you hear stories about five hundred other homosexuals in a single case: acquaintances, friends or previous friends, and so forth.

Wingate: All right, Doctor. What about a man like Donald Webster Cory, author of the book, *The Homosexual in America—A Subjective Approach*? Mr. Cory says that he has both a happy marriage and a homosexual relationship. Does not his experience contradict your thesis that no homosexual can live a well-adjusted life?

Bergler: It doesn't contradict it at all, because, you see, Mr. Cory's book is a propaganda treatise and not a scientific book. Mr. Cory correctly said "a subjective approach." He could have said "an emotional approach." This is an emotional outburst in which a man, obviously under severest pressure of his own guilty feelings, presents an alibi. This proves nothing.

Wingate: Well, are you able to contradict his statement that he has a wife and does have homosexual relations, and is well adjusted? How could you do it?

Bergler: I couldn't, because I didn't analyze him. How could I?

Wingate: All right, Dr. Bergler. If the homosexual is a sick man, how does his illness affect the rest of the community? Is he, for example, prone to commit criminal offenses?

Bergler: No, provided he is not specialized on the specific "diet" which prefers only children. If he is specialized, he could commit a crime, but if we forget about this type, then the community need know nothing about a man's homosexuality if he is careful enough. But to be careful he must lead practically a double life. In other words, he will live in one part of a city and have his affairs in another part of the city. Still, he is in constant danger of being exposed, of being blackmailed. And also, he is always meeting someone at a party, someone he never suspected of belonging to this group in society. This is a very tragic, very insecure way of living. If you consider only the constant pressure, the peculiar requirements of conspiratorial living, you see the contradiction in the statement that somebody can be a homosexual and be well adjusted—not in the externals of his life, but in his inner life. These are very unhappy, very depressed, and very bitter people, regardless of their external attitudes. They are constantly laughing, constantly having a good time—seemingly. But if you look behind this mask you see a deeply unhappy, deeply depressed, deeply troubled person. If such a person says he is wonderfully adjusted, and tells me that I'm dogmatic—well, I can only be surprised at the self-deception. To give you a better argument—which I read in a homosexual journal: My problem, the argument runs, is that I have been extremely unhappy in my homosexual acquaintances. I just never met the normal homosexual. I describe neurotics. Yes, there are neurotics within the framework of homosexuality. But what about the healthy homosexual? My answer is: "That is a fantasy."

Wingate: You are stating categorically that there are no healthy homosexuals?

Bergler: Categorically.

Wingate: All right. A listener has given me this suggestion for a question to you. What do you, as a doctor, think when you hear someone use the phrase, "queer?"

Bergler: What *I* think about it?

Wingate: Yes.

Bergler: If somebody says this fellow is a "queer," then obviously I think he is a homosexual.

Wingate: Do you reject such a phrase, as a doctor?

Bergler: Of course I reject it; it is not a scientific term. It is a popular term. If someone asked me, "What would you say if you heard that Mr. X. calls his wife a frigidaire," I would tell him, "Interesting information, but this is not a scientific term. He obviously means his wife is frigid."

Wingate: All right. We heard your description, earlier, of typical homosexual behavior, internal attitudes, to some degree. I wonder, very briefly, in a layman's terms, if you could explain what you mean when you write that homosexuality is, and we quote you, Dr. Bergler, "the result of an unsolved masochistic conflict with the mother in earliest infancy." What do you mean by that?

Bergler: That is quite a complicated problem. What I mean is this: It goes without saying that every child must be educated. Education consists of the fact that certain things are forbidden. Every education, if you get down to brass tacks, consists of a series of don'ts. "Don't do this, don't do that, don't do this." There are certain compensations. If you are a good boy, you get the love of your parents, and other compensations. Now, some children are simply incapable of taking these constant don'ts. They react to the situation, not in a normal way, but in a neurotic way. For instance, if a child has an upset stomach, his mother will refuse to give him the candy which he normally gets before going to bed. The reason is completely logical, reasonable. It is explained to the child, and the mother believes the problem is solved. In some children, it is not. From the standpoint of these children, a "bad" person has refused them something they want. Now, if you take ten million incidents of this type—small everyday disappointments in early childhood—you see they have to be overcome. There are two possibilities. One is the normal way: one accepts reality with all its restrictions. Otherwise, one constantly reproaches the environment for its "injustice." Now, this reproach is inexpressible because of the weakness of the child. Therefore he internalizes this reproach and his aggression, and makes out of this constant displeasure in which he lives an unconscious pleasure. This is called psychic masochism, and this is all acquired in the first two or three years of life with the mother.

Wingate: Now, briefly, if the roots of homosexual behavior are found in infancy, what can a parent do to avoid having his son or daughter become homosexual?

Bergler: He can do two things. He can either be naive, or less naive. If he is naive, he will only look for what is now understood to be the precursor of homosexuality: whether the boy in a specific phase acts like a girl, or the girl like a boy. This is all wrong, because these are transitory and relatively harmless phases. If he is more informed, however, he will look out for one specific problem: whether the child is an injustice collector, whether he takes disappointments in this peculiar way, and constantly provokes disappointment. This does not mean that this child will become homosexual—

Wingate: So should he take the child to a psychiatrist?

Bergler: No, you cannot take every child to a psychiatrist. There are not enough psychiatrists around, and not enough money with which the parents can pay. The parent can explain to the child, first, in a friendly way, that certain things which he does are provocations for the purpose of getting himself into trouble. If this does not work, then in certain cases he should take the child to a psychiatrist, because that can prevent a neurosis. Whether the neurosis will also work out as a homosexual neurosis nobody can predict at that time.

Wingate: Dr. Bergler, let us press ahead because of time. According to the Kinsey Report, one man in three has homosexual experience with another man in his adult life. Would you agree that homosexuality is that widespread in the United States?

Bergler: No, I would not. I believe that Kinsey's statistics are completely misleading. Because, you see, Kinsey had some emotional tendency of wanting to "prove" that homosexuality is on the same level as heterosexuality. Whatever his reasons were, they are unknown to me. To get his high figures, he did something very peculiar. He included, as homosexuality, the typical homosexual play of boys in prepuberty and puberty. This is completely typical and has no later results. It simply means that the boy is more afraid of girls than of himself or another boy.

Wingate: Now, briefly, what about Dr. Kinsey's claim of latent homosexuality in every man?

Bergler: It is a fantasy.

Wingate: All right. Although many psychiatrists, Dr. Bergler, do not agree with you, you have written that homosexuals may be cured through analysis, and lose all desire, a man for a man, a Lesbian for another woman. Dr. Bergler, under what conditions do you believe such a complete cure, briefly, is possible?

Bergler: The cure is possible under one basic condition: that the patient really wants to change. The difficulty is that if somebody comes to us and tells us he wants to change, we have no possibility of judging whether this wish, this conscious wish—even if completely truthfully stated—has an unconscious basis. Consequently, we tell him to go into a "trial treatment" of four to six weeks' duration. Then we can see whether there is some unconscious guilt, stemming from other sources, which we can utilize.

Wingate: Doctor, briefly, let us talk about homosexuality and the law. In New York State, certain sexual acts between consenting parties over the age of eighteen are considered a misdemeanor, punishable by not more than a year in jail, a $500 fine, or both. Do you think the law should be changed and homosexual acts between parties who consent no longer be considered crimes?

Bergler: I don't believe that the psychiatrist is a social reformer. A psychiatrist can only say that certain attitudes are based on a specific illness. Consequently, we say homosexuality is an illness.

Wingate: Well, last month in Great Britain the Wolfenden Committee, a group of distinguished Britons, recommended that homosexual behavior in private between adults who consent no longer be classed as a crime. What do you think of that report?

Bergler: There is no objection to that. One thing is undoubtedly true: a jail sentence does not change a homosexual. The main problem is—

Wingate: The question is, do you approve the Wolfenden Report?

Bergler: No, I don't—Wait a minute, let me explain. I don't, because as far as I remember, there is no recommendation of psychiatric treatment. There is a great difference between saying that it is senseless to send these people to jail (that's no deterrent) and saying that these are sick people who are recommended for psychiatric treatment. As far as I know—but I am not fully informed, I read only excerpts—the English report says nothing about treatment.*

* Postscript: A few months after the interview, I read that the Wolfenden Report contains no objection to psychiatric treatment but expresses a pessimistic opinion with regard to the efficacy of psychiatric treatment in cases of homosexuality. Clearly, the Commission heard only negative testimony on this matter, and has swallowed Kinsey's opinions. In a recent issue of a medical journal, a British physician registered his protest against this unjustified pessimism.

Wingate: You say you don't. Then, doctor, let me ask you, if you don't believe in that, what is the point of making homosexuals liable to criminal prosecution?

Bergler: Well, you see, the psychiatrist does not do that; the law does that. Before you can change the law, you have to create a climate of opinion in which a great many people agree that homosexuality is an illness. What we see today is a conspiracy of silence. In other words, the big magazines and newspapers don't even dare to approach this problem. Creating a new climate is what should be done, and what has to be done before the law can be changed. First, one has to de-glamorize homosexuality, and start saying that this is an illness not more glamorous than typhoid fever. Secondly, one has to state that homosexuality is a curable disease, under specific circumstances. Third, a decisive point: Homosexuality is always connected with a personality difficulty and self-damaging tendencies, which are even more important than the sex act itself.

Wingate: All right. About your second contention: Many critics have said you don't know what you are talking about because you worked only with people who came to you with the desire to be cured. What about that?

Bergler: That is not true. Many people don't come to us because they want to be cured, but because the family drags them in. Then we see a young man or a young girl who says, "Under no circumstances do I want to be cured!" We are confronted with their parents, who are terribly unhappy about their children's homosexuality. We can either tell these people nothing can be done, or explain to them that homosexuality is connected with self-damaging tendencies, and state that sometime in the future the boy will, perhaps, want to go into treatment.

Wingate: One last question, Dr. Bergler. If a homosexual were to approach you on the street corner tonight, after this program, what would you do?

Bergler: (Laughing) You see, certain things just don't happen to certain people. Homosexuals have a very fine feeling about whom to approach.

Wingate: Thank you very much—I am sorry, time is up—for coming on *Nightbeat*.

The by-now familiar argument of the "normal homosexual" appeared on this occasion, too. What about him, and what is the claim that "happy" homosexuals exist based on?

Homosexuality, this story runs, is a direct parallel to heterosexuality. Homosexual love is just like heterosexual love; homosexual love (aside from the obvious technicalities) is the same but better. The argument continues: In addition to superiority in sex and love, homosexuals also tend to be superior in intelligence, outlook on life, artistic ability. The defenders of homosexuality, therefore, maintain that it is a normal and adjusted way of life and that its followers contribute as fully—if not more so—to the community as the heterosexual.

Recently I discussed homosexuality with a homosexual acquaintance who—though he thinks himself broadminded—was so outraged by my opinions on the subject that he was seriously considering breaking off all social contact with me. "Your last book definitely damages homosexuals," he charged in a letter. After writing the letter, he changed his mind: sacrificing himself for the "cause," he invited me to "a private and dispassionate discussion." Here is the gist of it; for the sake of clarity I am putting it in the form of a dialogue between A. (the homosexual apologist) and B. (myself).

A. What is your main objection to granting psychological parity to both heterosexuals and homosexuals?

B. The identical objection that pertains to granting parity to both the real product and the surrogate.

A. Will you admit that some synthetics are better, even more durable, than the originals?

B. Isn't this line of argument slightly in contradiction to your initial thesis: that both homo- and heterosexuality are original?

A. Touche. I was sidetracked by your comparison. How can you prove that homosexuality isn't just as much of a "real thing" as you say heterosexuality is?

B. That can be proved only by forgetting the naive viewpoint that takes phenomena at face value. In clinical analysis, I have found that homosexuals are, without exception, severe psychic masochists who unconsciously don't crave love, admiration, approval, kindness, but the exact opposites of these wishes: pain, humiliation, rejection, conflict. You understand, of course, that I'm not refering to their consciously proclaimed aims. This explains, also, why the best homosexual relationship has more conflicts than the worst heterosexual one.

A. I am glad to hear that you don't reserve the stigma of neurosis exclusively for homosexuals.

B. Your irony is unjustified. You knew from my books—when you still remembered reading them—that heterosexuality, per se, is no certificate of psychic health. There are innumerable neuroses in the framework of heterosexuality.

A. You claim, however, that there are some healthy heterosexuals?

B. Yes, some, provided you accept my definition of normality as "not-too-neurotic." Now, to simplify matters, I am going to answer your next question, the one you are about to ask. You want to know why I don't grant the same thing to homosexuals, instead of claiming that, unlike heterosexuals, *all* homosexuals are neurotics.

A. Exactly.

B. The answer hinges on clinical experience. If the homosexual's whole life is directed towards the duality: consciously warding off, and unconsciously living out, a severe inner masochistic conflict (as I claim homosexuals do), where is there room for healthily overcoming this conflict? Even if the attempt is made, it is shattered against the next obstacle: the masochism of the partner.

A. Two objections. First, your experiences are one-sided. In your consultation room you see only the neurotic sector of homosexuals. Second: your books say that psychic masochism is a universal human tendency, and still you make this psychic masochism into an exclusively homosexual prerogative.

B. Answer to objection No. 1: You are mistaken in assuming that I meet only the "neurotic sector" of homosexuals. What you obviously mean is that only the traitor to homosexuality wishes to change, and therefore only traitors consult the psychiatrist. May I remind you that in the past, before stringent criteria made it possible to tell which patients had a favorable prognosis, psychiatrists uncritically accepted for treatment any homosexual who presented himself? They made *no* selection. Frequently, these people came into analysis for reasons totally unrelated to even an official wish to be cured. Some of them were in conflict with the law, some with their families. Some wanted to reduce analysis to absurdity, so that they could later claim they had "tried everything"; this would diminish their guilt. Or the boy friend of a homosexual in analysis would also come into treatment, so that the psychiatrist's "dangerous influence" would be neutralized. There were even young people, incipient homosexuals who had already taken the decisive step in fantasy, but needed a permissive push, and knew that analysts don't forbid the execution of neurotic actions, but merely analyze them. These youngsters misused analysis for this purpose. In fact, they were delighted to be able to make it appear, to their families, that analysis had turned them into full-fledged homosexuals.

It was exactly this unsatisfactory state of affairs that prompted me to go before the New York Psychoanalytic Society in December, 1942, to plead for selectivity in the choice of homosexuals who presented themselves to us. The title of this lecture was "Eight Prerequisites for Psychoanalytic Treatment of Homosexuality." Please hand me my book, THE BASIC NEUROSIS:* the lecture is in part reproduced there.

My acquaintance went to his bookshelves (we were in his apartment) and found the book. He handed it to me, and I read from page 237:

* Grune & Stratton, New York, 1949.

I have listed the conditions which render prognosis possible and have brought forward the prerequisites which make it possible to pick out suitable cases. The ill repute enjoyed by our therapy among homosexuals is to be explained not only by analytical skepticism and the improper application of the analytical instrument. To all this we must add the unselective acceptance of homosexuals with bad prognosis for analysis, as turns out later. These cases then become the worst propagandists against us. The danger can be eliminated by a selection of suitable cases.

I then continued:

B. To finish up your objection No. 1: I also see numerous youngsters of both sexes whose parents insist that they come to me for one or two consultations. All of these youngsters keep telling me about "happy homosexuals." You must admit, therefore, that there is nothing to your claim that I see only the "neurotic sector."

Your second objection—if psychic masochism is, as I claim, a universal human trait, why burden homosexuals, exclusively, with it?—rests on a misunderstanding of yours. I have pointed out, time and again, that the homosexual is a deep-dyed psychic masochist—plus. That "plus" comprises a delegation of the power to mistreat: that power is taken from the woman (mother) and given to the man. Nobody calls the homosexual the only masochist in the world. On the contrary, he has two and a half billion confreres, the total population of the globe. What distinguishes him is not masochism, but his unconscious delegation of the executive power to mistreat to a member of the same sex.

A. Why should the homosexual have more of the "universal" stuff?

B. Unfavorable solution of the universal infantile conflict.

A. But you go much farther; in your recent enlarged edition of COUNTERFEIT-SEX you have added your offensive "twenty tell-tale indices of homosexuality." May I, this time, quote from one of your books *against* you?

My acquaintance fished out the "offensive" volume, and read to me from pages 204, 205 and 206:

> There are twenty tell-tale indices of homosexuality; some of these are unconscious; some have surface reverberations:
>
> 1. Personality structure; injustice collecting with all its concomitants: provocation, pseudo-aggression, self-pity.
> 2. Inwardly, fugitive from women, not renouncer of women.
> 3. Secondary elevation of the fear-antidote, man, to sexual attractiveness, executed with narcissistic safeguards.
> 4. Constant dissatisfaction, hence constant prowling, hence "mass consumption" of partners.
> 5. Inability to maintain long-range relations; when, in exceptional cases, these are attempted, insurmountable conflicts of the injustice-collecting type invariably appear.
> 6. Husband-wife camouflage, as "admission of the lesser intrapsychic crime," the greatest inner crime being psychic masochism.
> 7. Inordinate malice (pseudo-aggression), covering massive masochistic depression.
> 8. Megalomaniacal conviction of being "special" and set apart.
> 9. Unfounded conviction of the presence of homosexual trends in everyone.
> 10. Inner guilt, camouflaged, or visible in its reverberations.
> 11. Jealousy surpassing anything observable in heterosexual relationships; this jealousy is but window-dressing concealing masochistic injustice collecting.
> 12. Psychopathic trends, ranging from unreliability to instability to refusal to acknowledge accepted standards in nonsexual as well as sexual matters, on the assumption that the right to cut moral corners is bestowed as compensation for having "suffered so much."
> 13. Compensatory hyper-narcissism and hyper-superciliousness.
> 14. Flippant-cynical outlook on life, with special emphasis on tearing down accepted values.

15. Peculiar and neurotic attitude towards money; when in poverty, pathologic parasitic tendencies predominate and are built into injustice collecting—whatever they get is not enough; when wealthy, allow others to take advantage of them, but indignantly complain of the beneficiary's "ingratitude."

16. Conspiratorial attitude: hyper-suspicious, hyper-secretive, rather unscrupulous in execution of their aims.

17. Complaints about "constant tension": what appears consciously as sexual tension is inwardly but the inability to furnish an adequate defense against the superego's accusations of accumulation of psychic masochism. To cover up psychic masochism (inwardly always connected with the image of the "bad mother"), they resort to the defense of homosexuality.

18. "Artistic pose": Homosexuals consider themselves at least superior beings, possessing sensibility and sensitivity higher than the norm. In reality, their artistic gifts are preponderantly second-rate, and tend to be exhausted in "ornament, decoration, embroidery," as Somerset Maugham put it. When a homosexual is a first-rate artist, he is so not because of his homosexuality but despite it.

19. Superficiality and inability to mature: at fifty, a homosexual has not progressed beyond his teens emotionally.

20. Homosexuality is never an isolated area of illness in a healthy personality. The homosexual's whole personality is neurotically sick.

He concluded his recital with the statement: "Many of these 'tell-tale' indices are inacceptable and offensive to me."

B. For instance?

A. Take point 4: promiscuity. Isn't this an unwarranted exaggeration?

B. On the contrary, it is a simple statement of fact. Most homosexual contacts are five-minute affairs, passing contacts in public places or in men's rooms. On a different level, the rule is the one-night-stand. According to the information I get, homosexuals try steady relations with one partner, but always give up the attempt because of incessant injustice-collecting conflicts. Since you already have that 'offensive' COUNTERFEIT-SEX handy, let me quote you the statements of two fashion designers. This section begins with a short explanation.

I then read to him:

> All his defensive and unconscious tricks do not change the homosexual's basic structure: his deep oral-masochistic regression. This explains the fact that most homosexual encounters are five-minute "cruising" experiences in which the personality of the partner is simply obliterated and in which the partner is often not even seen. This also explains why, in the exceptional cases in which relations of some duration have been established, these relations are shattered by constant jealousy, reproaches, and a type of whining scene that can be described as "pulling a 'nobody loves me.' "

I went on to read the direct testimony of two patients, both homosexual fashion designers:

> Analyst: "Time and again we've discussed your quarrels with your boy friends. Weren't they all reducible to one common denominator, 'someone is unjust to you'? And isn't it true, as we established in many of your conflicts, that these 'injustices' were unconsciously self-created?"
>
> Patient A.: "That's what you claim."
>
> Analyst: "That's what the record shows. Take your present friend as example. You told me that you met him at a party where he flirted with you; another friend warned you that he was promiscuous to the nth degree. You yourself observed this, too. Still, you chose to have exactly this unreliable person for your friend. You go into tantrums every time the boy runs around with someone else. What reason did you have to assume that this psychopath was good material for a steady affair?"
>
> Patient A.: "Everybody can make an error in judgment."
>
> Analyst: "Make an error in judgment again and again? When this happens, the error is obviously part of a pattern, repeated ad nauseam."

In another case, a similar situation arose:

Analyst: "Why do you overlook the incessant conflicts with your long list of quick-change boy friends? Aren't these quarrels fashioned after the principle of injustice collecting?"

Patient B.: "Now you are blaming me for their neuroses!"

Analyst: "Far from it. I am holding you accountable for choosing, and not avoiding these neurotics."

Patient B.: "There aren't any others around."

Analyst: "And this doesn't make you skeptical of your repeated statements that homosexuality is just a way of life, an exact parallel to heterosexuality? Isn't the worst heterosexual relationship peaceful compared with the best homosexual one?"

Patient B.: "I'm not the sedate suburban type who's in search of quiet!"

Analyst: "Then why do you complain so bitterly about the injustice inflicted on you by your boy friends?"

Closing the book, I concluded: "To make it short and sweet: Do you seriously claim I'm wrong in stating that the 'steady affair' in homosexuality is the exception and not the rule?"

"Aren't heterosexuals promiscuous, too?"

"The neurotics frequently are. Take the celebrated example of the wolf," I answered. I gave him a description of the wolf as I see him:

The wolf is a neurotic who plumes himself on representing masculinity at its best. He thinks of himself as holding a patent on sex-enjoyment. Only a fool, he believes, can be content with only one woman. The sexual gourmet insists on variety. Since wolves move in circles dominated by neurotics, these men who are promiscuous on principle are sought after by frigid women who hope the "professional" will succeed in evoking feelings in them where the "amateur" has failed; they are admired by neurotic men who look up to them for daring to do what they cannot.

But the wolf is a palpable sexual impostor. Inwardly, he is consumed by fears. He is constantly aware of the danger of being proved impotent; to fight against this danger, he uses an unconscious preventive trick. He refuses to wait for the inevitable sexual fiasco. Instead, he discards the woman preventively. One could say that he makes his escape while the going is still good. In this way, he maintains the legend of his sexuality.

Some wolves have shortlived affairs; others go in exclusively for one-night-stands. The difference is merely between the ability to maintain potency during only one meeting, or throughout several.

Normal women instinctively realize that, at bottom, the wolf is merely an inflated neurotic weakling; they avoid him.

What makes a wolf? The basic reason is psychic masochism; the wolf's external defense consists of the standard unconscious alibi of the psychic masochist: pseudo-aggression. Under this offensive belligerence lies the stratum of injustice-collecting. He finds all his conquests "disappointing," which provides a convenient rationalization to justify his immediate flight to still another woman. The wolf's collection of scalps is in reality a collection of excuses—excuses which must perpetually be renewed. He is caught in the mill-race and must go on, with narcissistic satisfaction (derived from his self-attested belief that he is a "conqueror") as his only compensation.

The wolf's need for self-delusion about his exploits is so extensive that he blinds himself to the painful reality, and never realizes that he does not conquer his women at all but is merely used by them in their endless neurotic experimentations. The all-conquering wolf is a "cheated cheater," as I once told a patient in analysis: "Frigid, neurotic she-wolves try to use you as aphrodisiac, and discard you as bad medicine." The protests were eloquent, but the proof—in the form of a scrutiny of his last half-dozen affairs—was still more eloquent, and left him entirely deflated (though still protesting).

There is but one exception to the ironic rule that wolf always has a rendezvous with she-wolf. Every wolf treasures the memory of a few women who "really loved him." Of course, he did not love them; the wolf is incapable of love. But a sentimental recollection remains. The fact is that these alleged exceptions always prove to have been pitiful masochists, bent on disappointment. As a dispenser of disappointment, the wolf is well cast.

When the wolf's neurosis increases (as it inevitably does with time) he meets his Waterloo and can no longer hold his potency disturbance in check. He then tends to attach himself, making a typical neurotic "mistake," to a relatively normal woman who will have nothing to do with him. He cannot give up his unachievable object. He keeps trying, and her consistently negative response pushes him into a massive neurotic depression and a loss of interest in easy conquests. Another tendency also becomes manifest at this time: he may with advancing age show "a peculiar boredom with previous exploits." In plain English, this means that the old defenses have worn out, and the wolf finds himself impotent.

The wolf's opposite number, the neurotic promiscuous woman who declares that her principle is "sex on my own terms," is thoroughly engrossed in her never-ending search for the imaginary satisfier. Wolf and she-wolf meet and meet again, and are always disappointed in each other, regardless of their rationalizations. Where the wolf uses his promiscuity to fight impotence, the she-wolf uses hers to combat her frigidity. But frigidity is a neurosis that cannot be cured by repeated doses of the wrong medicine.

Our dialogue then resumed:

A. Agreed: heterosexuals are promiscuous. Why don't you concede the same right to homosexuals?

B. You seem not to understand that the wolf and the she-wolf are severe neurotics. Aren't you out to prove that homosexuals are "normal?"

A. I don't deny that there are neurotics among homosexuals.

B. You are begging the question. Would you deny that there are happy and stable heterosexual unions? And do you seriously claim that (proportionally) the number of happy and stable unions is the same among homosexuals?

A. Perhaps Kinsey was right when he wrote, in Volume I, that long-time relationships in the heterosexual world would probably be less frequent than they are if there were no social custom or legal restraint to enforce continued relationship in marriage.

B. Here I must charge you with taking a sentence out of context. Kinsey makes that statement (it's on page 633, Volume I) defiantly, to justify the fact—which he admits—that long-term *homosexual* relationships are "notably few." Where does that leave us? With a glorification of promiscuity?

A. Real life isn't so idealistic.

B. That may well be so, but to state as Kinsey does that the special police force of "social custom and legal restraint" alone guarantees long-lasting marriages, to disregard as he does such matters as love, companionship, sexual compatibility, children, similar likes and dislikes, seems to me a sheer parody of reality.

A. And what about your indices 7 and 12, where you claim that homosexuals are characterized by "inordinate malice" and "psychopathic trends"? Is this a compliment?

B. Let me point this out first: do you realize that you have again avoided coming to grips with my statements about the promiscuity typical of homosexuals? Instead, you jumped to indices 7 and 12. As for these statements: no, they are not compliments, nor were they intended to be. A description of scientific facts usually doesn't pave the way to a compliment. It is true that homosexuals show inordinate malice; that trait reflects the pseudo-aggression that follows every psychic masochist around like a duenna. And as for the statement about psychopathic trends that you found so offensive, this tendency towards unreliability or instability or refusal to acknowledge accepted standards is, again, typical of all severe psychic masochists. May I remind you once more that the homosexual is a psychic masochist, *plus*?

A. Why won't you admit that there are happy homosexuals?

B. How can someone be consciously happy if he inwardly wants misery?

A. Your whole approach has one purpose: to disparage the homosexual! Isn't it a well-known fact that many important writers (think of Shakespeare!), painters, sculptors, musicians, have been homosexual? You dispose of this whole body of evidence in cavalier fashion by saying, "When a homosexual is a first-rate artist, he is so not because of his homosexuality but despite it." That's your point 18.

B. To answer this question, I have to refer you to a full-length book, THE WRITER AND PSYCHOANALYSIS, which I first published in 1950.* That book describes the genetic basis of the artistic "gift"; this unconscious development takes place before the individual resorts to the homosexual "solution." Shakespeare, I will grant you, was undoubtedly a homosexual; his sonnets are unmistakable evidence. But do you seriously claim that he became the most famous poetic "circumnavigator of the soul"—as Herbert Trench so aptly called him, and as he actually was—only *because* he was a homosexual?

A. (Excitedly) Why do you hate homosexuals? Why is your whole book a bitter attack on homosexuals? Why don't you use your influence to change the antiquated laws, instead of making life harder for homosexuals? Why do you underestimate the social obstacles facing every homosexual?

B. Let's tone down your excitement; remember that you suggested a "dispassionate discussion." As to these four new questions: First, I don't hate homosexuals; a psychiatrist does not hate sick people. Second, my book (I assume you mean HOMOSEXUALITY: DISEASE OR WAY OF LIFE?) is not an attack on homosexuals, but a record of clinical data. I can obviously not be held responsible if homosexuals take offense at the presentation of clinical facts. Third, although a psychiatrist is neither a legislator nor a social reformer, I am doing a good deal to change prevailing prejudices: when enough people have been convinced that homosexuals are sick people in need of clinics and not jails, something can be done about it. Fourth, I am the last to underestimate the social obstacles facing homosexuals. But I am also aware that the social danger acts as an attraction: danger has its own neurotic allure. There is also a possible fifth point, though you didn't mention it. I must feel a very peculiar "hatred" for homosexuals, since I have presented them with the curability of a previously incurable disease. Why don't you add that to your indictment?

* Second enlarged edition, Brunner's Psychiatric Books, New York, 1954.

A. Who the hell told you that homosexuals want to be cured—how I hate that word!—in the first place?

B. Obviously, some of the nearly one thousand people who have consulted me over the years must have wanted to change; if they had not, I would never have been confronted with the problem. Or are you assuming that I had them shanghaied on the street, and brought to my office by force?

The "dispassionate" discussion with the "happy" homosexual ended as might have been expected: both parties remained firmly convinced of their original opinions.

The brilliantly witty poet, Heinrich Heine, observed of the Prussian officers of his day that these paragons of erect posture held themselves "as though they had swallowed the stick that beat them up in their early youth." One could apply this century-old simile to the "happy" homosexuals: they are so intransigent in their rejection of change, so dead-set on the "beauty" of homosexuality, because, having swallowed their specific defense against the imaginary "stick that beat them in early youth," they now cannot do without it. Fortunately (or rather, unfortunately) for them, they are not conscious of the basis for their "considered opinion" and mental "posture." The latter is—unconsciously—still but an im-posture.

8

"Special Cases" and Borderline Cases

THE TERM, "SPECIAL CASES," was originally applied by myself to describe a working hypothesis applied to homosexual patients whose behavior pattern appeared to be in contradiction to the assumptions I had gathered from observing and treating homosexuals. In each of the cases so designated, however, further treatment confirmed my basic theory and revealed that the traits which had seemed "special" were merely individual variations within the standard framework of the already deciphered.

The most puzzling cases among the "specials" fell into these three types:

1. Bisexuals who had extramarital homosexual affairs, but without the typical conflicts of homosexual relationships. These patients stated with great unanimity that their homosexual contacts were the only human relationships in which they found "real understanding" and "human warmth."

2. Homosexuals who "hated the typical homosexual," and were exclusively interested in seducing heterosexually married men

who were homosexual "virgins"; sometimes the seducers sent these men back to their wives, sometimes they did not.

3. Seemingly heterosexual married men who "sometimes" went on a "homosexual binge" (their terminology). Frequently this was an isolated experience; in other cases it was repeated a few times. After the "binge" these men would revert to heterosexuality; homosexuality did not seem to exercise any lasting attraction.

Here are cases illustrating these exceptions that turned out not to be exceptions:

Type I: *Bisexuals with the thesis: "Exclusive human warmth in casual homosexuality."*

This type of homosexual tells a tale completely at variance with the statements of all other homosexuals. Homosexual contacts, as already pointed out, fall into two categories: the five-minute affair or one-night-stand in which the personality of the partner is of no emotional importance, and in fact seems obliterated; the relationship of some duration, in which there is an attempt to forge an emotional link but the attempt fails because of the partner's "unreliability" and the consequent storms of jealousy and injustice collecting. This "special case" presents an extreme contrast: he stresses that his homosexual affairs give him human warmth *without* any conflicts. How is this possible? Who is giving false or at least misleading information?

It is impossible to doubt that injustice-collecting is the rule in homosexuality. In case after case after case, patients recite, in a matter-of-fact and resigned manner, stories of injustice-collecting conflicts. The two fashion designers quoted in Chapter Seven told typical stories. Mr. K., in Chapter Two, solved this problem in a drastic but logical way. He explained:

> "I have to make still another admission, and confirm another of your statements. It is true that there are more conflicts in the best homosexual relationship than in the worst heterosexual one."
>
> "If you go on making these admissions, you will find yourself acknowledging that homosexuality is your lost cause," I

remarked. "In the meantime, how do you manage, in the face of your disillusionments?"

Once more that thin smile appeared on Mr. K.'s face.

"I found a solution a couple of years ago: I retired into homosexual fantasy. Now my lovers are always kind and considerate; they never make trouble."

"That is the strongest argument against homosexuality—the strongest indictment of it—I have ever heard."

Even Mr. Y., the funereal lawyer described in Chapter Four, had to admit that constant conflicts had given him a distaste for long-term homosexual relationships, and that he had given them up.

It is hardly necessary to adduce additional testimony; the homosexual consensus of opinion declares that one cannot live in peace with a homosexual lover for any length of time.

The special type now under discussion apparently contradicts this thesis, although the relationships of which they speak are not imitations of marriage in which the two partners live together but merely a series of casual encounters with the same partner. These are continuing affairs, though within a framework of promiscuity, and in them, it is alleged, no conflicts arise and there is human warmth.

The case of Mr. T. is illustrative. He came from a social background similar to that of Mr. Y., who was just quoted above. He had been a member of a "good" fraternity at his "good" Eastern college, but after graduation made his own way, establishing a successful public relations firm. On his list he had eight or nine names of former classmates. At intervals in the course of many years he would revisit them all. This list was "elastic" and could be expanded.

As for his domestic situation, his parents had "married him off" to a woman who had been intellectual in her interests before marriage, but had since gone through a "shrinking process" and was now bored with ideas in general, and with those that appealed to her husband in particular. To this boredom she added acidity; her comments, Mr. T. said, "put cold water on every enthusiasm." She had a "positive genius for being a killjoy."

Mr. T. maintained his potency with her but put all his emotional dependence on his "list." They never failed him.

His marriage was different from the typical bisexual marriage, in which the wife is merely a social alibi and does not become part of the injustice-collecting game until the bisexual has used up his initial gratitude. (See the case of Mr. M., in Chapter Four.) When Mr. T. married, he had been confident that his adolescent homosexuality was a thing of the past. "Beautiful illusions" had accompanied him to the altar; he had every intention of making a good marriage.

His illusions, however, had proved to be without foundation. The girl was an "unsuitable type." Why had he married her? His mother had "pushed" him, he explained; the girl came from "the right circles." This willingness to be driven was in curious contradiction to the aggressive independence Mr. T. had shown in his business. In the matter of his marriage, he consented to be manipulated by his mother.

In inner reality, Mr. T.'s wife was by no means "unsuitable"—she was what he really wanted: an excellent provider of injustices who used the killjoy technique.

Mr. T.'s solution was to split his inner needs in two. He satisfied his masochism in his marriage; he provided himself with the inner alibi of really wanting "warmth and understanding" through his casual though repeated interludes with the men on his list.

Clearly, although there are different ways of executing the homosexual's masochistic purpose, the basis is always the same.

Mr. T. made one especially revealing statement. I asked him why he clung to his long list, instead of deciding on one lover. Cryptically, he answered: "It would not work."

"Why?"

"Personalities can't clash when meetings are spaced out. There's always time to cool down."

But Mr. T.—and two other "special cases" in his category—admitted that he was by no means above the allure of "casual bar acquaintances," and frequently had to fight off that "unhealthy desire." Q.E.D.

Type II. *"Scalp-hunters," pursuing heterosexually married homosexual "virgins."*

Emphatically and conspicuously, this type professes its rejection of the "typical" homosexual.

The rejection in itself means little; narcissistic homosexuals like Mr. L., who was described at length in Chapter Four, make the same claim. But refusal of contacts with "typical" homosexuals, plus specialization on "married homosexual virgins," presents a combination of traits that justifies a special classification.

Mr. U. was fifty. A man of leisure and many hobbies who kept a shrewd and knowing eye on his inherited capital, he came into analysis because of homosexuality. He was prompt to announce his "difference"; his first sentence declared: "I hate homosexuals; I never have any contact with them." His specialty was the heterosexually married "homosexual virgin," the young man who felt browbeaten by his wife and complained about her. He would introduce these young men to homosexuality, "give them a good time," and then send them back to their wives. The high point of his homosexual history was a triumph dating back many years. He had traveled halfway across the country on a nonstop bus, and in the course of the journey had slept with seven out of the eight drivers who had appeared for their successive shifts.

"A peculiar boredom with the whole business" had brought him into analysis. He had been brooding over his "change of heart," when a copy of HOMOSEXUALITY: DISEASE OR WAY OF LIFE? came into his hands. The book taught him something new: that homosexuality is always connected with self-damaging tendencies. He reviewed his life, and became concerned with the prospect of increasing self-damage playing him "new and damaging tricks." In spite of his wealth, he had always been stingy. Now he decided to "splurge for the first time" in his life, and indulge himself with an analysis.

Mr. U. described his relationship with his mother as "favorable" —he had nothing to complain about, since she had not denied him or interfered with him, he said. But his dreams immediately proved this judgment false: the theme of all his dreams dealt with a menace or at least a slight dealt him by a bad, cruel woman. These "self-made disclosures" astonished Mr. U., who had fancied himself an amateur psychologist. In his transference dreams, he faithfully repeated the same image of the "bad mother," although his external attitude towards me through his successful analysis was unvaryingly friendly. At times, in fact, Mr. U. was not so much friendly as fraternal; his inclusion of psychology among his many hobbies fostered in him the illusion that analysis is some kind of course of learning. Time punctured this face-saving device (which was responsible for one amusing scene in which he handed me his monthly check with the words, "Here is my tuition.").

It is unnecessary to go into the details of this complex analysis. As far as Mr. U.'s preference for "married homosexual virgins" is concerned, these facts are pertinent:

His mother had been the "soul" of the family business, and the actual creator of the family fortune. When she was forty (and the patient seven years old), she inaugurated a new policy: a training program for young men in their late teens or early twenties. These young men were taken on as business apprentices but treated like members of the family. After two or three years, they were set up in independent businesses in different parts of the country. Mr. U.'s mother supplied them with needed capital, charging no interest, and helped them in many other ways. This information was given me casually and incidentally; Mr. U. added that he had continued the family tradition of lending a helping hand to young men, but with one modification: he would first use them sexually. Afterwards, instead of setting them up independently, he would make them managers and fifty-per-cent partners in one of the chain of retail stores he had set up.

Here was another proof—if the amateur psychologist could only have seen it—of the impossibility of self-analysis. What he called "family tradition" was in inner reality the clue to one of his own deepest defeats in childhood, and the reason for his "scalp-hunting."

Although no recollections remained in consciousness, Mr. U. must have been, as a child, deeply hurt by his mother's interest in a succession of young men. Utilizing previous masochistic fantasies about witches (these were still evident in his dreams), he later unconsciously used the "training program" to prove to himself that woman really had a "devouring" nature (one young man had followed another in an apparently endless series). Mr. U. had no conscious memory of having suspected his mother of sexual relations with these young men, but his subsequent actions proved conclusively that he had done so. In taking over the "training program," he simply "outdid" his mother. The formula ran this way: "Any woman can seduce an inexperienced boy. That's what mother did. I can do better. I will seduce heterosexuals and married men, make them into homosexuals for as long as I want them, and then contemptuously send them back to their wives. Those bitchy women will find out that their husbands will never be what they were before I worked them over!"

Mr. U.'s was a complex inner "solution." In his homosexuality, he ran away from the "witch," his mother. In his specialized homosexual tastes, he pseudo-aggressively revenged himself on his mother (and, incidentally, on the wives of the men he seduced) by outdoing and outshining her as a "devourer." He even improved on his mother's trick of exploitation: instead of rewarding these young men by setting them up in business for themselves, he merely made them managers and gave them half-interests in one of his many stores. As already mentioned, he was very shrewd about money, but it pleased him to know that his ex- boy friends were all "prosperous and happy."

Specific determinants enter every case, and notably the "special cases." The scalp-hunting technique, directed exclusively at heterosexual men, appears with a variety of rationalizations. Patients have explained it as being "more fun"; as giving "less trouble afterwards—no extortion, maybe some scenes"; as providing "a way of poking fun at established standards"; as being "the same thing as heterosexual preference for virgins"; as a protective device—"a way of making sure there will be no criticism of my sex technique." But the basic determinant remains invariable despite the plethora of cover stories. This is always pseudo-aggressive hatred directed originally at the mother image, then shifted to the mothers (and wives) of the scalped. Unconsciously, this thought predominates: "What would that stupid woman say if she knew?" One such patient, after coming to an understanding of the interconnections, cynically quoted the old quip: "It takes a mother twenty years to bring up a boy, and a woman twenty seconds to undo it all."

"I'm just doing it in reverse," he added. "I make them homosexuals."

"Nothing to brag about," I answered. "You had better analyze the panic behind your truly pathological hatred of mothers."

Type III. *The occasional "homosexual binge" of the married heterosexual.*

In a study published in 1954, entitled "Spurious Homosexuality,"* I enumerated a dozen types which give to the uninitiated the impression of being homosexuals although actually they are not. Among others, I mentioned this category:

> Another type of neurotic, unjustly classed as homosexual, is represented by a specific division of masochists who associate with female termagants, and—in a shortlived rebellion—escape into sporadic homosexuality. This exceptional situation has this basis: these neurotics fortify themselves, so to speak, with doses of homosexuality, before reverting to their predilection —the heterosexual termagant who mistreats them, as unconsciously requested. The external appearances point in the direction of homosexuality; in inner reality these neurotics gain temporary immunity via the desperate defense of homosexuality. They admit *inwardly* to the "lesser crime" (in this case, paradoxically, homosexuality), to avoid being charged with the unconscious code's *crime of crimes*—psychic masochism. Of course, the remedy is worse than the disease; but masochists are adepts at getting themselves into trouble.

* * *

In the past, I also classified as "special cases" patients who had come to me as their second, third, or fourth analyst. I discontinued that classification for the obvious reason: the term does not apply. The colleagues who had treated these people previously had simply misjudged the depth of the neurosis involved in homosexuality; they had handled deep masochistic regressions like

* *The Psychiatric Quarterly Supplement* 28:68-77, 1954. The study is partially reproduced in HOMOSEXUALITY: DISEASE OR WAY OF LIFE?

superficial Oedipal cases. If one drills for oil in a specific spot (where oil actually is present a thousand feet below the surface) but never goes beyond a depth of one hundred feet, it is not exactly fair to blame the soil for one's oversight.

In a long series of continuations of analyses previously conducted by colleagues for four, six, seven, and even eight years, the technique advocated in HOMOSEXUALITY: DISEASE OR WAY OF LIFE? (e.g. the case of Mr. O. in that book, pp. 224-238) has repeatedly proved successful. Some of these ex-patients have since become so well known or prominent in their fields that it is out of the question to reproduce their case histories: no possible disguise would eliminate the possibility of recognition. In many of these cases the alteration of facts would invalidate the data; some of these patients, for example, had conflicts intimately connected with their professions and the story would be meaningless without this highly revealing information. Regretfully, I must deny myself the opportunity to present my most "famous" cases.

One example of how the masochistic, pseudo-aggressive *modus operandi* in homosexuals capitalizes on analytic naivete can be presented, however. Mr. V. was a spectacularly successful industrialist who had been in analysis with a colleague for four years before he interrupted his treatment and came into analysis with me. While still with the colleague he reported on the following incident: on the previous day, Mr. V. had taken a rather primitive young man, employed in one of his establishments, to his apartment. There they had sexual relations. Mr. V. had no intention of continuing the relationship. The colleague objected: Mr. V. could not act that way, he declared, after "establishing normal feelings as a normal human being." The patient was rather astonished. Feelings or no feelings, he told the analyst, "You seem to have misunderstood. This was not a hetero- but a homosexual affair."—"That's immaterial," was the answer.

That was all the patient needed: he attached himself, with fantastic submissiveness, to this primitive and psychopathic fellow. Hadn't the analyst recommended "feelings"? By reducing this pronouncement to absurdity, the patient twisted it into blanket permission to live out the greatest masochistic fiesta of his life.

This affair was not a "normal" rediscovery of feelings, as the analyst assumed, but an outlet for masochistic propensities, untouched and uninfluenced by analysis. As to "normality" in sex, the image was provided by Mr. V.'s bisexuality—that had existed *before* analysis, as well.

There was more to Mr. V.'s choice of "the primitive young man," too, than the analyst had seen. This was what I have called "a caricaturistic relationship." Encountered both in hetero- and homosexuality, it is a pairing (of husband and wife, girl friend and boy friend, two friends or acquaintances) in which one of the pair is chosen because he portrays for the other an unconsciously produced caricature of some infantile image, or because his traits include an exaggeration or distortion of the chooser's own unconsciously rejected qualities.

The person chosen may unconsciously appear as a caricature of mother, father, sister or brother, or else may represent a distorted and satirically overstated "oneself"—in projection. In the former type, the purpose of the choice is masochistic suffering with a slight overlay of defensive, pseudo-aggressive irony. In the latter type, the choice has the purpose of outdistancing a reproach of the inner conscience by dramatizing the alibi: "I hate, reject, and make fun of these impossible traits."

Mr. V.'s slavish attachment may very well have paralleled that of another homosexual patient, a man of forty-two who maintained in luxury a psychopathic man seven years his junior. This "friend" exploited him financially and emotionally on a grand scale. The patient suffered intensely from his jealousy of the other man—evidently for good reason—but would not leave him. Their life together consisted only of turbulent scenes, followed by reconciliations. The patient took the lead in starting both the conflicts and the peace conferences. Moreover, there was no evidence that he was approaching the usual "point of no return," where even the psychic masochist has had (temporarily) enough of the inner wish for humiliation and mistreatment. In this case, the friend's impossible behavior seemed to cement the relationship more firmly.

It seemed reasonable to assume that the patient's masochism had no limit, but before accepting that conclusion, this reconstruction was attempted: The patient's mother had been a personality who "acted the grande dame, made scenes, was full of snobbish whims, neglected the children emotionally." There was reason to assume that the patient's masochistic propensities had been built up in his relationship with his mother and that the parasitic boy friend was fashioned after the maternal model: essentially a neurotic, self-assured taker, never a giver.

Though the boy friend recalled the maternal model, he was by no means an exact copy. The patient caricatured his mother in this identification. He degraded her socially (the boy friend was, he said, "scum and slum"); he made her into an outright parasite and half-prostitute; he subjected her to his own whims (thus, in identification, actively reversing the passive situation of his childhood). At the same time, this thinly-veiled pseudo-aggression covered an almost slavish devotion to his boy friend. The patient took a great deal of "intolerable nonsense" from this man; clearly, his unreliability, "worthlessness and rottenness" (his own words) were alluring rather than repelling.

The repetition of the infantile situation was so exact that it cast light on one of the patient's peculiar routines. Repeatedly, he would break off his affair, and then start it again. This was an unconscious recapitulation of his feeling that his irrational mother had repeatedly let her child down, and then after some time resumed her loving attitude and acted as if nothing had happened.

Like all homosexuals, the patient was masochistically attached to the earliest image of his mother; the image he had created, however, was a decidedly malicious caricature. Simultaneously, and ironically, he created a "pseudo-moral alibi" for sexual attachment: by taking the blame for the "lesser intrapsychic crime" of incest, he covered up the more deeply repressed masochistic attachment. (The second camouflage was, of course, the switch from hetero- to homosexuality.)

The patient was quite aware of his friend's "worthlessness," but he did not realize that this was precisely the quality he cherished in his friend. These unsavory attributes provided the patient with an alibi for his pseudo-aggression, and with guilt-relieving confirmation of his opinion of his mother's pleasure, and gave him the "moral right" to have sex with a shifted mother image.

To return to Mr. V.: when he read HOMOSEXUALITY: DISEASE OR WAY OF LIFE? the similarity between his own case and the masochistic cases described in the book stunned him. Without delay, he left his therapist and presented himself to me, saying, "Though we never met before, we are old acquaintances—you described me perfectly in your book."

His second analysis was successful.

* * *

"Borderline cases" call for a brief mention. These are schizoid or psychotic people who present themselves for cure of homosexuality if this symptom, too, happens to be one on their extensive list. These cases are unsuitable for treatment.

9

Truth and Misconceptions about "Disagreeable" Homosexuals

In HOMOSEXUALITY: DISEASE OR WAY OF LIFE? I summed up my attitude towards homosexuals in this way:

> For nearly thirty years now I have been treating homosexuals, spending many hours with them in the course of their analyses. I can say with some justification that I have no bias against homosexuals; for me they are sick people requiring medical help. I have had a good many therapeutic successes with them, and some failures and some disappointments. I am obliged to them for having provided the opportunity to study their psychic structure, and the genesis and curability of their disease. A number of my papers and books have dealt with homosexuality. I have received a good many compliments for lectures and publications on the topic. All in all, I have no reason to complain of homosexuals.
>
> Still, though I have no bias, if I were asked what kind of

person the homosexual is, I would say: "Homosexuals are essentially disagreeable people, regardless of their pleasant or unpleasant outward manner. True, they are not responsible for their unconscious conflicts. However, these conflicts sap so much of their inner energy that the shell is a mixture of superciliousness, fake aggression, and whimpering. Like all psychic masochists, they are subservient when confronted with a stronger person, merciless when in power, unscrupulous about trampling on a weaker person. The only language their unconscious understands is brute force. What is most discouraging, you seldom find an intact ego (what is popularly called 'a correct person') among them."

Wary of my own impressions, I have repeatedly checked them against the opinions of my cured homosexual patients, asking them to sum up their opinions of homosexuals years after their cures. (I should add that I have frequently been amazed by the radical alteration in attitude achieved in successful analysis of homosexuals; the gulf between the traits described above and the normal "live and let live" philosophy is enormous, but often it is fully spanned.) The impressions of their former confreres I have received from cured homosexuals were deadly criticisms that made mine appear mild by comparison (pp. 28 ff.).

These paragraphs prompted a good many letters from readers; approximately half confirmed my findings, the rest abused me for them. A good deal of resentment, evidently, was aroused by a single sentence: the one in which I stated that homosexuals are "essentially disagreeable people." These letters were similar both in manner and reasoning to a complaint printed in the "Bergler issue" of the homosexual publication, *The Mattachine Review*. After quoting the same fatal sentence, that article continued:

The entire book displays so obvious an animus against the homosexual that one is led to suspect that Dr. Bergler brings out the worst in any homosexual who comes to him for treatment. It is no wonder that he is convinced that all homosexuals are masochists. What other kind would go to a man so aggressively anti-homosexual as he? Is it remarkable that homosexuals in analysis with such a person should become very "disagreeable" in sheer self-defense? Is it pathological for a man to defend himself if under attack? (p. 13)

The identical sore point has been brought up repeatedly by homosexuals during their first interviews with me; these would-be patients excitedly dispute my conclusion and hopefully invite an argument. Other homosexuals, those who come to their first interview inwardly ready for treatment, often single out the same quotation—giving it their full approval, and amplifying it with convincing examples.

What are the facts?

To begin with, it should be understood that I was not refering to homosexuals' behavior while in treatment. All analytic patients—heterosexual and homosexual—defend their neuroses to the last ditch. In doing so, they seize whatever weapons they know how to wield. More or less successfully, but always forcefully, they employ irony, cynicism, abuse. They throw temper tantrums and give vent to obscene language. These patterns are all part and parcel of the resistance situation. Chapter Three reproduces, verbatim, a discussion between myself and a heterosexual patient in treatment because of compulsive infidelity. This discussion took place during a relatively mild stage of resistance. Nevertheless, the patient's manner could not—outside the analytic appointment room—pass as "pleasant."

The entire argument put forward by the writer in the *Mattachine Review* symposium must therefore be dismissed; it is based on ignorance of the real facts, and has no pertinence. It may be amusing to observe the poverty of the argument, but that is its only value.

Only the analytically informed reader can connect my judgment of the "disagreeable" homosexual with its psychological substratum: the undeniable fact that homosexuality has psychic masochism at its core, and all psychic masochists are "disagreeable." The psychic masochist's life is studded with invisible-to-others slights, with injustices contrived out of thin air, with apparently harmless situations which to him convey an unmistakable call to arms. In consequence, he is always on guard, blade unsheathed. Where another person suspecting a slight or a minor injustice, or discovering that he has actually been wronged, suits his retort to the circumstances, the masochist has no reply less drastic than an intercontinental ballistic missile. He is incapable of defending himself with a mere palliative, like a cutting remark.

This does not mean that all psychic masochists carry the same earmarks, that the rigid inner pattern appears on the surface in a similarly rigid and unmistakable stereotype of external behavior. Psychic masochists come in a variety of forms. In my book, *The Superego,* I attempted a typology of these neurotics, and arrived at the following subdivisions:

The Injustice Collecting Type. This is a person who at all times is potentially or actually enraged because he is the victim of some terrible wrong. He will provoke an actual—or if necessary, a potential—enemy until he succeeds in getting his badly needed dose of daily—if not hourly—injustice. Between doses, he will accept as substitute a diet of impersonal, universal injustice. Since the world is what it is, the injustice collector is in no danger of remaining unsatisfied. This type is characterized by an air of hyper-excitement, hyper-touchiness, hyper-bellicosity.

The Coldly Detached Type. Phenomenologically, he seems to represent the opposite of the injustice collector. He is an icicle personified—distant, cold, unmoved, frequently so taciturn that he is classed with the "he gives me the creeps" variety. His presence makes other people uncomfortable. His pose is that of a visitor from another planet. He pays no compliments and is never guilty of making a moderately friendly-laudatory remark. Inwardly, of course, he is the same erupting volcano as his brother (or sister) under the skin, the clearly visible injustice collector.

The "Nice" Masochist. It is stretching the truth only slightly to call these people the only "nice" human beings. They are interested in your troubles, and eager to be helpful. They excel in magic gestures. Under this ingratiating surface is a hopelessly entangled masochist, suffering for reasons which he cannot understand (namely, his or her construction of the unhappy situation). In general, this type accepts his conscious unhappiness with stoicism and resignation. It is hopeless to try to help these people with common-sense advice. Their inexhaustible stock of rationalizations assures the permanence of the painful situation.

If they are women, the epitheton ornans "charming" is often applicable. In clinical analysis, these "nice" and "charming" masochists present specific difficulties: they use these qualities as a defense, the latter sometimes impenetrable. They also claim that the standard three-act drama of injustice collecting does not apply to them, since they do not show the typical pseudo-aggressive defense. In inner reality, they do make use of this defense; evidence of its presence can easily be found in their dreams and conflicts. Practically speaking, this "charm" means that the analyst must perform an *additional* task; he must uncover the hidden pseudo-aggression. Once this is done—and it may take months—a secondary difficulty arises. These patients consider their newly-retrieved pseudo-aggression a "great step forward."

The next step in analysis is to prove that these pseudo-aggressions are self-damaging, too. The "charming" psychic masochist's failure to build up the typical defense of pseudo-aggression has made him a "nicer" person, but no less of a masochist.

The Every-day Type. It might be more precise to designate this masochist "the unsuspected type." One meets an energetic business man, full of ideas and initiative; his private life, surprisingly enough, reveals him as the (self-created) victim of a shrewish wife. One meets a woman with the proverbial "calculating machine instead of a heart," a woman whose behavior seems to indicate that she has no "feelings" whatever; actually, she tortures herself with envy, the wrong boy friends, and other injustices.

The "Heaping-Coals-of-Fire-upon-His-Head" Technique (Self-Creation of an Artificial Victim Through Silence). One of the masochistic techniques merits special attention, not because of its frequency, but because it is an example of the depth to which the inner scourge can penetrate. This is the silence with which some masochists prefer to meet reproaches. Instead of defending themselves, they choose to be unjustly accused. Allegedly, they look forward to the malefactor's tearful acknowledgment of his injustice and cruelty. Many of these injustices, it goes without saying, are unconsciously provoked by the victim.

The homosexual, since he is a pronounced psychic masochist, plus, obviously belongs in one of these categories. By and large, unfortunately, he is the patent injustice collector, or the coldly detached type. I have seldom, if ever, encountered a homosexual who was a "nice" masochist.

This is not all. The "plus" which, added to psychic masochism, constitutes the basis of homosexuality, gives rise to additional difficulties. No homosexual ever feels safe; he must always be on guard against "them," the outsiders. Conspiratorial living cannot but foster not-too-pleasant inner characteristics. The homosexual's bitterness and malice, for which *internal* reasons exist, is constantly shifted to *external* difficulties.

This attitude permeates every detail of daily life. In the same issue of *The Mattachine Review* that has already been quoted, another contributor wrote under the heading, "Insult Added to Injury":

> Dr. Bergler's thesis, at least inferentially, seems to imply that homosexuality is indeed a disease and that treatment will invariably be successful if there is a sincere desire for a cure. I do not believe that experience bears this out. The law describes the practicing homosexual as a felon. Should Dr. Bergler's assumptions become universal all practicing homosexuals would also be classified as *wilfully diseased.* This adds insult to injury (p. 10; my italics).

This cannot be charitably dismissed as an absurd misunderstanding. It is malice concentrated. The homosexual who wrote these sentences meant to imply that I wish to make the lot of the homosexual more difficult than it is. One gathers from them that I recommend a double penalty for a homosexual who refuses to promise to enter analysis, when the Court offers him this alternative to sentencing under the law. This misunderstanding, an amalgam of naivete and malice, rests on the failure to distinguish between the conscious and the unconscious.

10

The Tragedy of Parents of Young Homosexuals

WHENEVER PARENTS OF teenagers or of young men and women in their early twenties discover that these "children" are homosexuals, unmitigated tragedy is in the making. With remarkable unanimity, these parents accuse themselves of being in some way responsible.

Are these parents in fact responsible? My answer is a definite "no." In my opinion, no parent—not even the parent who directed the affairs of the nursery foolishly—has the power to induce neurosis in his or her children.

This answer does not, I concede, accord with the attitude that has been orthodox in the last few decades. Popular opinion, based on statements made by psychiatrists and psychologists, has made the parent into the sculptor and the child into the clay. Nobody has gone so far as to use the Bible as authority—"The fathers have eaten a sour grape, and the teeth of the children are set on edge"—but in dealing with neurotic children the theory has called for investigating their problems primarily in terms of what their parents have done or failed to do. However, neurosis is *not* a photographic copy of reality, and what the parents do or do not do is not necessarily what the child perceives them as doing or neglecting to do.

The essentially superficial approach which shifts responsibility entirely to the parents overlooks a vital fact. Four troublemakers conduce to neurosis, and these operate in the baby and infant independently of parental influence. These troublemakers are:

1. Desperate clinging to infantile megalomania;
2. Desperate fight with passivity;
3. Desperate though futile attempts to express and implement aggressive countermeasures against this passivity;
4. Rebounding of aggression against the child himself when it cannot (because of the child's immaturity and because of parental taboos) be expended outwardly, and the accumulation of this unused aggression in the pre-stages of the inner tyrant, the superego.

Not even perfect parental care (a Utopian aim) can prevent these inner conflicts from arising, or solve them by external means. The end result of the infantile conflict—in my opinion, invariably a psychic masochistic solution to a greater or lesser degree—is made inevitable by the inner situation. The parents' stupidities do not create the child's intrapsychic conflicts, though they can aggravate these by pushing the child into the creation of specific neurotic defenses. But the infant's misconceptions, which constitute the kernel of his over-all problem, are beyond the reach of either perfect or imperfect upbringers.

All children create inner defenses; the important question is whether the individual child discards these defenses when they no longer fit the specific situation, or whether he persists in using his outdated, neurotic defenses when the situation for which they were tailored has become a part of his outlived past. Psychic masochism figures in both techniques, but it is pre-eminent only for the child who clings, like a miser, to every neurotic "asset."

We cannot yet state why two children brought up under

identical circumstances do not acquire identical addictions to psychic masochism, although both the inner and the outer attributes (the genetic and clinical pictures) which accompany this acquisition can be described, and the neurosis changed analytically. However, in exploring its genesis, it seems to me justifiable to start from a basic point which is to be found in Freud's statement in *Civilization and Its Discontents* (pp. 110 ff. German edition) partially accepting findings of the English group of analysts. This statement declares that the severity of the superego is not the direct result of the educational process, but can develop independently of the educators. The obvious conclusion from Freud's statement is that that guilt and the always unsatisfied need to appease the cruel inner tyrant of conscience accounts for the creation of all neurotic defenses (including, as I believe, the psychic masochistic "solution.")

Stated more simply: The inner tyrant's appetite for torture does not reproduce the external atmosphere of the nursery, but arises from other circumstances. (As I see it, some children have difficulties in coming to terms with inborn megalomania; they desperately rescue themselves, as their last resort, with psychic masochism. By provoking punishment and later accepting the punishment imposed for the provocation, they cast themselves in the role of primum movens. In this way the weak child triumphs over the strongest adversary—but at a fantastic price.)

Moreover, the child does not see reality as it really is, but through the spectacles of "projection." If the child produces great amounts of aggression against the parents, and attempts to get rid of these disagreeable feelings via unconscious shift, he attributes his *own* aggression *to the parents.* Via this unconscious falsification of facts, even kind parents are "perceived" by the child as—"cruel."

The general tendency to oversimplify the problem of the neurotic child has also distorted the real meaning of the term, "traumatic experience." Popularly, this is taken to refer to a single shocking experience which inevitably leaves its disfiguring marks on the child. But no experience in itself will produce a traumatic effect if the soil is not fertile to begin with, nor can a single experience do so. Where there has been a genuine traumatic effect, the starting point may have been the child's fantasy and not a real fact, and in any case it will have been the last of a series of small incidents and not merely a culmination without a preamble.

It is a common experience to see siblings reacting differently when exposed to the same shock. Neurosis may result in one and not in the other; two different neuroses may be established in the two children; the "trauma" may not register because the neurosis has already formed and taken root.

The effect of any external circumstance on a child seems to be primarily a matter of how it is unconsciously interpreted and elaborated on. This deduction applies in general and to the presumably traumatic experience as well. The two sons of a neurotic mother may retain an equally disagreeable memory of their childhood, but it is not uncommon to find one of them *correcting* the past by marrying a warm, affectionate woman, and the other *perpetuating* it by marrying a carbon copy of his mother.

Here is an example of a child undergoing an objectively tragic and shocking experience which left no decisive marks on him.

This event was part of the past history of a man of thirty-two who had come into analysis with me because of writer's block. His family background was aristocratic; his father was imperious, his mother "gentle and kind." He "lost" his mother when he was seven; "lost" here is not the usual euphemism for death. His father had discovered that his wife was unfaithful to him and had had their marriage annulled. The mother left the house, presumably to visit friends. When the time came to announce the situation to the children, the father had the patient and his slightly older brother summoned to his room by a servant. They found their father seated at a table, his army pistol before him. He told the children that their mother would not return; they were to forget her completely. Now he was asking them for "absolute loyalty" to him. If they were less "loyal" than he required, he would kill himself with the pistol lying on the table. Of course the children promised everything, although all they understood of the scene was that they were deprived of their mother.

The incident could be used to illustrate the high point of all traumatic experiences. Nevertheless, *it had no impact at all* on the patient's neurosis. It was clear in analysis that all his neurotic difficulties—his writing block, his potency disorder—had their roots in the earliest years of life, before he "lost" his mother so dramatically. Both disturbances arose from his masochistic attachment to the mother image, and from his futile attempts to prove to the inner tyrant that he did not want, masochistically, to be refused, but did the refusing himself. He refused words, and refused sex.

This case proves that no experience can have traumatic effects unless it coincides with the requirements of the child's inner conflict. The boy's neurosis was already established at the time of the revolver episode; the experience did not affect it. The episode did, however, produce other minor scars: his tendency towards hypocrisy could be traced back to his peculiar oath.

Psychic masochism is present in quantitatively different degrees in every human being, and the protracted maturation time of the human child inexorably sets the stage for its first appearance. The child's helpless first years see the dictatorship of the inner conscience established, and the pattern of pleasure-in-displeasure acquired.

As already stated, the inner situation dominates; the externalities that are part of the educational process do not alter unconscious results. Lenient education does not produce an indulgent inner conscience, nor severe education a harsh one.

This would be a painful admission for either parents or educators to make, aside from the entirely understandable need, on the part of upbringers, to overestimate the importance of their roles. The end result of overestimation, however, is that upbringers query every move they make, perpetually intimidated by what they fear may be a lasting, unchangeable and disastrous effect on the child. These parents, faithfully following the hyper-modern precepts of child psychology, have used love, understanding, persuasion and kindness as their only educational media. And yet, many report that this regime has produced an "unmanageable" child who always seems to be "asking for a spanking."

The child's plight cannot be ignored. A diet restricted to love and kindness provides him with no outlet for his psychic masochism. This does not mean that the once-commonplace techniques of intimidation, harsh words and corporal punishment should be reinstated. But the limitations of "love, understanding, persuasion and kindness" should be understood. In addition to all these, the child needs to accept a certain discipline, and he needs some external provision for his psychic masochism. Underestimating the latter need can lead to tragicomic consequences.

One patient, the mother of a three-year-old, was a firm believer in the anti-deterrence theory of education. I asked her, once, what she would do if her child established a routine that contravened accepted practice in every area of daily life: if he slept in the daytime, ate like an animal, repeatedly set fire to the house, repeatedly attacked his infant brother. If love, persuasion, etcetera proved ineffective, would she not have to impose some kind of punishment? And how could she prevent the child from construing her restrictions as "deprivations," and therefore injustices? And how could she prevent the child from remaining unimpressed by her punishment, and provocatively continuing his routine?

The child's reaction to rules or even to the absence of rules depends on the results of his inner conflicts. If a child is an avid psychic masochist, he will extract punishment from even the most lenient and loving of upbringers.

In an attempt to compromise between "permissiveness" and the obvious necessity of imposing restrictions, the so-called authorities have recommended that disapproval be frankly expressed, but always in a way that will make it clear to the child that the parents love him even when they are condemning one of his acts. There are many obstacles to the success of this method, aside from the dramatic proficience needed to perform such a feat of facial and vocal control. Even the parents who successfully censor covert as well as overt exasperation and carefully stress their unchanging love before forbidding a specific naughtiness cannot prevent the child from ignoring the love and concentrating on the disapproval.

There are many ways of making one's life miserable. Ignorance of the fact that parents do not dominate the psychic development of the child is one sure way. It makes parents easy dupes of what has become a standard modern grievance: young people who go into analysis confront their mothers and fathers with the accusation, "My analysis proves that you are responsible for my neurosis."

No one will deny that few parents have been perfect. But they acted as their neurotic difficulties forced them to act. Logic cannot defend the acquittal of the children because of the impersonal nature of their neuroses when at the same time the parents are personally blamed for both their children's neuroses and their own. The injustice here is as apparent as the illogic.

This point must be clarified in one's own mind: Of the three influences molding the child—biology, environment, unconscious elaboration on the part of the child's ego—the last is the decisive factor.

Parents are incapable of "producing" neurosis in their children. Shifting the blame to them is naive as well as unfair: how many generations are to be included in the shifting process? In every neurosis one can see that the child has used a parental trait as basic material for a neurotic elaboration, but one cannot conclude from this that the trait, in itself, prompted the neurosis.

It has been my experience that many parents, when thus accused, combine conscious indignation with what can be recognized as an unconscious willingness to plead guilty. When informed that the blame could not be put on them they say, "This is very consoling," and go right on enjoying—unconsciously—the masochistic tidbit supplied by their children.

Here is a clinical example which demonstrates that environmental influences are *not* decisive:

Recently a commercial artist, aged twenty-eight, consulted me. In great excitement, he informed me that he could explain his homosexuality. He then proceeded to parade his half-digested psychological "knowledge." He had acquired a distaste for women at an early age, he explained, because of his mother. She was a cruel person whose disposition had "reduced poor father to a pulp." He enlarged on this: "The best way of describing her attitude towards him would be the comparison of a cat playing with a mouse before devouring it." The patient and his *twin* brother had suffered severely in the emotional Siberia which was their home. At about the age of eleven they began homosexual practices. These were continued until they were eighteen, when they left home to attend different colleges. I asked what had happened to the brother. The patient did not know much about him. For years there had been no contact and little communication between the two. A short time before seeing me, however, the patient had taken the long trip back to his home town to attend his brother's wedding.

"So your brother isn't a homosexual?"

"No. He married a rather nice girl."

"Where does this leave your theory that your mother is responsible for your homosexuality? Wasn't your twin brother under the identical influence and for the identical period of time?"

The young man looked startled. But he recovered quickly, and resumed his railing against the mother.

Here is an assortment of parental tragedies caused by children's homosexuality.*

A New England industrialist and his wife—Mr. and Mrs. W.—consulted me on behalf of their son, a young man of twenty-three. Mrs. W. had been the first to suspect the actual state of affairs. She had worried and wondered about the unreasonably late hours her son kept, and then had found a diary containing his explicit descriptions of homosexual affairs. She "nearly had a nervous breakdown," and Mr. W. then confronted their son with the evidence. Obviously uncomfortable at the revelation of his perversion, the son nevertheless was firm in maintaining that "there is nothing wrong with homosexuality."

Mr. W. now had a double-barreled dilemma to solve: the problems of his homosexual son and his hysterical wife. Common sense told him that he had to protect his family and himself; he therefore decided to ask his son to leave home and change his name** as a precaution against scandal. Mrs. W. objected violently, and made scenes. The W.s' peaceful existence was shattered.

Some time after my interview with his parents, I saw young W. His was an impenetrable shell. I pointed out the legal dangers of homosexuality; he replied, with naive assurance, "I'm too smart for them." His outlook on life was cynical: "Father will not let me down because Mother cannot live without me." I described the inner dangers of self-damage; he shrugged his shoulders and informed me loftily that these dangers could not affect him.

* The case of Mr. and Mrs. A. has already been touched on, in Chapters One and Two.

** I have heard of this suggestion several times; it seems to be a device proposed by family lawyers.

I asked him: "Are you so sure you are invulnerable to self-damage? How about the infection you described in your diary?"

"Accidents will happen."

"I wouldn't be so sure this was just an accident. Is your promiscuity an accident, also?"

"No. That's my fun."

"You are an immature boy who is bound to get into trouble. I wouldn't put too much reliance on your mother's attachment to you; your father will convince her that self-protection comes first."

"I don't think so."

"We shall see. If you deny that you have any self-damaging tendencies, how do you account for the fact that you indirectly informed your parents about your homosexuality? Why did you leave your diary where it could be found?"

"I took it for granted they wouldn't dare touch any of my personal possessions!"

"That pseudo-naivete of yours is exactly what will get you into trouble again and again."

Her son's homosexuality was a major tragedy, as Mrs. W. saw it. Equally painful was the fact that she was devoting her life to an unanswerable query: what was the "mistake" she had made that led to her son's "disgrace"? Every attempt to clarify the issue failed.

Mrs. X., a widow who lived in Baltimore, consulted me because of her twenty-five-year-old son. The "boy" had always been a reasonable fellow, she told me, before going into the armed forces. In the service, he became a homosexual. "When he got home again, I found out. He got suspicious telephone calls, and I read some of his letters."

"Did you discuss the problem with him?"

"Yes. He said that I'm still living in the last century, and don't know what's going on. I insisted that he see a minister or a psychiatrist. He became indignant and gave me an ultimatum: if I didn't leave him alone, he would move out."

"Well, he is obviously not ready for a change. But I believe he should know about the self-damage always present in homosexuality. You could tell him that you consulted me about your own nervous state, and I asked that he give me information about you. This might be a way of persuading him to listen to information about self-damage."

"I will try that. Please, please tell me: Am I responsible?"

"Homosexuality is an illness, and you are *not* responsible."

Mrs. X. did not appear to be either convinced or relieved. It seemed likely that her masochism would have welcomed a different answer.

I never saw young X.

Mr. Z. was an oil magnate from a Southern state. He came to my office, under the protection of an alias, to "hear from the horse's mouth" all about "the dirty business" of homosexuality.

He explained his reasons: "My son is twenty-eight. He got into bad company, and now he is a fairy. Imagine that!"

"Bad company does not make a homosexual."

"What else would? Where did he pick it up? Certainly not from me."

"Homosexuality is an illness, but not an infectious one. No one 'picks it up.' It is an unfavorable unconscious elaboration of an inner conflict that faces every child."

"But the boy had the happiest childhood!"

"How did you find out about his homosexuality?"

"Through my lawyer—he has a son in the same crowd. My lawyer's idea is that I give my boy a choice—either he gives up his homosexuality, or I change my will and am through with him for good; he takes another name and gets out of the house. What do you think of that?"

"Threats are useless. Every homosexual is unconsciously aiming at self-damage. What would be a deterrent to the ordinary, normal person is unconsciously alluring to him."

"That's crazy!"

"No, only neurotic-masochistic."

"You haven't heard the rest of it. Besides making trouble for me, the boy has sent his mother off on a crazy binge. She calls it 'soul-searching.'"

"Soul-searching for mistakes she made in bringing up her son?"

"You got it. My God, she goes over every move she made or didn't make when he was a baby, trying to decide when and how she committed her 'crime.' I told her to stop or she'd end in a nuthouse."

"Please give your wife this message: even if she made educational mistakes, these cannot account for a child's subsequent homosexuality."

"I'll tell her. Whether she'll believe it is another thing. By the way, would I be able to force the boy into treatment?"

"If you could, it wouldn't be any use. Nothing can be achieved unless he *inwardly* wishes to change."

"Look, I'm old fashioned. I'll put him under pressure and he'll be here in your office!"

"I'm trying to dissuade you from taking dramatic steps: disinheriting him, or throwing him out of your house, or forcing him into treatment will all be futile."

"In God's name, what will help him?"

"His own defeats and disappointments, if anything. They may make him ready for treatment."

"I'll think that over. As of now, I still think I ought to cut the bastard out of my will."

I have never heard another chapter of this story.

Mr. and Mrs. AA. came from the Midwest to tell me the familiar tale about their twenty-three-year-old son. Mr. AA., a business man, took it rather resignedly; his wife did not. Hers was a fighting mood, though streaked with self-reproach.

"First I heard rumors," she said. "Then I overheard some telephone conversations, and then I caught a peculiar look my son gave another boy. That was disgusting and heart-breaking: the kind of look a boy gives a beautiful girl. It turned my stomach and broke my heart. What can be done for him?"

"Nothing, without his inner cooperation. How does he feel about it?"

"He's one hundred per cent for that dirty business. I have only one explanation for the whole dirty mess: I was forty-one when he was born, and I had toxemia. Is God punishing me?"

"Neither toxemia nor the age of the mother can account for homosexuality. You are torturing yourself needlessly."

"If I could only believe that!"

I suggested to them, as I had to Mrs. X., that their son be

told his mother had consulted me about her own condition, and that I had asked to talk to him about her.

After Mr. AA. had exerted a good deal of pressure, the son came down from college to see me. He scoffed at my information about self-damage; his entire attitude was one of anger and irony combined.

A few weeks later I heard through his mother that his boy friend (and roommate) had been arrested. Although the college year had just ended, the boy had stayed on in the college town. The parents now tried to force him to leave, but the boy insisted on remaining, despite his own danger, so that he could help his friend.

Over the telephone his desperate mother asked me: "Now that he's face to face with *real* danger, will this be frightening enough to push him into treatment?"

"I believe he needs a few more shocks," I replied.

So far I have not heard from this young man, who had told me with much assurance that he "did not believe there was danger."

Another case of miserable, perplexed parents and recalcitrant, resentful son was that of the BB. family. Like Mr. and Mrs. A. (see Chapter One), these parents had recorded some of their son's telephone conversations with his boy friends, having first overheard suspicious phrases on an extension. The facts made clear in these conversations horrified them, but they never mentioned their specific knowledge to their son. Instead, they spoke to him in general terms, disparaging his friends. He defended his friends hotly. Given his mother's health as an excuse, he eventually agreed to see me.

This young man was not too clever; he talked himself into many partial admissions. When I told him that self-damage was a basic element in homosexuality, he seemed alarmed and became thoughtful. I had the impression that the information had registered, and might—some day in the future—sink in.

Mr. CC.'s problem was his twenty-year-old daughter, the child of his first wife. The girl was a Lesbian; after her graduation from a West Coast college she and another girl had set up an apartment together in the college town. Her parents had been divorced when the girl was eleven; Mr. CC. now wanted to know whether he was responsible for his daughter's "tragedy."

After I explained that masochism is built up in the first eighteen months of life, Mr. CC. calmed down sufficiently to discuss his daughter in some detail. During her last winter vacation as an undergraduate, the girl had brought a guest home with her. The guest was a boy: Mr. CC. saw at once that he was a homosexual. Ironically, the girl—"unconsciously on purpose"—failed to realize this, although the evidence was blatant. The boy was living with another homosexual, and the girl used to visit them on Sunday mornings and cook breakfast for them. A short time after the winter vacation, the girl was "taken over" by a masculine-looking Lesbian.

"I read your book," Mr. CC. said, "and I understand what you mean by self-damage. Look what this child did!"

Example after example could be cited of desperate, self-accusing parents and recalcitrant children. The rationalizations which the parents present to excuse their alleged guilt are so inane, so far-fetched, that they must be taken as evidence of the existence of some kind of *guilt-proneness.* Often these parents appear to have found and to be exploiting a new source of masochism.

It is pertinent to ask whether the parents' discovery of a child's homosexuality is actually, as reported, due only to the child's stupidity, indiscretion, carelessness and thoughtlessness. I doubt this; I believe that two superimposed processes promote these revelations. Superficially, these young people are actuated by pseudo-aggressive revenge wishes ("See what you made of me!"). In a deeper layer, they are increasing their masochistic stakes, "bidding up" their allotment of trouble.

Although in general it is futile to use a ruse in order to persuade a neurotic to consult an analyst, I believe that in the cases of these young recalcitrants the one suggested is both justified and advisable. Seeing the analyst, even reluctantly and in response to parental pressure, serves two purposes. To begin with, it reassures the parents—who are also people, and also in need of help. In their despairing mood, any move is better than inactivity and a therapeutic shrug of the shoulders. Secondly, the information imparted to the young homosexual—the fact that inner self-damage and homosexuality are twins—*may* take root and have effect some time in the future. No one can tell, but even a faint possibility is worth trying for.

11

Homosexuality, Shakespeare's "Hamlet" and D. H. Lawrence's "The Fox"

FOR MORE THAN three hundred and fifty years, *Hamlet* has been a staple item in the repertory of the theater in that part of the world influenced by Western thinking. Even a staple item, of course, passes through periods of neglect and revival, and *Hamlet* has been no exception to this rule. Nevertheless, it has been called—and with some justification—the most famous play in world literature. In a classic, or in other words a venerable and time-honored work, neither fame nor respect automatically ensures real interest. Some people consider an appreciation of the classics a cultural "must"; to admit their boredom would be to betray a cultural lack, and so they keep their absence of interest cautiously to themselves. Others misuse the classics by turning them into an exercise in self-aggrandizement. Happy in the recognition of phrases or passages made familiar in their school days, they make no attempt to understand the work of art as a whole. The ability to quote phrases, even when misapplied, serves as a satisfactory substitute.

Despite all these unavoidable and often ludicrous concomitants, *Hamlet* has moved and impressed millions of spectators. This is not the full extent of its claim to a special niche; in addition it contains a series of paradoxes and a series of brilliant psychological solutions.*

To name a few paradoxes:

First, the main psychological problem—Hamlet's motiveless indecision (he gets a commission and delivers an omission)—is not explained by Shakespeare, nor can it be *consciously* understood by the spectator. The paradoxical fact that an incomprehensible play could hold the attention of generations of spectators has disturbed generations of scholars—all who worked exclusively on the conscious level. It is true that some admixture of the mysterious-incomprehensible has seldom damaged an author. Andersen's fairy tale of the emperor's new clothes alludes to that human frailty, applicable to all human endeavors. Still, it would be an exaggeration to say that conscious incomprehensibility *alone* makes for success.

The second paradox in *Hamlet* has not so far even been formulated, to my knowledge: it pertains to the *specificity of Hamlet's conflict with inner conscience.* As already pointed out, inner conscience is in general a restrictive internal force, specializing exclusively in the veto. Its stock in trade consists of the terms, "Don't" and "It is positively forbidden." In those few cases in which inner conscience expresses itself in terms of "Do" and "It is allowed," permission is always granted *for* a disagreeable duty and *against* some pleasure. Regardless of whether the restriction is aimed at aggressive or libidinous tendencies, instinctual fantasies and deeds are always hit. No wonder that Mark Twain in *The Mysterious Stranger* called conscience "a misery machine."

Now, the plot of *Hamlet* exactly reverses this rule: conscience, represented by the ghost of the murdered king, Hamlet's father, directly orders a deed typically forbidden: murder. What does this mean? Isn't it paradoxical that conscience, the forbidder of

* "Seven Paradoxes in Shakespeare's 'Hamlet'" a shortened version of a lecture delivered at The Institute of Arts and Sciences, Columbia University, New York, February 14, 1957.

the instinctual, should in this case reverse itself?

Of course, one could object that in Hamlet's time the abdication of individual revenge to orderly judicial procedure was not so common as it is today. But it is clear from Hamlet's great popularity among his subjects—a factor repeatedly stressed in the play—that he could have saved himself the trouble of a personally executed revenge, *provided* he had a case. But did he? He was acting in fulfillment of a ghost's command. Translated into modern terms, the ghost-scene in *Hamlet* is comparable to the situation of a man who wakes up one morning and "just knows" that his recently deceased father had been poisoned by the adulterous pair: mother and uncle. Intuition is not a legal argument. Exhumation and the contemporary equivalent of chemical analysis (or even inspection of the body) are never mentioned in the play.

There is another flaw in the argument that justifiable revenge, going as far as murder, was countenanced in Hamlet's day, especially among the nobility. Respect for law is not the only deterrent. Hamlet's was an era of devout and unquestioning religious belief, and Hamlet, too, was devout. In his first monologue Hamlet regrets that God forbids suicide. Later in the play, when Hamlet comes upon the king at his devotions, he rationalizes his failure to seize the opportunity of killing him: killed while on his knees at prayer, the uncle-king would automatically have gone to heaven.

Still, all this but adds to the paradox, for Shakespeare mentions no religious scruples in connection with executing the ghost's command. The mystery deepens, therefore: how can *inner* conscience order and condone murder?

The third paradox is the *disproportion between crime and punishment*. Hamlet's crime, as Freud explained in 1899, is one of the banal and unavoidable "heartaches and natural shocks that flesh is heir to" (to quote from Hamlet's great soliloquy). The Oedipal wishes common to every child during a certain stage in development constitute his crime. Boys who remain glued to these fantasies instead of overcoming them must, as adults, pay the penalty of psychogenically induced potency disturbance, not-too-dangerous depression and dissatisfaction. They are unaware, of course, of the reasons for this. But the penalty of impotence and the penalty of death (as in Hamlet's case) are not quite comparable. Why should so great an intuitive psychologist as Shakespeare have represented these facts incorrectly?

The players' scenes make it obvious that Hamlet seeks death. His provocations succeed in arousing the king, who then makes three moves which live up to Hamlet's inner expectations: he sends a mission to England bearing letters ordering Hamlet's execution; he makes a pact with Laertes to kill Hamlet with a poisoned rapier; he prepares a poisoned drink for Hamlet. Hamlet's unremitting provocations are inwardly intended as pleas that he be killed. This is made clear by the amazing naivete of the reason he gives for arranging the greatest of his provocations: the re-enactment of a murder in the play within a play. Allegedly, his purpose is to study the king's facial expression. But in earlier scenes he had lamented the hypocrisy and inscrutability of the king's facial expressions ("That one may smile, and smile, and be a villain," Act I, Scene V).

Since the disproportion between crime and punishment is so patent in *Hamlet* are we confronted with a psychological error made by a psychological genius, or are we dealing with a description which appears to ring false but is actually correct because it covers something more deeply repressed?

The fourth paradox in *Hamlet* centers around this question: Does Hamlet indirectly commit suicide by "provocation and proxy," or is he really killed by Laertes, acting as the instrument of King Claudius? Hamlet is opposed to suicide for two reasons. In his first monologue he regrets that religion prohibits "self-slaughter":

> O! that this too too solid flesh would melt,
> Thaw, and resolve itself into a dew;
> Or that the everlasting had not fix'd
> His canon 'gainst self-slaughter! O God! O God!

And in his second great monologue ("To be or not to be . . .") he questions whether life after death is any better than life on earth; perhaps it may be worse:

To die,—to sleep;
To sleep! perchance to dream:—ay, there's the rub;
For in that sleep of death what dreams may come,
When we have shuffled off this mortal coil,
Must give us pause . . .
But that the dread of something after death,—
The undiscover'd country, from whose bourn
No traveller returns,—puzzles the will,
And makes us rather bear those ills we have
Than fly to others that we know not of?

Nevertheless, at the end of the play Hamlet naively allows himself to be killed. The king has made sure of his death by preparing both a poisoned rapier and a poisoned drink; as soon as Hamlet accepted the silly wager, the result became inevitable. Why did he have no suspicions of the king? Hamlet knew the treacherous contents of the sealed letter to England; he had just told Horatio that this letter decreed his death. And why does Hamlet make no move to prevent his mother from drinking the poison after the king warns her not to do so? Hamlet exchanges rapiers with Laertes (thus showing that he is on guard against treachery) but only *after* he himself had been wounded by the poisoned weapon. So contradictory is Hamlet's pseudo-naivete that Shakespeare feels obliged to explain it beforehand: in preparing the trick with the poisoned blades, the king calls Hamlet "most generous and free from all contriving" (Act IV, Scene VII).

How are we to explain Hamlet's paradoxical naivete?

The fifth paradox is the frequently overlooked fact that Hamlet *disobeys* not only his father's *first command*—to revenge the murder of the father by his wife and brother—but also his *second*—to leave Queen Gertrude in peace:

O horrible! O, horrible! most horrible!
If thou hast nature in thee, bear it not;
Let not the royal bed of Denmark be
A couch for luxury and damned incest.
But, howsoever thou pursu'st this act,
Taint not thy mind, nor let thy soul contrive
Against thy mother aught: leave her to Heaven,
And to those thorns that in her bosom lodge,
To prick and sting her.

What really happens is that Hamlet furiously attacks his mother in words, and ineffectually and silently plots against the uncle-king in his thoughts when in the company of the alleged malefactor. Moreover, in his cruel "get thee to a nunnery" scene with Ophelia, Hamlet develops an extreme anti-sex philosophy and names woman *the* prime culprit:

> . . . Or, if thou wilt needs marry, marry a fool; for *wise men*
> know well enough what monsters you make of them.

This gives the impression that Hamlet considered man merely the executive organ of woman's conspiratorial cruelty: a theme which does not fit at all into the Oedipal fantasy, where the mother is represented as weak, passive, and completely under the father's dominance.

Paradox No. 6, again, is a frequently neglected factor. Hamlet's ambivalence is not limited to his father's command to revenge his murder; it runs like a red thread through many of Hamlet's actions as well. Generalized ambivalence is not unusual in a doubt-torn individual. But in Hamlet, as in many of Shakespeare's characters, different persons appear to be used to express different aspects of the basic theme: love and hatred, felt for the same person, at the same time. The possibility arises, therefore, that Polonius depicts the father-image, caricatured and demoted, and that Ophelia represents a demoted mother-image. Cruelty dominates in Hamlet's treatment of these doubles: he kills Polonius and drives Ophelia into psychosis and suicide.

The seventh paradox is the most confusing of them all. Before psychoanalysis, it was taken for granted that a poet's work dramatized his *conscious* experiences or fantasies. Since Freud, this view has been modified; the stress now falls on *unconscious* wishes and fantasies. Hamlet has been adduced as a classical example of the Oedipus complex, and the play has not only been taken as a classical presentation of such a case but as a starting point for conclusions regarding the author himself, whoever the genius was who wrote under the name of Shakespeare. It has been asserted that *Hamlet* had been written as a reaction to the death of the poet's father; it has also been claimed that the poet represented his own self in Hamlet, for had not the name of his first-born been Hamnet?

There is only one flaw in this deduction. Shakespeare was a *bisexual.* It is true that he married at an early age; it is also true that he wrote the homosexually tinged sonnets. Oscar Wilde, himself a homosexual, used this fact in writing *The Portrait of Mr. W. H.* (Shakespeare had dedicated the sonnets to "Mr. W. H."; the initials are those of a young man mentioned by Shakespeare.) Since the roots of homosexuality are acquired before the Oedipus phase appears in children (as demonstrated in earlier chapters), it therefore follows that the Oedipal conflict could not have been Shakespeare's real problem.

The analytic microscope makes it possible to resolve this septet of paradoxes.

Parts of the first paradox—Hamlet's objectively senseless and totally unmotivated indecision—were admirably clarified by Freud in a footnote appended to the text of *The Interpretation of Dreams* (1899). Here are Freud's exact words:

> Another of the great creations of tragic poetry, Shakespeare's *Hamlet,* has its root in the same soil as *Oedipus Rex.* But the changed treatment of the material reveals the whole difference in the mental life of these two widely separated epochs of civilization: the secular advance of repression in the emotional life of mankind. In the *Oedipus* of Sophocles the child's underlying wishful fantasy is brought into the open and realized as it would be in a dream. In *Hamlet* it remains repressed, and—just as in the case of a neurosis—we only learn of its existence from its inhibiting consequences. Strangely enough, the overwhelming effect produced by the more modern tragedy has turned out to be compatible with the fact that people have remained completely in the dark as to the hero's character. The play is built up on Hamlet's hesitation over fulfilling the task of revenge that is assigned to him, but its text offers no reason or motives for these hesitations and an immense variety of attempts at interpreting them have failed to produce a result. According to the view which originated with Goethe and is still the prevailing one today, Hamlet represents the type of

man whose power of direct action is paralyzed by an excessive development of his intellect. (He is "sicklied o'er with the pale cast of thought.") According to another view, the dramatist has tried to portray a pathologically irresolute character, one which may be classed as neurasthenic. The plot of the drama shows us, however, that Hamlet is far from being represented as a person incapable of taking any action. We see him in action on two occasions: first, in a sudden outburst of temper, when he runs his sword through the eavesdropper behind the arras, and secondly in a premeditated and even crafty fashion, when, with all the callousness of a Renaissance prince, he sends the two courtiers to the death that has been planned for himself. What is it, then, that inhibits him in fulfilling the task set to him by his father's ghost? The answer, once more, is that it is the peculiar nature of the task. Hamlet is able to do anything —except take vengeance on the man who did away with his father and took the father's place with his mother, the man who shows him the repressed wishes of his own childhood realized. Thus the loathing which should drive him on to revenge is replaced in him by self-reproaches, by scruples of conscience, which remind him that he himself is literally no better than the sinner whom he is to punish. Here I have translated into conscious terms what was bound to remain unconscious in Hamlet's mind; and if anyone is inclined to call him a hysteric, I can only accept the fact as one that is implied by my interpretation. The distaste for sexuality expressed by Hamlet in his conversation with Ophelia fits in very well with this: the same distaste which was destined to take possession of the poet's mind more and more during the years that followed, and which reached its extreme expression in *Timon of Athens*. For it can of course only be the poet's own mind which confronts us in Hamlet. I observe in a book on Shakespeare by George Brandes (1896) a statement that *Hamlet* was written immediately after the death of Shakespeare's father (in 1601), that is, under the immediate impact of his bereavement and, as we may assume, while his childhood feelings about his father had been freshly revived. It is known, too, that Shakespeare's own son who died at an early age bore the name of "Hamnet," which is identical with "Hamlet." Just as *Hamlet* deals with the relation of a son to his parents, so *Macbeth* (written at approximately the same period) is concerned with the subject of childlessness. But just as all neurotic symptoms, and, for that matter, dreams are capable of being "interpreted in different layers" ("ueberdeterminiert") and indeed need to be, if they are to be fully understood, so all genuine creative writings are the product of more than a single impulse in the poet's mind, and are open to more than a single interpretation. In what I have written I have only attempted to interpret the deepest layer of impulses in the mind of the creative writer.

In 1919, in a later edition of *The Interpretation of Dreams,* Freud added:

> The above indications of a psychoanalytic explanation of *Hamlet* have since been amplified by Ernest Jones and defended against the alternative views put forward in the literature on the subject.

Freud's discovery of the "dynamic unconscious"—which changed a nebulous philosophical concept into a clinically provable, dynamically effective and therapeutically accessible fact—also explained why (to use Freud's words) "the overwhelming effect (of *Hamlet*) turned out to be compatible with the fact that people remained completely in the dark as to the hero's character." Since every human being has gone through the Oedipal conflict, communication between the author's unconscious and that of the spectator is established.

Paradox No. 2—the specificity of Hamlet's conflict with inner conscience—resolves itself when we view Hamlet's indecision in terms of its unconscious beginnings. We know that the inner conscience is not a single force, but two opposed forces of unequal power. One, the ego ideal (called in this book the "department of don'ts and great expectations"), is a benevolent force which has absorbed, and identified with, precepts pronounced by the parents. The other, daimonion (the "department of torture," the inner tyrant), has a single function: the imposition of torture. As already pointed out in Chapter One, the proof that one has acted in accordance with parental precepts can ward off punishment imposed by the inner tyrant.

It is my opinion that Shakespeare intuitively anticipated these scientific discoveries regarding the inner conscience. The ghost in Hamlet represents the department of don'ts; the torture Hamlet inflicts on himself shows the inner tyrant at work.

Hamlet's department of don'ts commands revenge. If Hamlet had obeyed the command, he would have avoided the conflict, since it is laudable to revenge one's father's murderer. Exactly at this point, the inner tyrant makes the possible solution impossible by pointing out ironically that Hamlet is just as guilty as the murderer, Claudius. Hence Hamlet's hopeless conflict.

So beaten down is Hamlet's ego that he does not even ask the pertinent question: what right does conscience have to demand that he become a murderer, in the first place? Only one hint is included in the play. Hamlet asks Horatio to observe the king's facial expression during the players' performance:

> Observe mine uncle: if his occulted guilt
> Do not itself unkennel in one speech,
> *It is a damned ghost that we have seen,*
> *And my imaginations are as foul*
> *As Vulcan's stithy.*

The transition from "venerable" ghost to "damned"—soon after, in the bedroom scene with his mother, Hamlet reverts again to veneration of the ghost—represents a hopeless attempt to devalue the department of don'ts.

At the same time, Hamlet reveals his masochism by mercilessly provoking the king. This typical masochistic technique is, as usual, a success. Isn't it strange that it never occurs to Hamlet that no murderer hesitates to commit a *second* murder to conceal the fact that he is guilty of the first?

The whole ghost problem in *Hamlet* is intimately connected with intuition. Hamlet's exclamation, when the ghost tells him of the murder, "O my prophetic soul!," points clearly in the direction of previous subjective and insoluble inner suspicions. In dealing with this topic in several scientific papers and in my book, PRINCIPLES OF SELF-DAMAGE,* I have pointed out that intuition never manifests itself in periods of emotional calm. For intuition, this "knowledge above and beyond our

* The Philosophical Library, New York, 1959.

intelligence," to appear, the prerequisite is a severe "pseudo-incompetence attack" in which the inner tyrant launches an accusation of ignorance and pursues it whether or not the charge is justified. Generally, masochistic depression follows. In exceptional and rare situations, the individual unconsciously mobilizes his last reserves, producing a split-second of "intelligence beyond his intelligence." Thus an intuitive thought is born.

An intuitive thought may be productive, but is not always so. At times one gathers the impression that the malicious inner tyrant half-condescendingly permits the perception of knowledge otherwise hidden, purely for the sake of subsequently reducing the individual to absurdity. "Now you know," runs the deflating comment. "And what do you propose to do with this knowledge?" In short, the tables are unexpectedly turned and the wisdom retrieved in the act of intuition becomes a new source of torture. This seems to be the case in *Hamlet*.

These assumptions lead directly to the central problem: *What is Hamlet's real inner crime?* The answer to this question will dispose of a few of the paradoxes enumerated earlier: the discrepancy between Oedipal fantasies and self-destruction; the reason for and technique of self-destruction; the charge that woman is the main malefactor; the splitting-off technique in ambivalence.

It seems to me that Hamlet's crime of Oedipal fantasies, so brilliantly elucidated by Freud, is but camouflage obscuring a deeper conflict which antedates the Oedipal one. Freud wrote his opinion at a time when he was still exploring the most superficial layers of the unconscious; in later years he probed the deeper layer. This is the reverse of the child's actual development, which does not begin on the apex but at the base of the psychic pyramid. In 1931, Freud himself discovered the precursors of the triangular Oedipus complex: the duality of mother and child. Freud named this the "pre-Oedipal phase."

This phase is characterized by misconceptions, fears and projections. The child imputes all possible sinister designs to his objectively benevolent mother, unaware of the fact that he would die of hunger or exposure without loving motherly care. Barricaded behind his unfamiliarity with objective facts, living emotionally on the basis of his illusion of omnipotence and magical power, the child projects parts of his own inexpressible aggression (the portion that is not stored up in inner conscience to be used against himself later) on to his innocent mother. As a result, he is caught in a severe conflict of ambivalence. Strong fears are counter-balanced by the belated realization that mother is "also" good. Freud suspected that this painful ambivalence provides the impetus which pushes the child into the Oedipal phase. In this new stage (taking the boy as example), the positive emotional part of the child's ambivalent attitude is fastened to the mother, who is loved, while the negative part is attached to the father, the "bad" competitor, who is hated.

My own opinion is that the process does not stop there. The Oedipus complex represents a *rescue station* from unbearable fears centered around the mother of earliest infancy. By borrowing strength from his identification with the father, the boy—in an active repetition of a passively endured experience—completely reverses the roles. He now sees in his mother an image of his own helpless self, thus making the father (in identification with him, as well) into the alleged torturer. The rest of the story is more familiar. The new view of the father as the "torturer" leads only to further fears of retaliation ("castration fear"). After a few short years of attempting to cope with fears to end all fears, the Oedipal fantasy, too, collapses when the child is four or five. As a result, the attachment to the mother becomes desexualized; what is left is filial affection. In the same way, the attitude towards the father changes. Aggression is eliminated, leaving comradery and the wish to be father's "pal."

It is in the earliest level of development, before the Oedipal phase sets in, that the child lays the foundation for the most dangerous and most widespread of all defense mechanisms: psychic masochism.

These considerations explain some of the paradoxes in *Hamlet*. We can understand now why Hamlet sees in woman the main malefactor; one of his first reactions to the ghost's revelation is the exclamation: "O most pernicious woman!" It is perhaps pertinent, since we are not dealing with Hamlet as an independent character but as an author's creation, to cite another Shakespearian line: in *Twelfth Night* (Act I, Scene V, line 259) we find the words: "Lady, you are the cruell'st she alive." It may be that this anti-woman attitude explains even the official version of the murder of Hamlet's father. Allegedly, he is bitten by a snake while sleeping. The snake of the Garden of Eden is emotionally associated with Eve's daughters.

It is quite possible that Shakespeare's tendency to see woman as "the great enemy" also accounted for his coolness towards Queen Elizabeth. Georg Brandes, on page 41 of his biography of Shakespeare, remarked: "Shakespeare was the only poet of the period who absolutely refused to comply with the Queen's demand for incessant homage." The late Ludwig Jekels pointed out how different was Shakespeare's attitude towards Elizabeth's successor, James I, son of Mary Stuart, whom Elizabeth had executed. Some scholars (including Jekels) believed that *Macbeth* represents an apotheosis of James upon his succession to the throne. In this tragedy, Malcolm, son of the murdered King Duncan, finally becomes king. Once more, Lady Macbeth, the instigator, is thwarted.

If, as assumed, undigested masochistic attachment to the mother image is the core of Hamlet's "crime," many of his pseudo-naive actions are seen as purposeful. Unconsciously bent on suicide by provocation and proxy—a not infrequent occurrence in direct and indirect forms in these deeply regressed neurotics—he provokes the king, and the king acts the part assigned to him. Hamlet's aggression towards the minor images of his ambivalence, Polonius and Ophelia, is pseudo-aggression. The so-exaggeratedly pronounced Oedipal conflict, though also repressed, has the purpose of disguising the real, more deeply repressed problem. The extensive literature proves how successful a camouflage it is.

As is to be expected, Shakespeare clung to the usual pseudo-aggressive defense, *on the conscious level.* He presented at face value Hamlet's inhibited revenge fantasies (in reality, pseudo-aggression). This is visible in Hamlet's other double, Fortinbras. The late Ella F. Sharpe, a British analyst, brought this point out:

> Fortinbras had a father killed by King Hamlet (Hamlet's father). However, he does not succeed to the throne of Norway but remains in tutelage to an old uncle, harboring his resentment against King Hamlet's successor, Claudius. Thus Hamlet

and Fortinbras are in the same relationship to Claudius. Fortinbras gathers up "in the skirts of Norway" (Act I, Scene I) a set of wild unruly youth to make war on Claudius. It is to repel young Fortinbras that the war-like preparations are made and the close watch kept at the beginning of the play. But when, at Claudius' request, the old uncle rebukes Fortinbras, the latter obediently gives up his plan to avenge his father's death and asks instead only for a quest of honor elsewhere. It is only honor he covets. It is this valiant but obedient young man, *who has given up his thirst for revenge,* who returns in the final scene, when the orgy of death is over, to hear that Hamlet has named him as his successor. Fortinbras, the Knight sans peur et sans reproche, ascends without bloodshed to the throne of Denmark as soon as the wicked king and queen and the *revengeful* Hamlet have been disposed of by no deed of his (p. 256, my italics).*

No, Hamlet was not revengeful; he was but a depressed fugitive from a hopeless conflict with inner conscience. What appears as revengefulness is but pseudo-aggression covering the more deeply repressed masochistic infantile solution of his inner conflict.

Finally, we arrive at the last and most puzzling paradox: the charting of Shakespeare's inner psychic makeup on the basis of conclusions drawn from *Hamlet.*

In my clinical studies on writers—thirty-six clinical analyses are reported in my book, THE WRITER AND PSYCHOANALYSIS, first published in 1950, and that number has by now more than doubled—I pointed out that the writer is a chronic defendant standing before the tribunal of his inner conscience. His work of art represents his defense, in the form of a sublimation. However, he never admits to his real wishes but only to secondary defenses—meaning the defense against the defense—covering these wishes. The writer admits to the *lesser* intrapsychic crime to conceal and deny the *greater* intrapsychic crime.

To adduce an example:

In one of his unpublished novels, a French writer in analysis with me described a man who, after breaking off a relationship

* Collected Papers on Psychoanalysis, The Hogarth Press, London, 1950.

with a girl, wonders about the reasons. He cannot blame the girl; he just feels suddenly that he is "through" with her. No feeling is left. He perceives only a great emptiness, indifference, and the conviction that he must leave the girl. In a flash of insight the man understands that he is incapable of real love. A moment afterwards he represses his understanding and begins pursuing another woman. The reader is left with the impression that the neurotic hero will endlessly repeat the same pattern of falling in pseudo-love, being disappointed without obvious reason, and so forth.

During the preparation of that novel my patient found himself faced with the following conflict. His wife, the victim of a chronic incurable malady, had just suffered a new relapse. Although he desired to leave her, he found this plan unacceptable under the tragic circumstances. The marital conflict, however, was in no way connected with his wife's relapses since the family doctor had informed him, on behalf of the wife's family and before the marriage, of the girl's illness. The patient showed me the entry in his diary on the day on which the discussion with the physician took place. It reported the facts and the patient's decision: "I decided to gamble with destiny." This wish to overtrump medical destiny was a masochistic action, unconsciously motivated, and had exactly the results inwardly intended. Every time his wife had to enter a sanitarium for some months—and this happened with regularity—he complained bitterly about the injustice she had done him. He was not consciously aware that he had unconsciously provoked the whole situation by marrying her. This complaining about self-created ill luck was supplemented by self-commiseration.

As can be imagined, the patient did not understand his real conflict. He believed that he remained with his wife *despite* the suffering she inflicted on him. In unconscious reality, he was staying with her *because* of this unconsciously self-created and inwardly sought-for unhappiness. The situation was tailored to order for a psychic masochist.

In the patient's novel, his hero leaves a woman without having any reason to do so. This was exactly the patient's alibi: "If there are men who leave their wives without adequate reasons, I certainly can do it, for I have every justification."

The neurotic hero of his own story played the part of appeaser of the patient's inner conscience. This also explains why a less important element in his neurosis—his inability to love—was permitted to rise to consciousness, although typically repressed. Actually the patient's main conflict was induced by the wish to *remain* with his wife despite all logical reasons to the contrary; he wanted to stay with her because she gratified his masochistic, neurotic needs. His conflict appeared to be an aggressive one—whether or not to leave his wife; his defenses and alibis were produced in answer to the inner tyrant's accusation of masochism. But this pseudo-aggressive conflict covered the masochistic wish to suffer, which was his real problem. In the same way guilt was shifted from the masochistic to the pseudo-aggressive problem. Blame for the *lesser* intrapsychic crime was accepted in order to cover up the *greater* inner crime.

Another unconscious subterfuge is apparent. A flash of insight told the patient that he was incapable of love, and therefore neurotically ill. Significantly, no explanation was given for this inability. That omission, too, was an alibi. The inexplicable meant for the patient: "Neurosis is not under conscious volition, hence I cannot be held responsible."

Freudian psychoanalysis was originally interested in literature for a comparatively selfish reason—to prove its own point. Attacked again and again by so-called practical people as nonsensical and fantastic, the science of psychoanalysis has defended itself by various means: for instance, by pointing out the result of repressions and resistances making up the wasteland of the minds of the "practical" mediocrities. An unimportant argument against the self-righteousness of the "practical realists" was that great writers have known intuitively everything that psychoanalysis has discovered and proved scientifically. Therefore the writer's intuitive knowledge has been adduced in arguments pro analysis in hundreds of scientific papers.

In a lecture on the psychology of writers, I delivered before the New York Psychoanalytic Society on January 27, 1942,* I said:

* Later published in *The Psychoanalytic Review*, 31:40-70, 1944. Elaborated in THE WRITER AND PSYCHOANALYSIS (Second, enlarged edition, Brunner's Psychiatric Books, New York).

From an historical point of view, it is interesting to note that even the most complete of psychological doctrines, psychoanalysis, has to a certain extent been taken in by the artist. The original analytic formulation on this subject ran as follows: The artist expresses in his work his *unconscious* fantasies. This was a great improvement on the one previously accepted by the world in general, which assumed that the work represented his *conscious* wishes and experiences in modified form. Despite this, our increased understanding of the artistic personality was only relative. We still failed to distinguish between the unconscious wish and the unconscious mechanism of defense against this wish. My explanation for this is that very few *artists* were analyzed, and consequently early analytic assumptions were based upon the interpretation of the *work* of artists already dead. Analysis, in the first three decades of its existence, was struggling for a recognition of the Oedipus complex. It was indeed gratifying then to be able to point to the work and statements of great artists, which seemed to corroborate our findings.

To approach this in another way, let us consider Freud's well-known remarks about *Hamlet* . . . * It is truly an astounding and impressive explanation of Hamlet's character, but not a proof that Shakespeare was suffering from an unresolved Oedipus conflict at the time the tragedy was written. It could just as well have been, as has been evidenced in clinical material, that this problem originated as a means of defense against a more deeply imbedded conflict. This erroneous assumption, however, is the foundation for many analytic biographies. (The subtitle of this paragraph in my original paper was "Fallacy of Approach by Analogy.")

Six years after I delivered this paper, the late Ernest Jones—who, after publishing his biography of Freud, became as well known to the general public as he had for years been to students of psychoanalysis—indirectly confirmed my opinions. In a paper entitled "The Death of Hamlet's Father,"** he wrote:

* This refers to the footnote in "Interpretation of Dreams" quoted earlier in this chapter.

***International Journal of Psycho-Analysis*, 29:174-176, 1948.

> The theme of homosexuality does not surprise us in Shakespeare . . . I have argued (in *Hamlet and Oedipus,* a book published in 1949) that Shakespeare wrote *Hamlet* as a more or less successful abreaction of his intolerable emotions aroused by the painful situation he depicts in his Sonnets, his betrayal by both his beloved young noble and his mistress.

That Shakespeare himself saw male homosexuality only in terms of femininity is one of the poet's rationalizations (for example, the queen in *Hamlet* compares her son with a "female dove"). The same holds true of Shakespeare's misunderstanding of the reasons for his mistress' betrayal of him, so eloquently and so whiningly described in the Sonnets. He blames her more violently than the young man. In the paper on Shakespeare already cited, Ernest Jones quite justifiably suspected that Mary Fitton, the Dark Lady of the Sonnets, was unconsciously and indirectly induced to interest herself in W. H. (William Herbert, who later became Earl of Pembroke) by Shakespeare himself, perhaps by "boring her with praise of his beloved handsome youth." Jones concluded: "According to the Sonnets it was *she* who led young Herbert astray. . . . I venture to express the surmise that Shakespeare played an active part in bringing about the misfortunes that then so deeply affected him." This fits in with my conclusion that Hamlet considered his mother the chief malefactor.

We ask of a writer *psychologically correct* actions on the part of his dramatis personae, arrived at intuitively. We do not ask for conscious knowledge of these unconscious interconnections. Even the greatest writers have their conscious naivetes and rationalizations: they are as other mortals are.

Seldom in world literature has the accolade of fame been bestowed with more justification than in the case of the poet who wrote Hamlet. What Goethe said of him is still partly true: "Whatever can be known of the heart of man can be found in Shakespeare's plays." Had Goethe said "*intuitively* known," he would have come nearer the truth. It required another genius—a psychological genius—to bring the intuitively and vaguely understood to the stream of conscious awareness. That was

Freud's contribution. Although some modifications are required to bring Freud's opinions on *Hamlet,* expressed in 1899, to the level of today's knowledge, and although in my opinion the most important facts in *Hamlet*—the intuitive understanding of a masochistically provocative candidate for suicide and his submissive relationship to the inner conscience—remain unmentioned in Freud's famous footnote, the fact remains that Freud's analysis of Hamlet's superficial layer of unconscious defenses represents a unique bull's-eye. It opened a new era in analytic literary criticism. It is remarkable how the psychological genius met the poetic genius halfway.

* * *

To the average man, Lesbianism is a great mystery. Actually, it is no more of a "mystery" than male homosexuality: it is merely a different neurotic elaboration of the same inner problem. In HOMOSEXUALITY: DISEASE OR WAY OF LIFE? I presented extensive clinical material on Lesbianism. Another, and perhaps simpler, approach is also possible: presenting literary material dealing with Lesbians, and contrasting this with clinical experiences. A brilliant literary example is available; it is D. H. Lawrence's short story, *The Fox.**

This is a comparatively obscure novelette about two semi-intellectual Lesbians living on a farm in England at the end of the first World War. They are unsuccessfully trying to raise chickens. Their main obstacles are a fox which repeatedly raids the barnyard, a number of strange illnesses, and their flock's "obstinate refusal to lay eggs." The fox gradually becomes the most serious of their problems. The women plan to shoot him, but he is too elusive for them. At length one of the women, March, comes face to face with the fox:

> She lowered her eyes and suddenly saw the fox. He was looking up at her. His chin was pressed down, and his eyes were looking up. They met her eyes. And he knew her. She was spell-bound—she knew he knew her. So he looked into her

* This section is an abridged version of a paper first published in *Journal of Nervous and Mental Diseases,* May, 1958. The quotations from Lawrence's story were used by permission of the Viking Press, New York, from *The Portable Lawrence.*

eyes, and her soul failed her. He knew her, he was not daunted . . . She struggled, confusedly she came to herself, and saw him making off, with slow leaps over some fallen boughs, slow, impudent jumps . . . (Later) she took her gun again and went to look for the fox. For he had lifted his eyes upon her, and his knowing look seemed to have entered her brain. She did not so much think of him; she was possessed by him. She saw his dark, shrewd, unabashed eye looking into her, knowing her. She felt him invisibly master her spirit . . . And again, she saw him glance over his shoulder at her, half-inviting, half contemptuous and cunning . . .

The fox invades March's reveries:

March also was not conscious that she thought of the fox. But whenever she fell into her half-musing, when she was half-rapt and half-intelligently aware of what passed under her vision, then it was the fox which somehow dominated her unconscious, possessed the blank half of her musing. And so it was for weeks, and months.

A young soldier then comes to the farm. The two women find out that he is the grandson of the previous owner, and had not known of his grandfather's death; he had enlisted in Canada. Lawrence describes March's reaction to the stranger:

The young man—or youth, for he would not be more than twenty—now advanced and stood in the inner doorway. March, already under the influence of his strange, soft, modulated voice, stared at him spell-bound. He had a ruddy, roundish face, with fairish hair, rather long, flattened to his forehead with sweat. His eyes were blue, and very bright and sharp. On his cheeks, on the fresh ruddy skin, were fine, fair hairs, like a down, but sharper. It gave him a slightly glistening look . . . But for March he was the fox. Whether it was the thrusting forward of his head, or the glisten of fine whitish hair on the ruddy cheek-bones, or the bright, keen eyes, that can never be said: but the boy was to her the fox, and she could not see him otherwise.

The young man spends his leave at the farm, and falls in love with March. For some time he cannot make out the relationship of the two young women: March acts the "man," and Banford, her companion, the "wife." Confronted with the boy's advances, March is quite helpless and evasively confused. Then the young man shoots the fox:

> The first thing that both she and Banford did in the morning was to go out to see the (dead) fox. It was a lovely dog-fox in his prime, with a handsome thick winter coat: a lovely golden-rod colour, with grey as it passed to the belly, and belly all white, and a great full brush with a delicate black and grey and pure white tip . . . "He's a beauty, isn't he? said Henry, standing by.—"Oh, yes, he's a fine big fox. I wonder how many chickens he's responsible for," she replied . . . "Are you going to skin him?" she asked.—"Yes, when I've had breakfast and got a board to peg him on." . . . "My word, what a strong smell he's got! Pooo! It'll take some washing off one's hands. I don't know why I was so silly as to handle him."—And she looked at her right hand, that had passed down his belly and along his tail, and had even got a tiny streak of blood from one dark place in his fur.—"Have you seen the chickens when they smell him, how frightened they are?" he said—"Yes, aren't they!" Later in the day she saw the fox's skin nailed flat on a board, as if crucified. It gave her an uneasy feeling.

At last March consents to marry Henry, but subsequently changes her mind again and again. Severe conflicts with Banford, her Lesbian friend, follow. Here is one scene involving the women:

> He heard Banford's fretful: "Why don't you let me help you with the parcel?" She had a queer plaintive hitch in her voice. Then came March's robust and reckless: "Oh, I can manage. Don't you bother about me. You've all you can do to get yourself over."—"Yes, that's all very well," said Banford fretfully. "You may say 'Don't bother about me' and then all the while you feel injured because nobody thinks of you." . . . "When do I feel injured?" said March.—"Always. You always feel injured. Now you're feeling injured because I won't have that boy to come and live on the farm."—"I'm not feeling

injured at all," said March.—"I know you are. When he's gone you'll sulk over it . . ."

In addition to "feeling injured," March enjoys the conflict between Banford and the young man:

> March seemed to flourish in this atmosphere. She seemed to sit between the two antagonists with a little wicked smile on her face, enjoying herself. There was even a sort of complacency in the way she laboriously crocheted, this evening.

The end of the story is that the young man "inadvertently" kills his Lesbian competitor while felling a tree ("No one saw what was happening besides himself"); March marries the young man, although the marriage does not seem to work out sexually because March still cannot accept her new passive role.

The Fox contains a series of observations and between-the-lines allusions that are clinically correct. Mingled with these are inaccuracies, but the clinically correct observations predominate.

1. Lawrence describes the typical husband-wife camouflage of Lesbians, and at the same time stresses the psychic-masochistic substructure of the camouflage. March places her masochism in fantasies, remains helpless against the "mocking fox" although she has a shotgun in her hands, is equally masochistic in her relationship with the young man after he has shot the fox.

2. Lawrence correctly describes March's constant injustice collecting, and therefore her hidden psychic masochism. Banford's specific reference to this, "You always feel injured," is quoted above.

3. Lawrence accurately depicts the two sets of unconscious identification in March: the "leading" masochistic identification with the victim, and the "misleading" masculine identification, deposited in the husband-wife (Oedipal) camouflage of her relationship with Banford.

4. Lawrence ingeniously hints that the fox, the devourer of chickens, symbolizes the "devouring" mother; we know that the fear of being devoured has priority in the "septet of baby fears."

5. With a combination of naivete (on a conscious level) and good intuition (on the unconscious level), Lawrence describes the unvarying inner defense of his masochistic heroine: the search

for love, which these sick women can find neither in the Lesbian nor in the connubial bed since injustice collecting is the real aim.

6. Finally, Lawrence presents with clinical correctness the defensive pseudo-aggression so predominant in Lesbians. March speaks harshly to Banford, enjoys the conflict between Banford and her male competitor, and even marries the man who has been directly or indirectly responsible for Banford's death. Moreover, in some "tender" manner, she is glad of the fox's death.

Lawrence's accurate observations outweigh in importance his cherished mystical ideas on sex-predominance, which are brought in at the end of the story when he explains March's frigidity in terms of the superficial defensive masculine camouflage. Lawrence also misunderstands March's reason for turning to the young man: he declares that March identified the fox with Henry ("The boy was to her the fox"), and claims that March had been helpless against the fox. Putting the two statements together, one sees that March lands exactly at the point she tried desperately to escape—the point of masochistic passivity on the part of the victim (the devoured "chicken").

The initial analytic theory on Lesbianism assumed that a specific elaboration of an Oedipal situation was involved. In 1927 Ernest Jones suggested that Lesbianism could be traced to two factors: "an unusually intensive oral eroticism and an unusually strong sadism." In 1931, in his study *On Female Sexuality*, Freud described the pre-Oedipal phase of the girl. Freud assumed that basically this attachment is shattered through ambivalence and hatred. In application of these ideas, H. Deutsch reported in 1932, in her study, *On Female Homosexuality*, that her Lesbian patients repeated the child-mother and not the Oedipal fixation in their perversion: should the hatred for the pre-Oedipal mother be too pronounced, the reactive feeling of guilt gives rise to an attempt to deny its contents, according to the formula: "I'm not the refused and rejected child; I'm a child loved and nourished by you."

In my papers and books on this subject,* I have pointed out the five-layer unconscious structure upon which Lesbianism is built:

* See COUNTERFEIT-SEX (l.c.); HOMOSEXUALITY: DISEASE OR WAY OF LIFE? (l.c.); KINSEY'S MYTH OF FEMALE SEXUALITY (in collaboration with W. Kroger), Grune & Stratton, New York, 1954.

First: the end result of the infantile conflict—masochistic attachment to the mother of earliest infancy.

Second: the veto inevitably interposed by the inner tyrant, which objects to the pleasure-in-displeasure pattern.

Third: the standard disclaimer of psychic masochism, expressed through a show of pseudo-aggression.

Fourth: the prompt veto of the inner tyrant, which points out that "hatred" is also forbidden.

Fifth: the final defense, which takes the form of pseudo-love, clothed in the husband-wife camouflage of Lesbianism.

It should be understood that this last defense, which is dramatized in consciousness, does not represent (as alleged) a re-enactment of the roles of good mother and beloved child, but an unconscious (and wholly concealed) depiction of the fantasy of the masochistically mistreated child and the cruel, denying mother.

The five-layer basis of Lesbianism explains a number of phenomenologically observable facts.

First, the typical high tension of the Lesbian relationship as well as the pathological jealousy. This jealousy, in inner reality, merely provides a point of departure for masochistic injustice collecting.

Second, the abundance of ever-ready hatred in Lesbian relationships, which becomes evident at the least excuse and often is expressed in physical attacks. The pseudo-love which is the final defense of the Lesbian is easily penetrated to reveal the pseudo-aggression beneath.

Third, the husband-wife drama enacted as Oedipal camouflage is merely an admission of the lesser intrapsychic crime, devised as a screen for the more guilt-laden (because masochistic) mother-child relationship, which dates back to pre-Oedipal conflicts.

Fourth, the inevitable failure of a relationship established within the framework of Lesbianism. A person unconsciously seeking constant psychic masochistic satisfaction is incapable of conscious happiness.

Fifth, the central point of the Lesbian's—like the male homosexual's—solution consists of a specific elaboration of psychic masochism. That means that the over-riding pattern of her existence is injustice collecting for the essential purpose of achieving self-damage. This prevails over any and all conscious aims.

The effectiveness of *The Fox* derives from Lawrence's predominantly correct—and obviously intuitive—observations of a series of clinically verifiable facts on Lesbianism.

12

"Deglamorize Homosexuality"— A Practical Program for Changing the Existing Unsatisfactory Situation

THERE IS ONLY one way of coping with the problem of homosexuality today. That is a program of "deglamorizing," which means stripping that neurotic disease of its aura of false allure. This can be done by undertaking a series of educational and therapeutic measures.

1. The prevailing agreement, whether tacit or deliberate, to keep homosexuality out of the press and other mass media has artificially muffled discussion of a topic involving millions. As a result, people without special sources of information (such as scientific books) approach the subject with an attitude that mixes ignorance with contempt and sly innuendo. At the same time, it has produced in homosexuals themselves the feeling that they are being misunderstood and discriminated against. Like every

other half-conspiratorial movement, homosexuality exercises a masochistic attraction over neurotic candidates who love to "be different" and "live dangerously." An official policy of silence intensifies and often helps to create this allure.

2. A widespread publicity campaign should hammer away at disseminating the important fact that there is nothing mysterious or glamorous about homosexuality, which is an *illness* as painful, as unpleasant and as disabling as any other serious affliction.

3. The only partially successful fight against venereal diseases shows that it is not sufficient merely to let the public know of the dangers of the situation. Therapeutic facilities must be provided at the same time. In the case of homosexuality, this would necessitate a training program in which young psychiatrists could be taught how to treat homosexuals. With this should be coupled the establishment of out-patient departments in large hospitals to handle psychiatric treatment of homosexuals who do not have the means to consult a psychiatrist in private practice.

This three-point program takes no account of possible legal changes. The success of any movement to alter the legal status of the homosexual would depend entirely on the attitude of the public at large. Today, homosexuality is popularly regarded as exclusively a moral-criminal problem. Once the public has to a large extent substituted the scientific outlook for its present uninformed point of view and a new climate of opinion has arisen, it will be possible to approach the legal situation.

Experiences with the attitude of the confirmed homosexual prove that no cooperation can be expected from him. *The fight is for the young generation of homosexuals*, for the individual who has not yet completely fallen under the spell of homosexuality's alleged "glamor." The confirmed present-day homosexual naively looks forward to a time when the heterosexual majority will become so "enlightened" that it will grant the homosexual full parity. This bubble of misplaced optimism is bound to explode: heterosexual "enlightenment," when it comes, will consist of a new clarity of vision which will reveal homosexuality as a curable disease.

Repeated attempts have been made in the past to cope with homosexuality by means of the law. This technique has failed because *a disease cannot be eradicated by legislation.* The threat of prison and social disgrace, though consciously feared, unconsciously acts as no deterrent at all when the offender is a severe psychic masochist. This has been pointed out previously: since all homosexuals are psychic masochists, the prospect of humiliation and disgrace fits into their unconscious aim. Moreover, all homosexuals know that the present policy of enforcing the laws regarding homosexuality leaves an escape-hatch half-open at all times. Except when sporadic morality drives push the police and the courts into greater activity and severity, the code remains largely a dead letter, especially in large centers of population. If the code were more strictly and consistently enforced, a few more personal tragedies would follow, but the incidence of homosexuality would not be affected.

A recognition that this identical situation prevailed in Great Britain led some years ago to the establishment of a commission to study the situation. The Wolfenden Report, a document of dubious value, embodies the findings and recommendations of this commission.

To homosexuals, and to well-meaning people ignorant of the curability of homosexuality, the great merit of the report lay in its suggestion that legal penalties be omitted. Still, I call it "dubious" because it contains a series of misapprehensions. The most regrettable of these is the fact that the Commission apparently heard only the testimony of pessimistic psychiatrists, those who doubt that homosexuality can be cured. Moreover, the Commission accepted Kinsey's erroneous conclusions on homosexuality.

*

There is another aspect of this neurotic disease that is hardly ever mentioned in the press. This is the link between homosexuality and venereal disease.

In a bold but convincing report prepared on the basis of the statistics of the Magistrates' Courts of New York City in 1957, Herman Goodman, B.S. and M.D., a noted physician connected with the New York City Department of Health, stated in a lecture that there was more danger of acquiring a venereal disease from a homosexual contact than from a heterosexual contact.

Dr. Goodman arrives at his conclusion by pursuing two different lines of reasoning. One is based on the findings of physicians who do routine blood tests for syphilis. These tests are not necessarily performed because the patient suspects an infection; it should be remembered that a test for syphilis is required when applying for a marriage license. His other proof consists of a rational analysis of arrests and convictions for sex offenses, from which he arrives at an estimate of the number of men and women in New York City who are chronic sex offenders and as such are knowing or unknowing transmitters of venereal disease.

The figures derived from a comparison of physicians' practices are especially startling. Dr. Goodman cites one physician whose patients are a typical cross-section of the New York population. He has four hundred male patients. One of these proves to have active syphilis. Dr. Goodman then cites another medical man whose practice is almost solely among male homosexuals. Out of four hundred and sixty blood samples which this physician submitted to a laboratory, forty (of whom twenty are from men already under treatment for syphilis) show positive results. In his practice, therefore, twenty patients out of four hundred and forty suffer from early infectious syphilis.

Through the results tabulated at a clinic treating venereal diseases, one gets a picture of how quickly these infections can be spread through homosexual exposure. Patients with recently acquired venereal diseases were asked to name their exposures. Those who claimed to have only male contacts reported exposures, at the time of acquiring the disease, which averaged 3.6 per patient. Those who claimed to have been exposed to both men and women averaged the astounding figure of 16.4 contacts per patient. This figure was verified in at least one case by the evidence of one patient's "little black book." This listed his "professional appointments" with one hundred and twenty-five men and thirteen women within one year. All except two of these were examined. Nine of the men had early infectious transmissible syphilis. "A number of others," Dr. Goodman declares, "had syphilis in a non-infectious form. Two had new gonorrhea."

This is the story he tells of one young patient at the clinic:

Will was a clerk-manager-secretary with part time employment. He had blood tests within a month of his hospitalization.

The results were negative. He believed he was perfectly healthy. Will enjoyed the company of young males. He had a little money. He was introduced to a social club group. He provided cigarettes and drinks. He entered into the homosexual practices of the members. He reported to the hospital because he had an eruption of the skin. The diagnosis was secondary widespread syphilis. The entering point of the disease was a sore on the penis. This was acquired by oral manipulation. However, Will admitted other modes of sexual gratification within the group of the social club. Will was certain he became infected within the club and within the time period of his association with the members.

We examined 18 members of the club. We examined 40 house contacts to these 18 men. We examined several non-familial female contacts. In due time, several men exposed by the two females were examined.

Eight members of the social club—not including Will—were found in the infectious, communicable stage of syphilis. These men and their comrades admitted homosexual practices, active and passive. This is important! The persons of this group generally insist each practices only one phase of the act. The truth is the active partner in one set up is the passive partner in another. Promiscuity and change are features of the association of homosexual people.

In addition, exposure to female companions is frequent. This is another facet of homosexual existence. It is important in the search for exposed persons.

The only available study of infection among women consists of the results of examinations made of women arrested in New York City for prostitution. During 1955, 1956 and 1957, a total of 7,381 arrests were made; this may not represent the same total of individuals, since the figures do not note multiple arrests. The compulsory medical examinations of these women revealed one infectious case of syphilis: one case in three years! Five per cent of the women showed positive gonorrhea.

The provisions of the law call for the administration of chemical prophylaxis through antibiotics whenever there is an arrest for prostitution.

Dr. Goodman points out that there is no census of male homosexuals; the only way of arriving at an approximation of their number in any given area would be by analyzing the arrests for sexual offenses within a specific period. Beginning with a grand total of 14,795 males arrested for a variety of sexual offenses in New York City in 1957, Dr. Goodman (after carefully eliminating arrests that ended in discharges and suspended sentences, after making a generous allowance for multiple arrests, after eliminating arrests for rape) arrives at a figure of 6,500 male homosexuals apprehended during that year. On the assumption that only one-half the offenders are apprehended by the police, he suggests that 13,000 would be a fair approximation of the number of promiscuous male homosexuals in New York City, adding that this figure takes no account of the non-promiscuous male homosexual who is rarely arrested.*

Using the same break-down system on the arrests of women during 1957, Dr. Goodman concludes that the "hard core" of chronic female offenders in New York City amounts to about one thousand. He sums up:

> The conclusion is the current infections of early syphilis and gonorrhea arise from about 1,000 women available for hire and from 6,500 men who wittingly or unwittingly transfer venereal disease by male to male sexual bodily contact.
>
> The female offender when arrested is subject to physical examination and blood test. She is given chemical sterilization through antibiotics. She is rid of her communicable syphilis and gonorrhea each time arrested.
>
> The male offender when arrested is NOT subject to physical examination and blood test. He is NOT given chemical sterilization through antibiotics. He is NOT rid of his communicable syphilis and gonorrhea.
>
> The solution: Charge the male sex offender under 887 Code of Criminal Procedure** in addition to any other charge. Examine each male arrested for sex offense each time arrested. Expose to curative dosage of antibiotics as penicillin each time arrested. No discrimination for or against the sex offender either male or female.

* I believe that Dr. Goodman's approximate figures are too low. E.B.
** This makes medical treatment for venereal disease mandatory.

* * *

This cannot be too strongly stressed: The conspiracy of silence which surrounds homosexuality, and is—with negligible exceptions—maintained by the daily press, magazines, radio, television, has the end effect of *promoting* homosexuality. If information is unavailable, if false statistics are left uncontradicted, if new recruits are not warned by dissemination of the fact that homosexuality is but a disease, the confirmed homosexual is presented with a clear field for his operations—and your teen-age children may be the victims.

Participation in the effort to deglamorize homosexuality through an energetic campaign of public enlightenment is, I firmly believe, the serious duty of all well-meaning citizens who are concerned about their children.